IMMIGRATION DIALECTIC: IMAGINING COMMUNITY, ECONOMY, AND NATION

Immigration is an integral part of national identity in settler societies such as Canada. But in countries where identity is defined more in ethnic terms, such as Germany, the presence of immigrants has only recently begun to be acknowledged. Taking these two countries as case studies, *Immigration Dialectic* explores national identity as imagined through media-based discourses of immigration.

Harald Bauder argues that while both countries rely on negative depictions of immigrants to construct a positive image of the national self, the ways in which Canada and Germany construct national identity in relation to representations of immigrants are significantly different. Bauder introduces a sophisticated framework of Hegelian and materialist dialectics for the growing interdisciplinary literature regarding media perspectives on immigration and national identity. Providing close analysis of themes such as belonging, economic impacts, and national security, *Immigration Dialectic* will appeal to anyone interested in contemporary discussions on immigration.

HARALD BAUDER is the Academic Director of the Ryerson Centre for Immigration and Settlement and an associate professor in the Graduate Program in Immigration and Settlement Studies and the Department of Geography at Ryerson University.

HARALD BAUDER

Immigration Dialectic

Imagining Community, Economy, and Nation

UNIVERSITY OF TORONTO PRESS
Toronto Buffalo London

Toronto Buffalo London
utorontopress.com

ISBN 978-1-4426-4161-7 (cloth)
ISBN 978-1-4426-1076-7 (paper)

Library and Archives Canada Cataloguing in Publication

Bauder, Harald, 1969–
Immigration dialectic : imagining community, economy, and nation / Harald Bauder.

Includes bibliographical references and index.
ISBN 978-1-4426-4161-7 (bound). – ISBN 978-1-4426-1076-7 (pbk.)

1. Germany – Emigration and immigration. 2. Canada – Emigration and immigration. 3. Identity politics – Germany. 4. Identity politics – Canada. 5. Nationalism – Germany. 6. Nationalism – Canada. I. Title.

JV8025.2.B39 2011 325.43 C2011-904137-5

Cover photograph: KingWu/iStockphoto

This book has been published with the help of a grant from the Canadian Federation for the Humanities and Social Sciences, through the Aid to Scholarly Publications Program, using funds provided by the Social Sciences and Humanities Research Council of Canada.

University of Toronto Press acknowledges the financial assistance to its publishing program of the Canada Council for the Arts and the Ontario Arts Council.

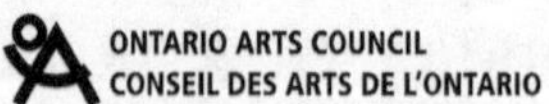

University of Toronto Press acknowledges the financial support of the Government of Canada through the Canada Book Fund for its publishing activities.

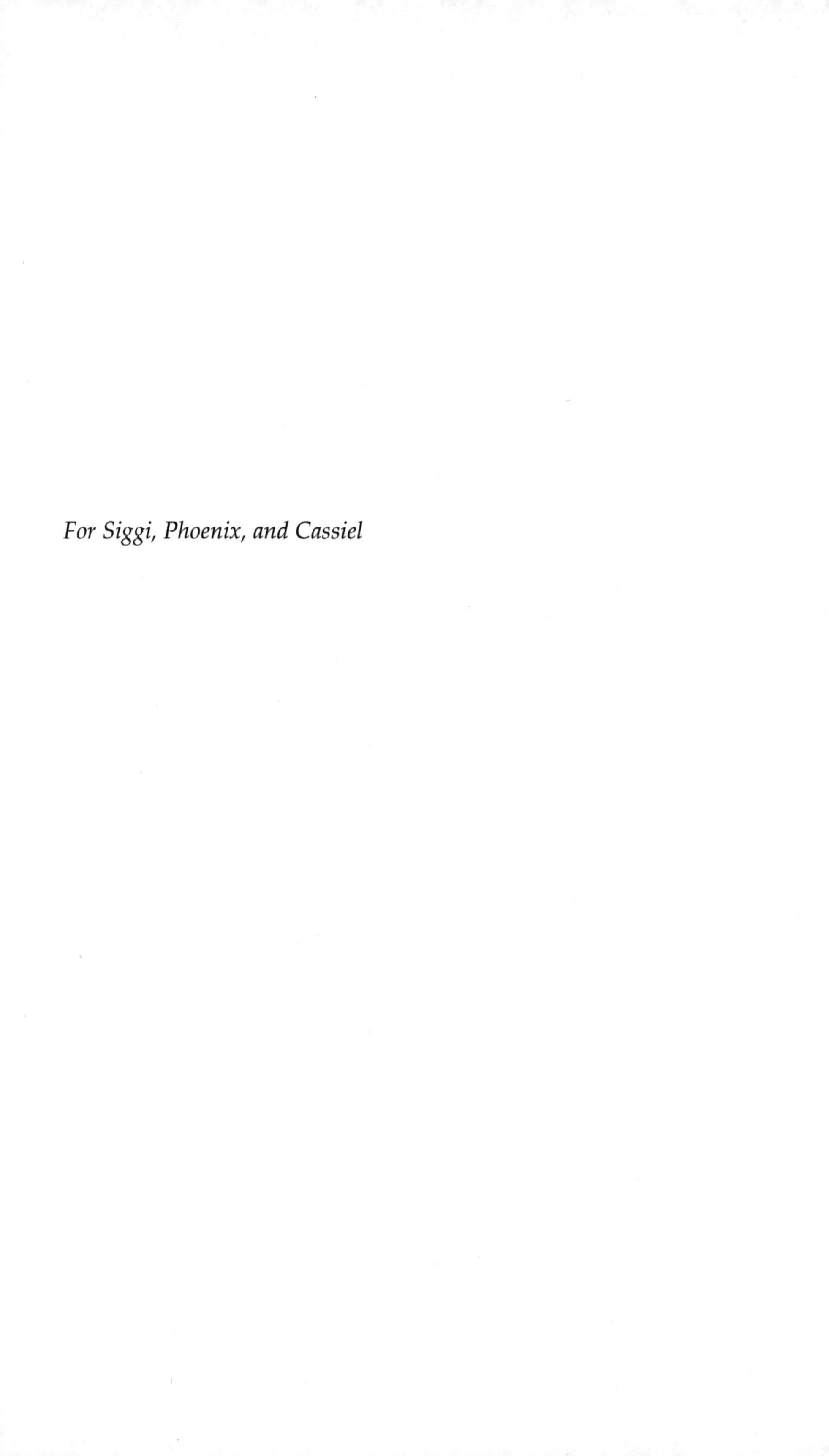

For Siggi, Phoenix, and Cassiel

Contents

Preface

This preface has been my favourite part of writing this book, as it is less constrained by the rigid scholarly practices and formulaic conventions that characterize the substantive parts of an academic book. The reviewers and the readers typically exclude the preface from the expectation of scientific method and scholarly rigour. Thus, it presents an opportunity to reflect on the research and writing process, and speak frankly about the subject matter in a way that otherwise may not have withstood the scepticism inherent in the peer-review process.

The idea of this book arose from a previous project that compared the integration of immigrants into the labour markets of Canada and Germany. I summarized this project in a different book, entitled *Labor Movement: How Migration Regulates Labor Markets* (Bauder, 2006b). I began the research for *Labor Movement* with the intention to compare both the situation of immigrant workers in the two countries and the cultural and institutional mechanisms that structure the labour market circumstances of these Canadian and German workers. Early in the research process I became aware of the difficulties of such a national comparison. While the cultural and institutional mechanisms differed to some degree between the two countries, they were not the leading explanation of the different situations of immigrants in Canada and Germany. Rather, the biggest difference consisted of legal contexts that encase cultural and institutional mechanisms. Furthermore, these legal contexts are rooted in radically different understandings of nationhood in Canada and Germany. When I published my research results in *Labor Movement,* I therefore refrained from making a direct comparison of immigrant workers in both countries. Rather, I used the two national contexts as examples of how various cultural and institutional mechanisms relate to the economic marginalization of immigrants. In *Immigration Dialectic,* I am now addressing the compelling questions that arose from this previous research: *what are the different conceptions of nationhood in Canada and Germany* and *how do they relate to the legal frameworks of immigration?* In a way, *Immigration Dialectic* should have preceded my earlier investigation of the cultural and institutional marginalization of immigrant labour. Unfortunately, the research process does not always progress in a linear fashion.

Immigration Dialectic, however, is in no way an afterthought. Although I began the project based on gaps that emerged in previous research, I also explore new ideas, which, I think, put a new spin on the way social scientists think of the relationship between immigration and nationhood. While the book is rather particular in empirical scope, some of the ideas developed in this book may be applicable to a range of other research contexts. In particular, I explore the notion of dialectics, which has been at the cornerstone of the enlightenment project and has a long tradition in 'Western' thought.[1] Yet, it seems to have fallen out of favour with many contemporary social scientists.

When I discussed the idea of dialectics at the dinner table – after my children demanded to know about this book I am writing that is causing me to neglect some of my family duties – I found myself struggling to provide a simple explanation. 'Dialectics is about everything and nothing,' I said.[2] After staring into bewildered faces, I elaborated that dialectics involves reciprocity between seemingly unrelated things (I spare you the details of the conversation that involved explaining words like 'reciprocity' to my nine-, seven-, and four-year-old children). But dialectics also means that identities are constantly changing; that they themselves may be children today, but soon they will be teenagers and adults. 'And,' I continued, 'dialectics describe how these identities relate to the way people act': when they sit nicely at the dinner table without throwing food or picking their noses, I am a proud father, but my identity will change if they begin to act differently. Although my children may still not see the use-value of dialectics, nor do they engage in a discussion of 'dialectics' with their classmates in the schoolyard, they saw that I am dealing with a complex concept.

My interest in dialectics stems largely from the desire to expand my learning experience and contribution to scholarship beyond the task of data collection while I conducted fieldwork in Germany. My impression of the Anglo-American social sciences – geography in particular – was that it borrowed heavily from French philosophy and

'Anglo-American' social theory. German philosophy and critical theory have much to offer, yet, for some reason, they have not penetrated the 'mainstream' Anglo-American social sciences to the same degree.[3] The location of my fieldwork provided plenty of opportunities to address this shortcoming, at least in my own work. Much of my fieldwork took place in the southern German city of Stuttgart, which happens to be the birth city of Georg Wilhelm Friedrich Hegel. In Stuttgart, I attended the Hegel lecture series, regularly held by Theodor Huett in the basement of Hegel's birthplace, now called the 'Hegel-Haus.' As I visited colleagues and universities in other parts of Germany, it was hard to escape Hegel's presence. In Berlin and Jena I was reminded of his activities in these cities and at the local universities, and in Bamberg I suddenly found myself standing in front of a house with a plaque noting that this was where Hegel wrote the famous preface to *Phenomenology of Spirit*. After these experiences triggered my interest, I realized that Hegel's philosophy could provide the missing link to understanding how immigration relates to nationhood. In *Immigration Dialectic* I apply many of Hegel's ideas. However, rather than embracing his entire philosophy, or system, I select elements of his work that suit the particular focus of my project and my quest for understanding the processes of national identity formation in the context of contemporary immigration. For example, I find a materialist perspective of dialectics much more appealing than Hegel's original idealist perspective.

Although this book is intended for a multidisciplinary audience with an interest in Canadian and European immigration and nation building, its contents and approach reflect my disciplinary background and training as a geographer. To me, one of the great benefits of being a geographer is the discipline's comprehensiveness[4] and remarkable dynamicism. Geographers are limited to neither a particular topic nor a particular perspective. The discipline provided me with the flexibility and freedom to look in unconventional places – including Hegelian dialectics – to find answers to the research questions I am asking.

If I nevertheless had to position myself within this comprehensive and dynamic discipline, I would call myself a 'critical geographer.' I associate this label with an approach to scholarship represented by critical theory, which Herbert Marcuse (1964: x) described as 'a theory which analyzes society in the light of its used and unused or abused capacities for improving the human condition.' Critical scholarship is part and parcel of the potential of progressive change.[5] I will say more about this role of critical scholarship again in the conclusion. Although some commentators critiqued the conclusion of my previous book, *Labor Movement,* as going too far for their taste beyond the original analysis to engage the reader in critical debate, I continue to point towards the possibility of progressive change in the conclusion of *Immigration Dialectic.* This time, however, I made an effort to link this discussion more closely with the analysis at hand, and I added a brief epilogue to raise a wider political question related to the dialectic of immigration.

Furthermore, I feel it is necessary to offer a disclaimer on my use of certain terminology in this book. The term 'discourse,' in particular, has created misunderstandings when I field-tested some of the ideas that I present in *Immigration Dialectic* during a series of lectures I gave in 2008 and 2009 at Canadian and German universities. The term discourse obviously does not have a uniform meaning. Rather, it has been applied in a variety of ways, reflecting different disciplinary traditions, scholarly approaches, and region- and language-particular scholarly conventions (Wodak, 2006). In the English-language social sciences of the last two decades, the study of discourse has heavily drawn on the work of Michel Foucault (e.g., 1972, 1977, 1984). In this context, the term discourse is typically associated with a truth regime that defines valid knowledge and establishes the parameters through which everyday communication and thought occur. Ernesto Laclau and Chantal Mouffe (1985) expand this understanding of discourse from purely linguistic processes to encompass the entire range of social, political, and cultural practices. The last decade has seen an explosion of empirical studies that apply the term discourse to examine relations of power that are articulated in taken-for-granted concepts, naturalized performances, and everyday practices.[6] Rather than seeking to define valid knowledge as it is framed by the entire range of human communication, thought, and practice, my empirical research is concerned with the use of language in particular texts and in the context of particular political settings. In the words of linguist and discourse scholar Ruth Wodak (2001: 64), my study explores the field of politics 'in the narrow sense.' It applies a version of an approach that Wodak and her colleagues would call 'critical discourse analysis,' which follows a tradition of critical theory and is compatible with my interpretation of Hegelian dialectics (e.g., Fairclough and Wodak, 1997; Wodak and Meyer, 2001; Wodak et al., 1999: 8–9).[7] The problem that I confronted during my lecture tour was that the audience associated the term discourse with particular disciplinary and sometimes research-group particular connotations, which often differed from my own use of the term. To avoid such misunderstandings in *Immigration Dialectic,* I use the term discourse sparsely and apply whenever possible more concrete language. For example, I typically refer to immigration 'debate,' although in some contexts the use of immigration 'discourse' may conform to scholarly convention.

This effort to keep the language clear and concise also supports my aim to make this book accessible to a wide audience. A core requirement of critical scholarship is that its content is effectively communicated to the audience. It is my hope that *Immigration Dialectic* succeeds in this effort.

Finally, all translations of German material in this book are my own.

Acknowledgments

The empirical research for this book was funded by a grant from the Social Sciences and Humanities Research Council of Canada and supported by the Alexander von Humboldt Foundation. The research began when I was a faculty member in the Geography Department at the University of Guelph. I developed the core theoretical ideas while I was a Humboldt Fellow – or 'Humboldian' – at the University of Stuttgart in 2007–8. I thank Wolf Gaebe, Simone Plahuta, and my colleagues at the now defunct Department of Geography at the University of Stuttgart for their hospitality and generosity. At the Alexander von Humboldt Foundation, I thank Maria-Bernadette Carstens-Behrens for outstanding assistance and support. After I returned from Germany, I joined Ryerson University, where I wrote the book manuscript. I thank my Ryerson colleagues in the Graduate Program in Immigration and Settlement Studies and the Geography Department for providing an extremely supportive, stimulating, and collegial environment; Brian Ceh, Myer Siemiatycki, John Shields, Vappu Tyyskä, and Shuguang Wang deserve special mention.

During my visit in Germany and after my return to Canada, I 'field-tested' many of the ideas presented in this book in a series of lectures. These lectures would not have been possible without the generous support and hospitality of the following persons: Dirk Gebhardt, who invited me to participate at the 'Ringvorlesung kritische Geographie' at the Humboldt University of Berlin, Hans Gebhardt of the Institute of Geography at the University of Heidelberg, Liette Gilbert of the Faculty of Environmental Studies at York University, Deborah Leslie of the Department of Geography and Planning at the University of Toronto, and Ludger Pries of the Department of Sociology at the Ruhr-University of Bochum. The feedback I was able to collect from these lectures proved enormously valuable for completing this book. In addition, I thank Friedrich Heckmann and Wolfgang Bosswick, directors of the *european forum for migration studies* at the Otto-Friedrich-University of Bamberg, for hosting me during the summer of 2009, while I continued working on the manuscript.

Many colleagues and friends provided comments, feedback, and support from the point when the ideas for this book were initially conceived until I submitted the final manuscript. In particular, I benefited from discussions with Ken Hewitt, Ulrike Ramming, Michael Samers, Christian Storr, and Michael Weingarten. Gillian Creese and Alan Simmons provided feedback on an earlier version of chapter 6. In addition, I was very fortunate to work with and supervise bright graduate students who provided intellectual inspiration. These include Carly Austin, Manvi Bista, Ashley Bradimore, Denise Chung Guerrero, Suhair Deeb, Ruby Dumais, Charity-Ann Hannan, Mabel Ho, Lida Moazzam, Sebastian Marian, Tom Lusis, Sandra Pehilj, Jan Semmelroggen, and Angelica Suorineni.

The empirical work for the book would not have been possible without an international team of exceptional research assistants. The Canadian team included James Christison, Genevieve Gilbert, Jennifer Herne, and Sophia Lowe. The German team consisted of Katharina Graeber (née Weyrewski), Aris Oreopoulos, and Till Rockenbauch. Muzzammil Beelut helped with formatting parts of the manuscript.

At the University of Toronto Press, I thank the commissioning editor, Daniel Quinlan, and managing editor, Wayne Herrington. Two anonymous reviewers read the entire draft version of the manuscript and provided important constructive criticism that enabled me to refine and strengthen my arguments. The book benefited greatly from thorough copy-editing by John St James.

Karen Uchic deserves very special thanks for reading the manuscript from cover to cover, providing feedback on the readability of the book and supporting me in various ways through the research and writing process. The book is dedicated to my three sons (listed in reverse alphabetical order), who are straddling their multiple national identities.

Many of the ideas that I present in this book are novel and have not been published elsewhere. However, the book also contains material that I published previously in peer-reviewed journals. This material was substantially revised and integrated into the wider framework of this book. I thank David Spenser, editor of the *Canadian Journal of Media Studies*.

Furthermore, I acknowledge the publishers for permission to use material from the following copyrighted articles: 'Media Discourse and the New German Immigration Law,' *Journal of Ethnic and Migration Studies* 34(1) (2008): 95–112, available at www.informaworld.com; 'Immigration Debate in Canada: How Newspapers Reported, 1996–2004,' *Journal of International Migration and Integration* 9(3) (2008): 289–310; 'Dialectics of Humanitarian Immigration and National Identity in Canadian Public Discourse,' *Refuge* 25(1) (2008): 84–93; 'The Economic Case for Immigration: Neoliberal and Regulatory Paradigms in Canada's Press,' *Studies in Political Economy* 82 (Autumn, 2008): 131–52; 'Neoliberalism and the Utility of Immigration: Media Perspectives of Germany's Immigration Law,' *Antipode* 40(1) (2008): 55–78; 'Humanitarian Immigration and German National Identity in the Media,' *National Identities* 11(3) (2009): 263–80, available at www.informaworld.com.

IMMIGRATION DIALECTIC: IMAGINING COMMUNITY, ECONOMY, AND NATION

Introduction

Since 1 January 2005, Germany has had, for the first time in its history, an immigration law. The new law was intended to mark a turning point in Germany's attitudes towards immigration. It was supposed to signify the beginning of a new era – an era in which Germany finally puts to rest its old identity as an ethnic nation and becomes an immigration country. The originally proposed law was modelled on similar laws in countries that have a long immigration history. Canada, in particular, served as a role model in the conception of the proposal. Accordingly, the initial proposal of the law contained a Canadian-style points system for the selection of economic immigrants, a clear commitment to humanitarian immigration, and provisions for the integration of newcomers. However, between the time the law was proposed, in August 2001, and when it was finally accepted by parliament, in July 2004, it lost many of its most groundbreaking features. The law that took effect in 2005 did not open the country's borders to immigration of any significant magnitude, nor did it become the desired symbol of Germany's departure from being a non-immigration country. Two years after the new law took effect, immigration scholar Dieter Oberndörfer concluded that 'Germany has not become an immigration country' (2007: 1). Instead, critics argue, Germany continues to embrace the ethnic national identity that it has held since the Wilhelmine Empire, and this identity does not include immigration. In the wake of a controversy following the publication of an anti-Muslim book in 2010 by board member of the German Bundesbank Thilo Sarrazin, the Bavarian president Horst Seehofer declared, 'We do not need additional immigration from other cultural regions' (Baur, 2010: 11) and German chancellor Angela Merkel claimed that multiculturalism had failed as a policy in Germany (Eddy, 2010: n.p.). Rather than converging on policies of immigration, Canada and Germany seem to maintain different attitudes towards immigration.

In this book, I explore the national identities of Canada and Germany through the lens of immigration. German immigration scholar Rainer Geißler describes Canada as an 'immigration country of classical type' (2003: 24–5) with a long tradition of immigrant inclusion. Germany, by contrast, is an 'immigration country of modern type' because historically it was not defined in terms of migration; only recently have Germans confronted the fact that immigration exists. In other words, Canada is a settler society – a society which consists predominantly of immigrants and their descendants.[1] Such a society embraces practices and institutions to integrate immigrants as self-evident, and immigration is deeply engrained in the national consciousness. Conversely, for much of its modern history, Germany has been described as an ethnic nation. The German name for 'Germany' illustrates this identity. *Deutschland* refers to the 'land' of the people who are 'deutsch' (i.e., German). In this way, the match between national territory and ethnic identity is explicit in the country's name; immigration does not occupy an important role in the manner in which the nation is defined. Recently, however, the fact that millions of non-Germans now live in the country has challenged Germany's historical identity as an ethnic nation.

The categories of settler society and ethnic nation provide two conceptual models of national identity that I explore in this book. These models could also be described through the terms *demos,* referring to civic understandings of national belonging, and *ethnos,* describing membership by descent.[2] Canada and Germany serve as case studies to address questions about the connection between immigration and nationhood in relation to both models. Immigration scholars rarely compare Canada and Germany,[3] although the two countries make for fascinating case studies because of their different historical attitudes towards immigration. Despite these differences, both countries possess highly advanced post-industrial economies that are similarly affected by forces of globalization, including international migration. In addition, both countries belong to a political-ideological configuration that could be described as the 'West.'

Although I am setting up the categories of settler society and ethnic nation as analytical 'hooks' for an empirical analysis of national identity, I recognize the limitations of these categories. For example, Christian Joppke has examined the practices of granting membership in settler societies and ethnic nations in greater detail. He suggests that the strict division between settler societies and ethnic nations is misleading. Rather,

> all nations are fundamentally defined by descent and origin; this makes them different from, say, class, age, sex, or lifestyle as alternative (and often competing) forms of allegiance and group organization. Conversely, all nations have a 'civic' element, because they are by definition associations of strangers that transcend the immediate kinship nexus. (Joppke, 2005: 17)

Countries that could be labelled settler societies also grant citizenship on the basis of ancestry. In fact, about four out of five Canadians never immigrated to Canada, but received their citizenship at birth.[4] By the same token, ethnic nations have processes in place to include new members who were neither born as citizens nor possess ancestral ties to the country. In Germany almost a fifth of the population possesses a background in migration.[5]

In addition, both settler societies and ethnic nations are affected by the similar trends of rising global mobility and global competition. Workers, families, refugees, and asylum seekers are increasingly mobile, able to move between countries and maintain transnational ties. In this climate of global migration and transnationalism, industrialized countries compete for skilled migrant labour while trying to close their borders to undesired migration. These tendencies coincide with efforts by both settler and ethnic nations to articulate rights and state membership in liberal terms that assume racial and ethnic equality.[6]

Nevertheless, the histories of many nation states gave rise to identities of their being a settler society or an ethnic nation. Such identities remain deeply engrained in the collective consciousness of these nations. Rita Süssmuth, the former president of the German Parliament and an advocate for implementing a Canadian-style immigration system in Germany, noted how historically derived identities still matter when she recently spoke at a conference of migration scholars and policymakers in Bonn, Germany. Süssmuth remarked that migration is now a global phenomenon that affects countries with such different histories as Canada and Germany in similar ways. Nevertheless, these different histories influence which policies a country adopts. Süssmuth elaborated that German policymakers had underestimated the public 'fear' of diversity. She suggested that the Canadian-style system was ultimately rejected because the adoption of such a system would have amounted to an admission that Germany is an immigration country (Süssmuth, 2008). The denial that Germany is an immigration country, however, does not necessarly mean that the ethnic conception of nationhood persevered in exactly the same manner as before. The public outcry that followed the publication of Thilo Sarrazin's book signifies that non-Christian immigrants are not universally constructed as unbelonging in Germany. In this book, I explore how conceptions of nationhood relate to the immigration policy.

Immigration and Nation

Immigration law has been called 'the last bastion of sovereignty' (e.g., Dauvergne, 2007a, 2008; Casey, 2009: 25) in light of the eroding influence of the state in other policy arenas. While nation states have lost significant control over the movement of goods, services, capital, and information, they are assertively regulating people's mobility across their borders and membership in their national communities. In this way, they practise sovereignty by determining who is able to cross the border into their national territories and deciding who will be allowed to claim citizenship. National identity can be an important factor in how these decisions are made. According to some liberal theorists, the nation state possesses the right to include and exclude new members in the national community based on criteria that reflect the collective identity of the national community (Walzer, 1983). In other words, a national community admits new members based on the envisioned identity of this community.

In this sense, settler societies and ethnic nations include and exclude new members based on similar principles of sovereignty and self-determination. In a Canadian context, legal scholar Catherine Dauvergne observes that 'national identity is the most powerful variable for giving an account of [immigration] law's features, changes, and applications' (Dauvergne, 2005: 26). In a German context, Christian Joppke remarks that the German state has responsibility to the people who are historically connected to it; otherwise 'it would be a nameless cash register for the transactions randomly occurring on its territory' (2005: 226).[7] National identity thus is an important variable in explaining the immigration policies of a country.

Let me return to the earlier example of Germany's first immigration law to illustrate the link between immigration law and national identity.

Germany's struggle with the new law was essentially a matter of identity politics. While the final law effectively blocks new immigration to Germany, it acknowledges the presence of millions of migrants in Germany and demands their integration. Wolfgang Bosswick astutely asks: 'Integration, yes, but to what? Old conflicts over the self-identity of German society . . . re-emerge in this new discourse' (2008: 131). Conversely, Canada's identity as a multicultural society appears to be much more aligned with the active selection of immigrants based on non-ethnic and non-racial criteria.

In this book, I reverse the logic of the argument that national identity explains immigration policy. Rather than examining national identity to understand immigration policy, I examine immigration debate and policy to explain national identity. In other words, I ask the question, What does immigration debate and policy say about how a nation is conceived? In seeking answers to this question, I realize of course that the relationship between immigration policy and national identity is neither one-dimensional nor linear. Attitudes and policies towards immigration are not the only variable that shapes national identity. In addition, immigration influences national identity just as national identity influences practices towards immigration. Nevertheless, as I will show here, the manner in which a national community debates immigration and justifies immigration policies provides meaningful and important insights into how this nation is imagined.

National Imagination

An identity is not something a nation naturally possesses or that is given to the nation by the grace of God or any other higher authority. Neither is the nation a category that was created by such a higher authority. Benedict Anderson has suggested that nationhood and nationalism are historically produced 'cultural artefacts' (Anderson 1991: 4). Other scholars concur that nations are historically, geographically, socially, politically, and culturally grounded constructions (see, e.g., Hobsbawn, 1989; Gellner, 1983).[8]

A danger of using the 'nation' as a unit of empirical analysis is to reify national communities and reproduce the nation state as a taken-for-granted category, a fallacy also known as 'methodological nationalism' (Wimmer and Glick Schiller, 2002). The nature of this fallacy can be illustrated by a debate that followed Rogers Brubaker's (1992) publication of *Citizenship and Nationhood in France and Germany.* In this influential book, Brubaker discussed the relationship between nationhood, state building, and national identity. The book's critics noted, among other things,[9] Brubaker's problematic starting position of theorizing the nation state and citizenship. In the words of Andreas Behnke (1997: 247): 'In Brubaker's historical study, we have to take the existence of a "state" in France as an unproblematic fact, in order to witness this state constructing a "nation." In the German case, we need to accept the prior existence of a "nation" as the foundation for the historical process of state-building.'

Christian Joppke extends this critique to an immigration context and argues that nation states cannot be taken 'as independent variable' to 'explain national variations of incorporating immigrants' (1998: 7). In other words, beginning a discussion of the national imagination with the assumption of the a priori existence of either a nation or a state uncritically reifies these concepts as natural occurrences.[10]

This critique of Brubaker's ontology is relevant to the research presented in this book. It would be problematic to assume that Germany's identity presupposed an ethnic community, or *Volk*. Similarly, it would be inappropriate to argue that Canadian identity rest solely on the pre-existing colonial state. Rather, the relationship between the nation and state is a dialectical one. This perspective of a dialectical relationship between nation and state is consistent with the general approach I have taken in this book, which focuses on dialectics and which I will elaborate upon further below.

The notion of dialectics is also reflected in Pierre Bourdieu's (1991: 224) conceptualization of ethnicity as a mental and performative construct that 'claims to bring about what it asserts' (223). Drawing in part on Bourdieu's work, Brubaker later refined his earlier position and speaks of the nation as a 'practice' (Brubaker, 2004b), and suggests 'thinking of ethnicity, race, and nation not in terms of substantial groups or entities but in terms of practical categories, cultural idioms, cognitive schemas, discursive frames, organizational routines, institutional forms, political projects, and contingent events' (2004a: 11). The idea of the nation as a discursive frame, in particular, resonates with the application of the national category in the empirical analysis which I present in this book.

The question of the national imagination emerges from the understanding that nations are not pre-existing entities. In a famous quote, Benedict Anderson explains that the nation 'is *imagined* because the members of even the smallest nation will never know most of their fellow-members, meet them, or even hear of them, yet in the minds of each lives the image of their communion' (1991: 6, original emphasis). Important questions that follow from the realization that nations are imagined are *how* they are imagined and *what* the contents, or substance, of this national imagination is supposed to be.

The historical perspective on the national imagination assumed by Anderson and others must be complemented by a contemporary perspective that emphasizes the practices with which national communities decide on who becomes a new member of the community and who should remain excluded from the community. Immigration is thus an important aspect of the national imagination. National immigration policies select people deemed worthy of inclusion in the national community; and public and media debates about immigration reveal who is imagined to belong to the nation and whose presence cannot be reconciled with the image of the nation.

National identity formation relates to practices of inclusion and exclusion. This relationship links again to long-established ideas of dialectics. For example, identities of national communities are established by defining who or what they are *not*. On the one hand, national communities select immigrants who reflect a desired image of the nation. On the other hand, they reject people based on characteristics that are represented as irreconcilable with the national identity. In contexts other than Canada and Germany, researchers have alluded to the dialectical relationship between representations of immigrants and racialized minorities as non-belonging and the construction of national identity (see, e.g., van Dijk, 1991; Blommaert and Verschueren, 1998). In addition, a literature exists that has been explicit about the dialectical relation between migration and nationhood (e.g., Wodak et al., 1999). A central theme of this book is that the process of national identity formation through immigration unfolds in a dialectical manner.

Dialectics

A particular contribution of this book is that it draws on the philosophy of Georg W.F. Hegel for understanding the nation–immigration dialectic. A conventional interpretation of dialectics relates to the juxtaposition of contradictory perspectives that negate each other. This interpretation of immigration as the negation of the national self is the starting point from which I develop a more nuanced understanding of national identity formation. In particular, I move beyond the conventional treatment of dialectics as simple dualisms and juxtapositions by applying Hegel's ideas of how the dialectical process prevails over these dualisms. In addition, the dialectic of national identity formation is a continual and geographically contingent process. National identities are never complete or finished, and immigration assumes different roles in shaping the national identities in Canada and Germany. Furthermore, I explore a series of nested 'dimensions' of dialectics which link the formation of national identity to internal processes of subject formation, the interaction between linguistic and material practices, and the nature of journalistic reporting.

In my eyes, dialectics are the most appealing conceptual approach currently available for exploring processes of national identity formation through immigration. The dialectical approach embraces the contradictions which inevitably characterize national (and other) identities. Furthermore, dialectics permits integrating various perspectives and approaches, ranging from material to discursive, from epistemological to ontological, and from positive to normative.

To operationalize the dialectical framework for my study, I had to make a number of important choices. Rather than embracing Hegel's idealism, I apply a materialist interpretation of dialectics. In particular, I investigate how national identities are dialectically referenced in the material circumstances related to immigration. These identities affirm and reproduce existing social and political structures of inequality. In addition, I focus on the particular substance–subject relation between immigration law and media debate. According to Hegel, the state and its laws are the highest forms of the material expression of human identity.[11] In the context of immigration, it is probably fair to say that laws and policies constitute the main material pathways or barriers that permit or deny migrants' entry to a country and membership in a national community. By observing the *debate* of these material laws and policies, I intend to obtain insights into the processes of identity formation from the perspective of the subject. The subject, in this case, is an assumed collective national community, represented by the media, which engages in this debate.[12]

My empirical approach to the nation–immigration dialectic is, in a way, itself dialectical. By comparing Canada, which can be described as a settler society, and Germany, an ethnic nation, I implement a dialectical method of discovery through juxtapositions and revealing contradictions. Furthermore, with each of these national contexts, I do not focus on one single 'story' of how immigration and national identity are related. Rather, I place multiple 'aspects' of immigration debate side by side. For example, in the context of both Canada and Germany, I discuss aspects of economy, humanitarianism, and danger independently from each other. I chose the term 'aspect' deliberately. Borrowing the term from Ludwig Wittgenstein, I use it to describe varying perspectives and viewpoints of the same topic of immigration.[13] Rather than claiming to produce an authoritative account of immigration debate from an Archimedean vantage point, my intention is to illustrate that multiple sets of material context, experiences of identity formation, and interpretations of immigration coexist. This treatment of the nation–immigration dialectic resonates with a literature on positionality and situatedness that has long recognized that knowledge is always partial and referenced in a particular set of experiences (see, e.g., Haraway, 1991; Rose, 1997).

Language

In the empirical analysis I examine the debate over immigration law in the daily newsprint media. Thus, I put language at the centre of the nation–immigration dialectic. This approach builds on exisiting research that examines how media representations mediate 'how newcomers imagine themselves and are imaged by the larger society in relation to the nation' (Chavez, 2008: 5). In addition, I focus on the link between linguistic and material practice. This link has received a significant amount of attention in recent years. Investigating the neoliberal turn in the economic and political fields, numerous scholars have emphasized the role of the media, and in particular the use of language by the media, in facilitating and legitimating this turn.[14] Norman Fairclough, for example, remarks that the struggle of neoliberalism's 'new order is partly a struggle over language' (2000: 147). Similarly, Andrew Herod argues that 'the articulation by neoliberals of a discourse of global threat to national and local competitiveness is presently serving as a potent device for transforming the nature of economic and political regulation' (2000: 1785). A central aim of critical discourse analysis has been to study this relationship between material and linguistic practice (see, e.g., Fairclough and Wodak, 1997; Wodak, 2006).

Migration scholars have followed suit in examining the link between language and material practice. For example, Canadian researchers have emphasized racial and ethnic prejudice in the media in the context of the material deprivation and subordination of immigrant groups

(Hier and Greenberg, 2002; Mahtani, 2001; Mahtani and Mountz, 2002). In my own research, I found parallels between media reports on temporary seasonal foreign workers in Canada and the material treatment of these 'off-shore' workers as exploited labour, their rejection by local communities, and their denial of citizenship (Bauder, 2005, 2008b). A recent study, which Ashely Bradimore and I co-authored, links changes in federal refugee policy to the media reporting on the arrival of a boat carrying Tamil refugees on Canada's west coast in 2010 (Bradimore and Bauder, 2011).

The field of the media should not be equated with public opinion. Rather, the media is a playground of the political, economic, and cultural elites. To a considerable degree, media debate reflects powerful political and economic interests (van Dijk, 1987, 1991). According to a strictly materialist interpretation of dialectics, the language deployed in the media would merely reflect existing power configurations related to national identity and immigration. Marx and Engels were explicit about the material basis of dominant ideology when they observed: 'The thoughts of the ruling class are in every epoch the dominating thought; this means the class which is the ruling *material* power of society is also the ruling *intellectual* power (*geistige Macht*)' (1953: 44, emphasis in original). I would not deny that the language of immigration debate and the related processes of national identity formation reflect the interests of the powerful. In fact, the empirical evidence which I present in this book illustrates precisely how media debate is embedded in existing power configurations.

In line with critical theory, however, I do not believe that the dialectic of national identity formation is a closed process in which human agency plays no role. Rather, this dialectic remains an unfinished and open project. As such it provides opportunities for intervention and intentional transformation. In fact, the critical theorists of the Frankfurt School found Hegel's own writing to be an illustration of the unfinished and open character of linguistic practice. Let me briefly review this interpretation of Hegel's text to illustrate – in an accessible way – the nature of the dialectic.

Many readers of Hegel find his texts ambiguous and sometimes difficult to follow because concepts and ideas are not always well defined. According to Theodor Adorno, these ambiguities of Hegel's texts signify precisely the impossibility and the undesirability of stabilizing language. Adorno interprets Hegel's written work as 'anti-texts' that do not seek to fix meanings, but rather encourage the reader to engage with the 'curves' (Adorno, 1963: 136, 140) of the dialectical movement of language. In addition, Hegel's work demonstrates the geographically particular nature of linguistic practice. Hegel was born in Stuttgart, the capital city of Württemberg in the southern German region of Swabia, where people still often speak in such a thick dialect that they sometimes have difficulties communicating with people from other parts of Germany. Although Hegel lived and worked for much of his adult life in other regions of Germany, he apparently refused to soften his Swabian dialect. This refusal had the effect that his students at the University of Berlin in Prussia had difficulties following his lectures and recorded very different lecture notes.[15] Max Horkheimer, who, like Hegel, was born in Stuttgart and was thus familiar with Hegel's native dialect and use of language, reportedly said that only a person able to speak the Swabian dialect can fully understand the meaning of Hegel's texts.[16]

These examples of Hegel's work and language use illustrate how linguistic practice and the associated dialectical process is open, unfinished, and geographically located. In the field of the media and in the context of immigration and national identity formation, linguistic practices are similarly open and geographical contingent. I will return to the possibility for critical intervention in the immigration–nation dialectic in the concluding chapter.

Outline of the Book

The book has three parts, each consisting of three chapters. In part 1, I develop the principles of the dialectic of immigration and national identity at a conceptual level. Chapter 1 establishes how immigration and national identity are dialectically related to each other. I draw especially on Hegel and critical theory, and expand on the significance of the ideas of negation, sublation, and agency in the nation–immigration dialectic. In chapter 2, I turn to the field of the media. In particular, I explore various dimensions of dialectics that characterize this field. While the journalistic method is fundamentally dialectical, in that discovery is a matter of juxtaposing and revealing contradiction, the media also links linguistic and material practice, and engages in Hegelian formations of meaning and identity. These interlocking dialectics structure the nation–immigration dialectic as it can be observed in the media. In chapter 3, I set the stage for the empirical analysis. I present an overview of the relevant historical, political, and cultural contexts that have shaped contemporary immigration policies and debates in Canada and

Germany. In addition, I review important milestones of recent immigration reforms in both countries and introduce the basic character and patterns of the media debate of these reforms.

Parts 2 and 3 apply the principles of the nation–immigration dialectic, which I developed in part 1, in an empirical case study of media reporting on immigration reform. Part 2 focuses on Canada, part 3 on Germany. I separate the discussion of the two countries because the dialectics unfold in fundamentally different ways in Canada, which the media represents as a settler society, and Germany, a country that is historically conceived as an ethnic nation. Each chapter addresses a particular aspect of immigration debate. Chapter 4 examines how the aspect of 'danger' appears to be a structural component in the construction of Canadian national identity vis-à-vis immigration. Chapter 5 explores the role of humanitarianism in presenting Canada as compassionate and welcoming. Chapter 6 investigates the economic utility of immigration and the material embeddedness of immigration debate. The analysis of German media debate on immigration begins with the economic aspect in chapter 7. This aspect relates to an economic national identity, which has featured very strongly in the German national imagination after the Second World War. Chapter 8 links the aspects of culture and danger to argue that German immigration debate has performed Hegelian dialectical twists and turns by presenting Germany as an immigration country, a non-immigration country, and finally an integration country. In chapter 9, I explore the representations of refugees and asylum seekers and outline important differences to the Canadian discussion of the humanitarian aspect of immigration. I end with a conclusion in which I discuss the empirical findings in light of contextual and theoretical considerations. From this discussion, I carry on to investigate the possibility of critical intervention in the nation–immigration dialectic.

PART ONE

Immigration and Identity Formation

1 The Nation–Immigration Dialectic

Similarly to a person who has an individual identity, a nation can be understood as a collective community that possesses a national identity. Although the nation is a political and social construct, the members of this construct usually recognize the nation's existence. In fact, this recognition marks the first step in the formation of national identity. The process through which this national identity unfolds can be understood in the terms of Georg W.F. Hegel's ideas of dialectics. According to Hegel, a dialectical relationship exists between two subject positions: inward-focused self-reflection and outward-searching observation of material circumstances. In the preface of his book *Phenomenology of Spirit* (Hegel, 2005 [1807]), Hegel argues that the contradictions between these two subject positions drive a dialectical movement of self-discovery and identity formation. For example, an individual may be aware of its own existence; however, to make sense of this existence the individual observes the world around it and situates itself relative to the people and things that exist in this world. Through interaction and engagement with its material surroundings, the individual acquires an identity for itself. Hegel's dialectical principle in the formation of the self has been widely applied to the study of individual identity.[1] This principle can also be applied to the formation of collective identities of nations. In this chapter, I discuss a general outline of the dialectical relationship between immigration and the formation of national identity. To set the stage for this discussion, I briefly review important critiques of Hegel's ideas that are relevant to my argument.

Dialectic of Identity Formation

The idealist position assumed by Hegel has been the focus of sustained critique. This critique is important for my argument on the dialectical relationship between immigration and the formation of national identity. In particular, Hegel suggested that material substance – including history, the constitutional state, and law (Hegel 1961 [1837], 1970 [1820]) – is a manifestation of human agency and reason. Along these lines, Hegel maintains that the 'spirit of a nation' (*Geist eines Volkes*) constitutes the foundation for a national consciousness and for the institutions of a particular nation state (1961 [1837]: 103–5).

Ludwig Feuerbach (1986 [1841]) generally opposed Hegel's idealist viewpoint. Feuerbach instead observed that the formation of human identity is a function of material conditions. Karl Marx and Friedrich Engels accepted Feuerbach's position. They famously sought to turn Hegel from his head onto his feet; or, in their words: 'In contrast to the German [i.e., Hegelian] philosophy, which descends from heaven to earth, here one ascends from earth to heaven' (Marx and Engels, 1953: 22). Marxian-inspired critical theory has generally adopted this materialist perspective of the dialectical process. It rejects the claim that human reason occupies a superior position over material substance in the dialectical process. Instead, it embraces the idea that identity formation has a material basis.[2] In the context of this book, this perspective entails that an examination of the dialectical process of national identity formation must acknowledge existing material practices and circumstances related to immigration. In addition, this perspective implies that the 'nation' cannot be assumed to be an a priori category, but is itself a historical and material product.

A Hegelian approach may also strike a discord with the followers of Foucauldian genealogy and understandings of discourse. Michel Foucault distanced himself from Hegel's philosophy[3] and suggested that discourse and social practice 'can never be reduced to a single system of differences [and] . . . leaves no privilege to any centre' (1972, 204; also 1984). While I share the viewpoint that some of Hegel's ideas are highly problematic, I also believe that aspects of his philosophy are very valuable to contemporary analysis. Rather than focusing on Hegel's system and his idealist position, I emphasize the nature of the Hegelian dialectical process. Theodor Adorno (1963), for example, remarked that Hegel's philosophy highlights precisely the unfinished and open character of the dialectical movement.

Contemporary critical scholarship embraces the idea of an unfinished and open dialectical relationship between identity formation and material substance. In particular, in the context of concrete processes of national identity formation through immigration, an understanding of Hegelian dialectics offers valuable insights; it informs how the process of identity formation unfolds. In other words, an understanding of Hegelian dialectics enables me to examine how the material relations and circumstances of immigration relate to the imagination of the national self.

The material circumstances that anchor the dialectic of collective identity formation often relate to territory and place.[4] In this sense, the dialectic of identity formation is deeply geographical in nature. The manner in which juxtaposition can define geographical identity illustrates the role of territory and place in this dialectic. For example, in his path-breaking work *Orientalism,* Edward Said (1978) demonstrates at a regional scale how the image of the 'Orient' has served as the negation of the 'Occident.'[5] The oriental image is not only a mechanism of control and subordination, but also a vital element in the construction of the collective self-image of the 'Occident.' At the neighbourhood scale, places like Chinatown reflect practices of the Othering of Chinese communities relative to a European-origin population (K. Anderson, 1991). At the national scale, modern nations are imagined through processes that involve similar dialectics of negation. For example, national identity in Turkey has been produced in opposition to an Armenian identity (Göl, 2005). In a similar way, in Central Europe in the eighteenth and nineteenth centuries, political and cultural elites sought to unite fragmented political territories by constructing a Pan-German national identity based on an ethnic imagination and in opposition to French nationhood, which, according to Brubaker (1992), was based on political principles. Canadian national identity linked to multiculturalism is often framed in opposition to the United States, which is associated with the 'melting pot.'[6] One could even argue that such dialectics of negation have contributed to bringing distinct German and Canadian national identities into existence in the first place.

Below, I will focus on this national scale and the nation state as a contemporary material configuration. I will argue that immigration is an important element in the formation of national identity. In fact, the very concepts of immigrant and immigration are dialectically related to the nation: people are considered immigrants when they enter and settle in the territorial nation state. Without a territorial manifestation of the nation, the concept of the immigrant could not be conceived in the way it currently is. In the next section, I explore the dialectical movement between immigration and national identity in greater detail.

The Dialectic of Immigration

A range of different practices illustrate the dialectical nature of national identity formation through immigration. Below, I first examine how discursive processes of *negation* shape national identities. Then, I discuss the Hegelian notion of *sublation,* which Hegel also called a second negation. According to this second negation, the dialectic of identity formation extends beyond the first negation to overcome the juxtaposition of the self and its oppositional reference point. I link this dialectical sequence of negation and sublation to the formation of national identity through the discursive and legal practices of identifying, selecting, and integrating immigrants.[7]

Negation

Negation is a basic principle of the Hegelian dialectic. This principle entails that people can only recognize a concept by grasping what it is not. A tree, for example, can only be recognized as such because it is not a rock or a bush (or any other thing for that matter). The concept of 'tree' is thus referenced in its material negations.[8] The same principle applies to the identity of people. In Hegel's terms, the awareness of the self (*Selbstbewusstsein*) depends on its material negation. In his famous master-servant comparison, Hegel (2005 [1807]: 153–64) articulated this dialectic of self-awareness in the following way: awareness occurs in two opposing forms. First, as the unending, immaterial, and self-reflecting 'master'; second, as the ending, embodied, and materially oriented 'servant.'[9] In this way, awareness exists as pure identity and as material experience. In a first negation the identity of the master requires the existence of the servant. Or, in other words, an abstract identity of the self necessitates a material reference point. If this material reference point did not exist, an identity of the self would not make any sense. The 'death' of the servant would also imply the master's end.[10]

In the context of national identity formation, the principle of negation does not apply to an individual but to a collective self. In this particular context, immigrants are represented as the negation of an imagined nation; in fact, they can serve to construct the nation, whose members become aware of it, in the first place. National communities can be imagined[11] in juxtaposition to the material characteristics of individuals and groups who do not belong to the nation or its territory. In this way, immigrants serve as material reference points for an abstract identity of the nation. This practice of national identity formation through negation involves the construction of 'impassable symbolic boundaries' (Hall, 1996 [1989]: 445) that homogenize diverse immigrant populations as outsiders, distinguish them from those who belong to the nation, and then fix these binary identities.[12]

The formation of national identity through negation by immigration can be observed in traditional settler societies. For example, in the United States, discursive practices tend to homogenize immigrants from Latin American countries under the label 'Hispanic' or 'Latino' and represent them as non-belonging (Oboler, 1995). In his investigation of the Clinton administration's policies towards migration practices across the border between Mexico and the United States, Joseph Nevins demonstrates how the racialization of 'Hispanic' immigrants and their demotion 'to a position of sociocultural, political and economic inferiority' signify their role as negated Others who do not belong in the United States (2002: 104).[13] The news media, in particular, depict immigrants as a threat (Chavez, 2008) and even as 'dangerous and destructive pollutants' (Cisneros, 2008: 570).[14] Through negation by representations of migrants as non-belonging, inferior, and polluting, the national self is implicitly imagined as 'white,' 'Anglo,' and superior.

Similar processes of identity formation through negation apply in Canada. Canadian case studies have uncovered racialized representations of immigrants in opinion polls, parliamentary debate, government documents, media reporting and even in academic scholarship (see, e.g., Li, 2001; Mahtani, 2001; Henry and Tator, 2002; Sharma, 2006). For example, in 1999 four boats carrying 599 migrants from the Chinese province of Fujian arrived at the coast of British Columbia. Sean Hier and Joshua Greenberg examined media reporting about the arrival of these migrants. They observed how the media emphasized that migrants 'were of "Chinese" or "Asian" origin, creating an instant epistemological distinction between "Chinese" and "Canadian," "Orient" and "Occident," "Us" and "Them"' (Hier and Greenberg, 2002: 498). Although the number of arrivals was negligible in comparison to the 24,398 refugees who arrived in Canada in the same year (Citizenship and Immigration Canada, 2007b), the media constructed the event as a crisis and migrants were represented as the quintessential symbol of non-belonging in Canada. Hier and Greenberg interpret the press coverage of these arrivals as a practice to construct and reproduce 'a racialised discourse of citizenship and national identity' of Canada (2002: 491). The representation of the Chinese refugees constituted the negation of an imagined Canadian nation that is situated in the Occident and defined by order and civility.[15] In chapter 4, I will show that the media devoted a significant share of its coverage of immigration reform to the dangers emanating from immigration, including terrorism, violence, and organized crime. The fear of immigrants associated with terror, subjugation, and crime reflects the negation of an imagined national identity of peace, freedom, and safety.

In traditional non-immigration countries, the presence of immigrants and foreigners and residents with a migration background assumes a similar role in the formation of identity. For example, Switzerland has a history – dating back to confederation in the thirteenth century, the legend of William Tell, and the country's struggle against the house of Habsburg in the fourteenth century – of defining national identity in relation to foreign threats. In more recent government debates and popular discourses of modern Switzerland, immigrants are identified as such a foreign threat. In particular, non–European Union nationals are represented as culturally distant, non-belonging, and foreign. These representations dialectically situate Switzerland in a European cultural context (Riaño and Wastl-Walter, 2006). In Switzerland's neighbouring country, Austria, similar practices exist. Media discourses portray non-EU immigrants and refugees as ultimate Others. Some metaphors that circulate through Austrian newspapers associate Kurdish refugees not even with human beings but with animals (El Refaie, 2001). In Scandinavian countries, similar practices of national identity formation through the negation of immigrants exist. For example, in Sweden, a range of discursive practices construct immigrants as 'an exception from the [Swedish] mainstream and a "deviation from the [Swedish] norm"' (Dahlstedt and Hertzberg, 2007: 191). The characteristics attributed to immigrants help define the cultural traits that Swedes are supposed to possess. Sweden's trade union movement, for example, represented immigrants as 'disorderly' and 'passionate,' in opposition to a presumed Swedish normality of order and calmness.

Germany is hardly exempt from these practices of negation and identity formation. Muslim immigrants have long been depicted as non-belonging in an imagined enlightened Christian German nation. When German talk-show hosts ask, 'How can "We" deal with Islam, must "We" be afraid of Muslims?' they distinguish the national community from Muslim immigrants and imply that a German Muslim is something 'almost unimaginable' (Kermani, 2008: 15). In particular, representations of Muslims as backward, oppressive against women, and religiously fanatical enable the imagination of a national German identity as modern, liberal, and enlightened. Even in German parliamentary debate, the conflation of immigrants with traditional and backward Muslims rests on the implicit assumption of a German national identity that is liberal-democratic and modern-Christian (Bauder and Semmelroggen, 2009). Acknowledging the dialectical nature of national identity formation, Navid Kermani suggests that the construction of identity through negation is a 'normal process' (2008: 15). However, he critiques the German media for uncritically drawing the symbolic boundary between the Other and the self along immigrant and religious lines. In part 3, I will elaborate on the role of immigrant Others in the formation of German national identity.

Legal categories are important in the formation of national identity through the negation by the immigrant Other. For example, in the United States, politicians and the media often speak of 'illegal immigrants' or 'aliens' when they refer to non-status and 'irregular' immigrants.[16] Often these terms are associated with 'Hispanics' and 'Latinos.' The use of these terms expresses the ultimate legal exclusion from the political community of the nation. The denial of rights, status, and recognition to these outsiders contrasts with the claims of rights, status, and recognition among citizens. The political and legal exclusion of migrants negate the privileges that come with American citizenship. The presence of 'illegal' 'Hispanics' and 'Latinos' helps maintain an identity of America that is associated with unique rights and privileges.

In addition to the use of the language of legality and illegality, legal procedures and policies towards migrants are also important material practices in the formation of national identity. In the context of Australia and Canada, Catherine Dauvergne examined humanitarian immigration law and policy. She found that humanitarianism is precisely 'reinforcing the boundary between an "us" group and a "them" group' (Dauvergne, 2005: 72). Evoking the language of negation, Dauvergne suggests that the refugee projects the 'photographic negative' of an imagined national self (124). The process of Othering refugees and migrants in need of protection enables a receiving society to construct itself in positive terms. By providing refuge to migrants who flee totalitarian and abusive societies, the receiving nation implicitly assumes an identity of possessing the opposite characteristics of the refugee's country of origin.

The case of humanitarianism illustrates that the dialectic of national identity formation has a material basis. This material basis is constituted in the various forms of deprivation experienced by eligible refugees, including the lack of security and safety, and the denial of gender equality and human rights. Based on her research, Dauvergne confirms that humanitarian admission of refugees 'is grounded in a specific type of difference created by material inequality' (2005: 72). This inequality identifies the receiving national community as a place where opposite conditions exist – in this case a place that is secure and safe and that respects gender equality and human rights.[17]

Another example of the material basis of the Othering of migrants relates to temporary migration. Many industrialized countries maintain a labour force of temporary and seasonal migrant labour that is denied the prospect of citizenship or permanent residence. In these cases, the material demand for vulnerable and exploitable labour can be the origin of discursive representations of migrants as foreign and non-belonging. For example, Canada's Seasonal Agricultural Workers Program has become an economic necessity to the Canadian horticultural industry, because it supplies Canadian growers with a labour force of vulnerable and seasonally exchangeable workers (Satzewich, 1991; Basok, 2002).[18] In my research on the media representations of this program and the participating workers, I found that newspapers acknowledge the economic importance of the migrant workers. However, they also represent the workers as non-belonging and racialized Others, thereby legitimating their exclusion from the imagined community and ultimately justifying their unequal treatment and exploitation (Bauder, 2005, 2008b). Many other countries of Europe and North America also rely heavily on a seasonal and temporary foreign workforce that is legally excluded from the national community. In these countries, corresponding images of exclusion from the imagined national community exist, such as 'Hispanic' workers in the United States, Polish foreigners in Germany, and Africans in Spain (Mitchell, 1996; Bade, 2004; Suárez-Navaz, 2007).

The formation of national identity through immigration is intimately linked to material geographical inequalities. These inequalities are the material substance in which national identify is referenced. The discursive demotion and exclusion of the migrant Other reproduce the material structures of deprivation, subordination, and exploitation. By the same token, the dialectical construction of national identity in opposition to migrants and immigrants reifies the privileges that the members of the nation possess. The deprived, subordinated, and exploited immigrant provides the material basis for a national identity of privilege.

Sublation

The dialectical movement does not end with the first negation. Despite the dialectical interdependence of immigration and national identity, the national self contructed through this interdependence remains 'unhappy' because of the continuing separation of abstract identity and material experience. A second negation, or sublation, mediates between the two positions. In Hegelian terms, this second negation facilitates the continuation of the process of self-discovery (*zu sich selbst kommen*) (Hegel, 2005 [1807], 162–3) by embracing the very contradiction between both positions. In the context of immigration, national identity incorporates precisely the tension between the nation and the immigrant Other.[19]

This second negation can be observed in traditional immigration countries. In reference to the United States, Bonnie Honig (2001) argues that immigrants, although constructed as Others, also replenish the nation. They are not only the external source of identity formation, but they also constitute an integral component of the construction of the nation. According to Honig, foreigners are 'founders' of the nation:

> The foreign-founder may be a way of making the novelty that is necessarily a feature of any (re)founding. The same mythic figure may be a way of illustrating psychological insight that stale or corrupt patterns cannot be broken without the injection of something new. The novelties of foreignness, the mysteries of strangeness, the perspective of an outsider may represent the departure or disruption that is necessary for change. (2001: 4)

The United States is defined not only in opposition to immigrants, but it also absorbs the immigrants into the national community, thereby constructing a national identity of dynamic transformation and change. The incorporation of immigrants into the nation surpasses the first negation of constructing the immigrant as Other. This second negation entails that the *tension* between the material substance of immigration and an abstract national identity constitutes the national self. This second negation of the dialectical process of subject formation elevates national identity to a higher meaning.

In traditional immigration countries, material interests are a driving force behind immigration discourses and national identity formation through immigrant sublation. Australia and Canada, for example, proactively select immigrants based on their human capital and domestic-labour-market needs (Walsh, 2008). The selection of new residents and their integration by granting them citizenship after a few years reflect the country's material interest in economic growth and demographic development. In the case of Canada, Peter Li confirms that 'immigration debate is primarily framed from the standpoint of Canada's self-interest, on which the merits of immigration and the contributions of immigrants are articulated in terms of benefits to Canada' (2003: 163). These benefits and the expectation that immigration makes the country a highly competitive contender in the global economy shape how the national community is envisioned.

Humanitarian immigration further exemplifies the formation of national identity through negation and sublation. After identifying refugees as the Other and selecting them as eligible for resettlement, the countries in which the refugees are allowed to settle permanently accept them as members of the national community. By welcoming immigrants in need, these countries acquire a positive national image. For example, in the context of Canadian and Australian immigration policy and law, humanitarianism and refugee admission defines 'the nation as compassionate and caring' (Dauvergne, 2005: 75) and projects an image of the nation as 'good' and performing an 'act of grace' (ibid.: 161). 'Humanitarianism is about identity. The individual identity of the other who benefits from our grace is important, but only because of the light it reflects back on us. When we admit the deserving, we are good' (164).

Minelle Mahtani and Alison Mountz observed a similar situation in the context of the coverage of the admission and settlement of Kosovar civil-war refugees in the British Columbia press: 'Clearly, Canadian immigration officials are looked upon favourably in the media when welcoming Kosovar refugees. We suggest that Canadians felt good about themselves vis-à-vis the press, the actions of government, and the contributions of citizens through that immigration event' (Mahtani and Mountz, 2002: 29). In chapter 5, I will elaborate on the Canadian newsprint media's representation of humanitarian immigration and refugees and its role in the formation of Canada's national identity.

The dialectic of immigration and national identity further involves overcoming the apparent contradiction between the Otherness of immigrants and refugees and their inclusion into the national community. Once they arrive in the country, newcomers are asked to shed their identity as the Other and adopt a new identity of belonging. In fact, to become a Canadian citizen, immigrants must pass a citizenship test that asks the new citizen to endorse symbols and concepts that represent the Canadian nation. The booklet to prepare for this test requests would-be Canadians, for example, to endorse 'freedom of conscience and religion' (and other Magna Carta rights), 'mobility rights,' 'aboriginal peoples' rights,' 'official language rights,' 'multiculturalism,' and the 'equality of men and women,' and to reject contrary 'barbaric cultural practices.' The booklet further identifies 'obeying the law,' 'taking responsibility for oneself and one's family,' 'serving on a jury,' 'voting in elections,' 'helping others,' and protecting Canada's 'heritage and environment' as distinct responsibilities of members of the Canadian national community (Citizenship and Immigration Canada, 2010: 8–9).[20] At the subsequent citizenship ceremony (for those who passed the citizenship test), the new Canadians affirm their allegiance to the Canadian state and sing the national anthem, 'O Canada.'

In this way, immigrants can be conceived as 'both other and not-other' (Dauvergne, 2005: 162). Again, Catherine Dauvergne has been a leading researcher articulating such an argument in the context of refugee law and humanitarian legal practice. In her words: 'When refugees are admitted as permanent members of the community, they are literally invited to change their national identity. This shift in identity is facilitated through a process that judges the old nation as bad and emphasizes the goodness of the new nation' (ibid.: 124). Immigrant and refugee Others become formative elements in the manner in which the nation is imagined through negation *and* sublation. Sublation entails the inclusion of immigrants and refugees into the national self and their redefinition from outsiders to members of the national community.

A thesis that I will explore in the empirical parts of this book is this: in non-immigration countries, the second negation does not occur. For example, although Switzerland is a multi-ethnic nation, consisting of Swiss-German, Swiss-French, Swiss-Italian, and Swiss-Romanic populations, foreigners continued to be excluded from the imagination of the nation. The fact that legal discourse has continued to refer to residents without Swiss citizenship as 'foreigners' rather than immigrants attests to the role of these residents as outsiders – rather than members – of the national community (Riaño and Wastl-Walter, 2006). Similarly, in Austria the imagination of the nation has long excluded the foreigner (Wodak et al., 1999).

I anticipate that in a traditional non-immigration country with a history of endorsing an ethnic identity, the absence of the second negation will be especially observable. A question I pursue in the empirical analysis in parts 2 and 3 is whether Germany fits this model of a non-immigration country. The post-war migration history of Germany raises the question of whether indeed a truncated dialectic of national identity formation lacks the incorporation of the immigrant Other into the national community. After the disasterous Nazi regime had ended, new political circumstances required the hate-driven ethnio-racial understanding of German nationhood to be questioned and rejected. In light of the astonishing post-war economic recovery, Germany's identity was rescripted into an *economic* identity. The so-called economic miracle became a symbolic marker for rearticulating West Germany's national identity away from an ethnic and towards an economic identity. In response to the German economy's thirst for labour, the federal German state created a 'guest-worker' program that enabled millions of migrants from Mediterranean counties to enter and work in Germany between 1955 and 1973.[21] The German media equated these migrants with an economic utility[22] and enshrined images of migrants as disposable low-skill labourers in the national 'collective memory' (Hell, 2005: 88). Since Germany was not imagined as an immigration country, migrants remained 'foreigners' even after they had settled in Germany for decades and generations. Immigrants contributed to the economy-centred national identity through the first negation, which is characterized by the Othering of foreign workers and their use as vulnerable labour to the benefit of the national economy. However, as they were not invited to join the national community, the second negation never occurred.

Although, in the aftermath of the Second World War, Germans have gererally been rather uneasy with an ethnic identity of Germany, people of non-ethnic German origin continued to be imagined as non-belonging. Klusmeyer and Papademetriou suggest that there was a high degree of continuation between the Wilhelmine Empire and the post-war period in terms of the recruitment of foreign workers, their denial of permanency, and their differential treatment based on ethnicity, race, nationality, and 'cultural' markers (2009: 86–96).[23]

A similar continuation of ethnic principles of inclusion and exclusion is evident in (West) Germany's post-war refugee and asylum policies. In light of the political atrocities committed by Nazi Germany, the new Federal Republic of Germany set high moral standards and enshrined generous asylum legislation in its constitutional law (*Grundgesetz*).[24] Asylum seekers, however, were never imagined as prospective members of the German nation. Instead, they were excluded from participation in the German labour market and political life. The exclusion on ethnic and national grounds is clearly expressed in the post-war legal distinction between 'refugees,'[25] referring to ethnic Germans who 'returned' to Germany after the war and who were included in the national imagination, and 'asylum seekers,' referring to non-Germans who were considered foreigners.

Changes in material circumstances, however, affect the way in which national communities, including traditional non-immigrant nations, are imagined. For example, in light of the non-European origin of a significant proportion of Sweden's current population, authorities declared Sweden a multicultural society, extended membership in the national community to immigrants, and invited them to actively participate in Sweden's liberal democracy (Dahlstedt and Hetzberg, 2007). Similarly, in Switzerland the continuing presence of 'foreigners' of the second and third generation has increasingly raised awareness of the need to include immigrants in the national imaginary. This realization led to the federal Decree on the Integration of Foreigners, which took effect in the year 2000 and outlined principles for the integration of non-citizens into Swiss society (Riaño and Wastl-Walter, 2006).

Similarly, the presence of millions of foreigners in Germany affected the way in which the German nation was imagined. This situation challenged Germany's identity as both an immigrant country and an ethnic nation. As I will discuss in greater detail in chapter 3, the realization that Germany is de facto an immigration country triggered a public debate in the 1990s on policies and laws that would formalize this material reality into Germany's first immigration law. In the debate of this law, the integration of immigrants who already lived in Germany became a major issue. The acknowledgment of the need to integrate foreigners went hand-in-hand with the recognition of diversity within the German national community (Hell, 2005; Müller, 2005). As public debate embraced the tension between the foreignness of immigrants and the national self, new narratives of immigrant integration emerged. These narratives aimed to overcome the contradiction between immigrant Others and their continuing physical presence in Germany. The inclusion of immigrants has been enacted by a variety of practices, ranging from government-funded German-language programs for immigrants to the media's celebration of the election of the second-generation Turkish-German politician Chem Özdemir as first leader of a major federal party, the Greens, in the fall of 2008. Practices towards immigrants seem to affirm a national identity that follows the material circumstances of post-war Germany. In part 3 I will examine the identities that have been constructed through the debate of the immigration law in detail.

An important question is whether the differences between traditional settler societies and non-immigrant nations are as clear-cut as the argument I have constructed in this chapter suggests. A danger is to assume that essential differences exist in the way nation states incorporate outsiders, and that the cateogries of settler and non-immigrant nations accurately capture theses differences. According to some commentators, the commitment to incorporating immigrants and refugees in settler societies represents neither successful inclusion nor equal integration of the Other into the national self. Rather, the 'multiculturalism' of traditional immigrant nations, such as Australia and Canada, continues to be beset by inequality and exclusion. In the case of Australia, Ghassan Hage (1998) argued more than a decade ago that tolerance and multiculturalism continues to represent non-white immigrants and aboriginal peoples as objects of exoticism, defining whiteness as the implicit but prevailing norm.

This argument can be extended to the case of Canada. Along these lines, Richard Day (2000) and Cecil Foster (2007) have applied a Hegelian approach to the phenomena of multiculturalism and diversity in Canada. Although both scholars do not engage directly with immigration policy as such, their contributions are highly relevant to the discussion of immigrant incorporation in Canada. Day argues that multicultural policies in Canada project the *fantasy* of a unified Canadian society. This fantasy caters to the Canadian national desire to overcome disharmony and disunity. In Hegelian terms, the fantasy of unity promises to cure the nation suffering from 'unhappiness.' As a fantasy, however, multiculturalism fails to deliver on this promise. While multicultural policy recognizes fragmentation, it is unable to reconcile it – that is, it fails to sublate the opposition between master and servant (Day, 2000: 178). By providing the illusion that 'multiculturalism as a state policy of recognition . . . would solve, once and for all, the problem of Canadian diversity' (38), the fantasy of unity actually perpetuates inequalities along ethnocultural lines. Day suggests that Canadian multiculturalism does not even engage in a dialectical movement, and concludes: 'If there is no dialectic in progress, it seems quite unlikely that there will ever be an *Aufhebung*' (217, emphasis in original). In a way, this conclusion echoes my earlier thesis that the second negation of immigrant integration never occurs. However, in this case it applies to Canada, a country that can be described as a settler society.

Cecil Foster has also applied a distinctly Hegelian lens to examine issues of identity in Canada, but reaches a different conclusion. Like Day, Foster evokes Hegel to suggest that multiculturalism 'is part of the consciousness of Blackness' that aspires to be idealized and ethnically pure Whiteness (Foster, 2007: xiv). Under contemporary Canadian multiculturalism, images of non-whiteness trap immigrant populations in their roles of the Other and continue to serve as the reference category for the formation of an abstract national Canadian identity. The continued separation between material Other and abstract liberalism cause the national consciousness to remain 'unhappy.' Unlike Day, however, Foster has faith in dialectical progress: existing contradictions of multiculturalism provide the conditions for new configurations of meaning, and for reaching a higher level of national awareness and thus the possibility of genuine multiculturalism.[26]

The different interpretations of Canadian multiculturalism raise the question whether a settler society is perhaps no different than a traditional non-immigration country with respect to the dialectical formation of national identity through immigration? The literature suggests that similar problems may exist in traditional non-immigration countries that have recently begun to embrace identities of inclusion that mirror those of traditional settler societies. Germany is an example of such a country. Similarly to the Canadian situation described by Hage and Day, the inclusion of immigrants into the national community of Germany is not unconditional. Rather, it is contingent on the adoption of the German language and engagement with civic and public life. While the German state provides government-sponsored German-language programs and offers incentives to civic and political participation, immigrants who do not adapt to certain cultural, social, and political norms remain excluded from the imagined nation. This exclusion is evidenced by debates that lament the 'ghettoization' of immigrants and accuse immigrant communities of establishing 'parallel societies' (see, e.g., Beck-Gernsheim, 2007).

The case of Germany seems not to be unique in this respect. Swedish society invites immigrants to become members of the national community through participation in civic and political institutions. To accomplish participation, however, it expects immigrants to shed their cultural identities and liberate themselves from their cultural backwardness by adopting Swedish norms of political practice (Dahlstedt and Hertzberg, 2007). The existence of such unresolved contradictions between immigration and national identity points to the continuing and unfinished nature of the dialectic of immigration and national identity.

Conclusion

Traditional immigrant and non-immigrant nations share the principle of dialectical movement of identity formation through immigration. This dialectical principle of immigration and national identity formation applies in different historical and geographical contexts. However, the contents of the dialectical movement, the circumstances of immigration, and the meanings of nationhood vary. As I have shown in this chapter, *how* immigration relates to processes of national identity formation differs between national contexts.[27]

The preliminary distinction between settler societies and non-immigration countries can offer interesting perspectives on the dialectic between immigration and national identity. In traditional settler societies, such as Australia, Canada, and the United States, immigrants have historically served as a source of demographic and economic development. This material necessity of immigration is associated with discourses of immigration that follow a dialectic of negation and sublation. In these countries, immigrants may be constructed as Others, but they are also included into the imagination of the national community. Settler societies rely on immigration as an important ingredient in the dialectical imagination of the nation. This dialectical formation of national identity through immigrant inclusion, however, does not mean that an endpoint in the dialectic or a contradiction-free national identity has been achieved. Even in a country with a strong commitment to multiculturalism, such as Canada, immigrants can remain the material embodiment of the Other.

In traditional non-immigration countries, the dialectic of national identity formation seems to follow a different path. Foreigners constitute the Other, but are not considered a resource to replenish the nation. Examples include post-war Austria, Sweden, Switzerland, and

Germany. In recent decades, however, debates of the social, cultural, and economic integration of immigrants have unfolded in Germany and other traditional non-immigration countries.[28] In Germany, this debate has predominantly involved immigrants who are already in the country – many of them for decades and generations – and signifies the progression of the dialectic of national identity formation along the path of settler societies, towards the incorporation of immigrants into the imagined nation.

Nevertheless, even as German national identity has begun to accommodate the millions of immigrants who live permanently in the country, Germany's relation to immigration differs drastically from that of traditional immigration countries like Canada. In particular, Germany's new immigration law permits entry to only a minute trickle of newcomers, while Canadian policy admits close to 1 per cent of its population as immigrants every year. Apparently, German identity is not defined through the active selection of significant numbers of new immigrants. In later chapters, I will explore these contradictions in greater detail.

An important point, which I have made in this chapter, is that immigration discourses are grounded in material and historical circumstances. In my view, the dialectic of national identity formation through immigration follows the materialist understandings of dialectics that many contemporary critical theorists also favour. Obviously, the very concept of immigration, whether defined in legal or symbolic terms, is dialectically linked to the material category of the nation state. Immigration discourses therefore necessarily affirm territorially existing states. Through negation by immigration and immigrants, these political configurations acquire and enshrine national identities. Discourses of immigrant integration, in turn, derive from the material need of a nation for newcomers or the material fact that immigrants have settled in a national territory.

This materialist understanding of dialectics should not imply that I dismiss human agency. In fact, the dialectic of immigration illustrates effectively the role of agency in the formation of national identity. Immigration policies define the parameters for selecting immigrants worthy of inclusion in the national community, and the debate of these policies scrutinizes the characteristics that immigrants and the desired national community are supposed to possess. In this way, immigration policies and debates serve to imagine the nation. In the dialectical process of national identity formation, immigrant selection can thus be interpreted as 'doing' (*Tun*). According to Hegel (2005 [1807]: 162–3), the knowing subject mediates between the abstract self and the material world by modifying the material world; that is, through action, or 'doing.' The subject thereby facilitates the dialectical formation of identity.[29] In the context of national identity formation, 'doing' involves legal and discursive practices towards immigration that may enable a nation to 'discover' itself. While for Hegel this process of discovery originates with the abstract self that acts on material substance, critical theory has reversed the direction of this process. For example, in the context of the immigration dialectic, the material need for economic and demographic development may involve active immigration selection and incorporation, leading to a national identity as a settler society. Nevertheless, the imagination of a national identity that embraces immigration is a collective act of agency. The critical issue of this book is how this collective agency is exercised.

The dialectic of immigration and national identity formation has not reached a point of stability at which the national self is in a state of 'happiness.' In fact, a utopian endpoint to the dialectical processes would be impossible to reach. Even in a traditional immigration country and multicultural society like Canada, the immigrant Other and the nation seem to remain separated subjects. In addition, the material context, on which the dialectic of national identity formation rests, changes continuously. For example, in an immigration-related study of Germany, Marianne Takle observes that material changes to Germany's situation in Europe have 'undermined how the concept of "otherness" could be understood' (2007b: 179). The continuing and contingent nature of the immigration–nation dialectic in Canada and Germany will be the central topic of parts 2 and 3.

2 The Field of the Media

Dialectics come in many different forms and can be observed in a nearly infinite range of contexts. It would be a hopeless endeavour to search for *the* dialectics that completely explain the relationship between nation and immigration. For example, in the previous chapter, I showed that the immigration–nation dialectic differs between national contexts. A single nation–immigration dialectic that applies universally does not exist. In addition, variable, interlocking dialectical processes apply in contexts such as parliamentary politics, law, education, and the everyday. The dialectic of national identity formation is immeasurably complex.

The media is only one of many fields in which dialectics of national identity formation can be observed. Nevertheless, the media also occupies a privileged position in the formation of national identity because it has a mandate to inform and educate the general public about the activities and events that affect the nation state. In other words, the media operates at the intersection of national identity formation and the material world of news and national politics. With this connecting role, the media is an important site at which the nation–immigration dialectic occurs.

Restricting the empirical exploration of the nation–immigration dialectic to the particular field of the media, however, does not make it an easy undertaking. Far from it. Rather, than performing a single dialectic, the media is characterized by a series of nested and interlocking dialectics.[1] Ruth Wodak (2001) has referred to different 'dimensions' of dialectics that structure the media and its practices. In this chapter I discuss three such dimensions. These three dimensions relate to the journalistic use of language, the connection between media debate and material context, and the construction of meaning and identity.[2]

As a separate field, the media operates according to principles that differ from other fields, such as the political field or the legal field. Below, I argue that the media is an inherently dialectical field. The dialectics that characterize the media, however, cannot be generalized. They do not apply in the same way in other fields. Thus, an investigation of the media cannot offer a general theory of dialectics and national identity formation that applies and can be tested across fields. It can, however, provide insights into the usefulness of the dialectical framework in examining the formation of meanings and identities.

The chapter is structured as follows. First, I show that the media is a separate field and argue that dialectics represent a set of 'rules' that structure this field. I develop these arguments by drawing on Pierre Bourdieu and his work on the journalistic field. Second, I examine the three dimensions of dialectics in the context of media practice. In this discussion, I follow the tradition of critical discourse analysis, which treats the use of language in the media as a 'form of "social practice"' (Fairclough and Wodak, 1997: 258) that contributes not only to the production of meaning and identity, but also links meaning and identity to material circumstances. Third, I examine the geographically contingent nature of these dialectics and discuss how they can be expected to differ between Canada and Germany.

The Media Field

In his work on television and journalism, Pierre Bourdieu (1998a) separates the field of the media from other social, political, and cultural fields. Bourdieu describes the journalistic field[3] as independent or autonomous because it follows its own rules, or 'laws': 'Journalism is a microcosm with its own laws, defined both by its position in the world at large and by the attractions and repulsions to which it is subject from other such microcosms. To say that it is independent or autonomous, that it has its own laws, is to say that what happens cannot be understood by looking only at external factors' (39). As a separate field, journalism and the media possess distinct hierarchies and social practices that differ from the hierarchies and practices in other fields. Journalism and the media also follow a particular logic of cultural production and symbolic expression. In other words, they observe 'a set of shared assumptions and beliefs' and impose a 'mental grid' according to which journalists select and interpret information (ibid.: 47).[4]

The conceptualization of the media as an autonomous field does not mean, however, that this field is homogeneous. Rather, it contains several subfields that may vary to a degree with respect to their practices, laws, and structures. For example, the subfields of radio, television, and newsprint differ in terms of journalistic specialization, degrees of professionalization, and levels of commercialization and in their relations to fields other than the media (Marchetti, 2005). Bourdieu was mainly interested in the subfield of television. In the particular context of France, he observed that, in television, competition and risk-averse behaviour among media agents has led to a convergence of journalistic practices. In other subfields and in other national contexts, journalistic practices may be guided by different principles or variations thereof.

Despite the possibility of differences between radio, television, and newsprint journalism, these subfields also share certain characteristics and journalistic practices. For example, the mandate to inform and educate the public, to facilitate democratic debate, and to report truthfully on facts and events exists across radio, television, and newsprint journalism. Bourdieu drew parallels between television and print journalism with respect to the coverage of jingoism and racism (1998a: 10). To a degree, Bourdieu's ideas related to television as an independent subfield are transferrable to newsprint journalism and thus apply to the empirical study of the nation–immigration dialectic, which I present in subsequent chapters.

Although the media may be independent or autonomous, it is not isolated from other fields. Bourdieu suggests in the above quote that the field of journalism is defined 'by its position in the world at large.' It is not difficult to see that media professionals and their journalistic practices are influenced by the interests and intentions of other social, political, and cultural agents and institutions.[5] The media uses concepts and categories that are also used in other fields. In fact, the media does not produce and engage with concepts and categories in a purely independent or autonomous fashion. Rather, journalists and media professionals circulate and to a degree reproduce concepts and categories that represent the interests of powerful social, cultural, and political agents.[6] These interests penetrate multiple fields, including the media. For example, in the context of an analysis of ethnicity and race, Teun van Dijk has shown that the media draws on 'preformulations' of concepts and categories articulated by influential social and cultural elites (van Dijk, 1987: 361; van Dijk, 1991: 41). Rather than blindly reproducing racial concepts and categories, the media engages with these concepts and categories, and subsequently 'reformulates' existing ethnic and racial identities (van Dijk, 1991: 7). Thus, the media is embedded in a complex network of interests and material circumstances. It exercises independence and autonomy in the limited way in which it interprets and responds to these interests and circumstances.

The field of the media also connects to everyday practice. Journalism caters to an audience that listens to, views, or reads the information which journalists produce and present. For example, when journalists write articles for 'mainstream' newspapers, they consider how an audience of popular readers is likely to interpret and use this information. In this way, the media presents 'scripts' for the interpretation of news events and political affairs. In a similar way, it provides scripts for the everyday social interaction between individuals and social groups (Downing and Husband, 2005: 43). An audience, however, does not blindly accept these scripts. Rather, the audience decodes journalistic reporting and often critically interprets the information it receives from the media (Hall, 1980).[7]

Some researchers have proposed that journalism occupies a special, agenda-setting position relative to other fields. Nick Couldry, for example, argues that the media functions as a 'meta-field' because it influences other fields, such as politics. In particular, the media supplies other fields with the 'representations of, and categories for understanding, the social world' (Couldry, 2003b: 668). With such an influential position and agenda-setting function, the field of the media is of particular interest to the investigation of the nation–immigration dialectic, because it is located at the centre of representations of immigration and nationhood that occur in other fields, including politics, law, education, and the everyday.

So far I have illustrated that the field of the media is, on the one hand, connected to other fields, elite interests, and the everyday. On the other hand, it is an independent and autonomous field that follows distinct practices and possesses its own rules. In fact, the ethics of good journalism and the norms of professionalism demand that media reporting maintains a degree of distance from economic and political fields[8] (Hallin, 1996). Although Bourdieu's work on journalism focused mainly on the power relations and hierarchies particular to the media field, he also acknowledges that media production follows a distinct set of journalistic practices. For example, Bourdieu observes that print journalism generally follows the practice of being inoffensive and inclusive; he even calls this practice a 'law' of journalism (Bourdieu, 1998a: 44). In the same vein, journalism has a 'code of ethics' that constrains and structures the way the media produces its output (71). As an autonomous field, the media possesses an independent set of principles that guide its journalistic practices.

The idea that media practice follows distinct principles resonates with some of Bourdieu's work that predates his writing on journalism. In particular, the notion of *habitus*[9] can be very useful to understand the practices that exist in the journalistic field. According to Bourdieu, habitus is a system of dispositions, styles, and tastes that are shared among the members of a social or professional community and that guide this community's practices. In other words, habitus defines the 'rules' by which the 'game' of a given field is played; habitus bestows the player with 'a feel for the game.' Similarly to the way that rules differ between games, so do the practices differ between fields. Although Bourdieu did not apply the concept of habitus in his work on journalism (1998a),[10] it is not a far stretch to suggest that habitus defines the guiding principles for the practices that exist in journalism.

In fact, several scholars of journalism have applied the concept of habitus to the media (see, e.g., Couldry, 2003a; Downing and Husband, 2005). According to these scholars, a range of media practices represent the journalistic habitus. Editors, reporters, and media staff embrace common rules of news publishing, standards of journalistic integrity, norms of establishing legitimacy, practices of selecting information, styles of writing, and ways of constructing meaning. In other words, they share a professional habitus. For example, in news rooms and editorial meetings, media professionals rely on their journalistic 'gut feeling' to selecting newsworthy information (Schultz, 2007).[11] This gut feeling is a manifestation of the habitus that journalists have internalized. While this habitus is essential in the media field, it may be of little relevance in other fields.

In a similar way, the use of language follows particular principles that reflect habitus.[12] The journalistic habitus specifies conventions of how news is reported, how information is presented, and how a narrative is constructed in a way that meets journalistic expectations. In a review article of research on journalism and the media, Michael Schudson identifies an approach to media studies that recognizes 'that news is a form of culture' and 'a form of literature' (2002: 251, 262) that follows certain professional traditions and styles of storytelling, and which deploys particular journalistic strategies, such as presenting expert voices to establish authority. What Schudson characterizes as culture, tradition, and style can also be described as the journalistic habitus.

Let me present a final example of journalistic habitus. The practice of 'framing' is of central importance in the production and presentation of news. The term framing refers to the selection and interpretation of information by referencing it in a particular context of societal and political circumstances.[13] Bourdieu explains the practice of framing through a comparison to wearing a special set of eye-glasses: 'Journalists have special "glasses" through which they see certain things and not others, and through which they see the things they see in the special way they see them' (1998a: 19). These 'glasses' help journalists to emphasize the unusual, tone down the ordinary, integrate news in pre-existing categories, and relate them to other social and political events. In France, for example, these special journalistic 'glasses' have projected an association between the 'inner city' and the recent 'riots.' In other contexts, press reporting of immigration is often framed in the context of danger and crime, humanitarianism, or economic competition. According to John Downing and Charles Husband (2005: 36), the very practice of framing is 'habitual and . . . rarely reflected upon' by the media professionals who reproduce and apply these frames. Through framing, the journalistic habitus structures the way the media collects, interprets, and presents information.

In this section, I have illustrated that a distinct set of practices exist in the media field. In the next section, I explore practices of news reporting in greater detail. In particular, I suggest that dialectics is an important principle that structures the media field. To a degree, these dialectics relate to habitus, in that they represent a taken-for-granted convention of reporting.

Dialectics of Journalistic Practice

A system of nested dialectics characterizes the field of the media. In this section, I concentrate on the subfield of the print media to explore these dialectics in greater detail. In this particular context, journalistic practices are subject to at least three overlapping dimensions of dialectics. These dimensions relate to the practices of reporting news, analysing information, and constructing meaning.

The first dialectical dimension refers to a linguistic practice of presenting and analysing information through juxtaposing oppositional positions. This dialectical dimension has a long tradition in 'Western' society. It can be traced to the classical Greek practice of dialogue as the exchange of proposition and counter-proposition.[14] In the media, this first dialectical dimension reflects the manner in which journalists apply language and construct arguments. Douglas Walton (2007) suggests that journalists simulate a conversation between two speakers when they write texts. Walton argues that when journalists seek to persuade their audience, 'they imagine a dialogue to establish the initial position of the audience, and they then work within that framework to persuade the audience through dialectically secured claims' (2007: 4). Although there may be only one journalist writing the story, the story itself represents more than one position. The same practice is used when journalists seek to inform their audiences about news events and analyse these events by presenting multiple perspectives and viewpoints. Through this dialectical practice, the claims made in the media report acquire legitimacy.[15]

This presentation of contradictions and opposing positions is a common feature of media reporting. Journalist and editors often aspire to 'balanced reporting'[16] by offering oppositional perspectives of news events and by juxtaposing differing opinions and interpretations. This dialectical practice of journalistic reporting is a method of presenting a nuanced picture of an issue and of obtaining a deeper understanding of news events. Contradiction and negation – rather than linear thinking and harmony – are central elements of journalistic discovery.[17] In the words of John Merrill:

> Absolutes and extremes are unproductive in journalism if they are honored as static values. They must be looked at upon as *means* – as instruments of opposition and friction – that lead to a new better journalistic idea or essence . . . No journalist can afford to push aside the awareness that ideas and events have complex and contradictory natures and that all is constantly changing. Flux is king in journalism. Dynamic thinking and dialogue is essential to journalistic progress. (1989: 8, original emphasis)

When Merrill calls on journalists to embrace the 'habit of thinking dialectically' (1989: 11), he implies that this dialectical practice of news reporting is habitual. The presentation of contradictory viewpoints and the positions of the 'good guys and bad guys' (Bourdieu, 1998a: 35), reflects a tacit linguistic rule of the game of print journalism.[18]

This rule of dialectical linguistic practice is firmly established in the media field. Although some journalists may seek a synthesis of opposing viewpoints, they are never able to present a definite endpoint of the interpretation of news. Rather, breaking news and transforming circumstances continuously challenge existing positions. In this way, they perpetuate the dialectical movement of journalistic reporting (Merrill, 1989). News is a 'product that must be made fresh daily,' Gaye Tuchman (1978: 179) observed more than three decades ago. Journalistic discovery rests with the daily and dialectical reinterpretation of events and circumstances, not the fixing of concepts and meanings.

The dialectical nature of news reporting has not been lost on researchers who study media content. In fact, the empirical analysis of media debate often focuses on the very contradictions, juxtapositions, and opposing positions articulated in the media (see, e.g., Wodak and Meyer, 2001). Ruth Wodak observes that the critical analysis of media texts 'aims at discovering inconsistencies, (self-)contradictions, paradoxes and dilemmas in the text-internal or discourse-internal structures' (2001: 65). The linguistic practice of juxtaposing contradicting positions constitutes the first dimension of dialectics relevant to the study of immigration and national identity in the press.

The second dimension of dialectics applies to the interaction between linguistic and material practices. More than four decades ago, Raymond Williams recognized this second dimension when he noted the relationship between 'communication' and material 'reality' (1966: 19). He wrote:

> We have been wrong in taking communications as secondary. Many people seem to assume as a matter of course that there is, first, reality, and then, second, communications about it . . . We need to say what many of us know from experience . . . that the struggle to learn, to describe, to understand, to educateis a central and necessary part of our humanity. This struggle is not begun, at secondary hand, after reality has occurred. It is, in itself, a major way in which reality is continually formed and changed.

The proponents of critical discourse analysis explicitly situate this dialectical relationship at the centre of their investigations. For example, Wodak remarks: 'On the one hand, the situational, institutional and social settings shape and affect discourses, and on the other, discourses influence discursive as well as non-discursive social and political processes and actions' (2001: 66). In a jointly authored book chapter, Norman Fairclough and Ruth Wodak refer to this second dialectical dimension as a 'two-way relationship: the discursive event is shaped by situations, institutions and social structures, but it also shapes them' (1997: 258). Critical discourse analysis therefore examines the 'dialectical relationship between particular discursive acts and the situations, institutions and social structures in which they are embedded . . . In other words, discourse constitutes social practice and is at the same time constituted by it' (Wodak et al., 1999: 8). An extension of this argument is that media debate itself can be treated as a social practice that is not limited to the realm of language, thought, and abstract argument, but rather engages with the material world. Wodak speaks of 'scaffolding,' or mutually supporting, human practices that constitute a 'dialectic among institutions, culture, situations, and agents who perform activities produced and reproduced in these settings' (2006: 599, referring to James Paul Gee, 2003: 1). Media debate is an integral component in this scaffolding. In fact, the metaphor of scaffolding permits another way of describing the second dialectic of media practice: as the interdependency between the media field and other fields. Media debate is integral to the manner in which people engage with other fields, including politics, law or the everyday.

Corresponding to such an understanding of dialectics, empirical research employing critical discourse analysis has focused on the relationship between linguistic and material practices. The print media, in particular, has served as a site where the dialectic between discursive and material practices can be observed, where the mediation between social norms and material practices manifests itself, and where the interests of politicians, civic administrators, corporate leaders, media owners, and other groups are reflected (see, e.g., van Dijk, 1991, 1997a; Wodak and Meyer, 2001; Wodak and Menz, 1990; Fairclough, 1992a).

The third dimension of dialectics occurring in the media field relates to the Hegelian construction of meaning and identity. This dialectic deals with the relation between subject and substance. It focuses on the production of abstract concepts (*Begriffe*) through which people comprehend the world, and the formation of abstract identities through which they know about themselves and others.

This third dimension of media dialectics is related to the second dialectical dimension outlined above. Similarly to the second dimension, this third dialectical dimension is concerned with the interplay between media practice and material context. Abstract concepts and identities are referenced in material contexts. Unlike the second dimension, however, this third dimension concerns mostly the formation of abstract concepts and identities, rather than the impact of media practice on material practice.

Language and meaning, we know from Ludwig Wittgenstein (2001 [1945/6]), are always situated in a particular context. Without substantive reference points, texts would be impossible to interpret in a meaningful way. In regard to media practice, material context is central to understanding the meanings constructed by journalistic texts and debate. The news and the material events which journalists report on constitute the material matter for referencing the meanings which journalists convey with their reports. Moreover, journalistic professional ethics require that the material evidence they present is not fictional. Rather, in the words of Michael Schudson, journalists – and thus the journalistic production of meaning and identity – are constrained by 'having to write "accurately" about objectively real occurrences in the world' (2002: 255).

While the news media may be obligated to write accurately about material facts, it also follows particular practices to select, interpret, and order these facts (Tuchman, 1978). For example, media reporting can portray immigration as an economic asset and a catalyst that makes a national economy globally competitive, or as an economic burden that increases fiscal insecurity and displaces domestic workers in the labour market. Similarly, framing practices can represent immigration as a positive feature of multiculturalism or as a threat to national security and civic order. Other characteristics of immigrants that do not fit into conventional frames of representation are rarely reported on. The meanings of immigration and the identities of immigrants are a function of how the facts about immigration and immigrants are selected, interpreted, and ordered relative to these frames of reference.

Neither such frames nor the related meanings and identities are fixed or static. Rather, they change with the transformation of material contexts and circumstances. For example, throughout the post-war period, the German press painted shifting images of immigration and immigrants that followed the country's changing geopolitical situation and fluctuations in the demand for labour. Based on these geopolitical and labour market changes, the press reframed immigration from welcome infusion of necessary labour power to undesired and undeserving job stealing (Wengeler, 1995). Framing practices also responded to key news events, such as violent attacks on asylum seekers by racist German Neo-Nazis (Brosius, 1993/4).[19] Resonating with the first dialectical dimension of media practice, which relates to journalistic discovery through juxtaposition, this third dimension never reaches a fixed endpoint of stability. Rather, it remains unstable and transforms with the ongoing shifts in the material circumstances and the continual production and reproduction of news (Bencivenga, 2000: 48).

Conclusion

The triple dialectical dimensions that exist in the media field are geographically contingent; that is, they differ from one place to another. This contingency relates to the fact that the dialectics are referenced in material contexts. As material contexts change, so do the contents and character of the dialectics. The dialectical *principle* applies, however, across places. In this final section, I discuss how geographical, linguistic, and national contexts affect the nation–immigration dialectic. This discussion provides basic insights for the empirical investigation of Canadian and German immigration debate in the media in parts 2 and 3.

Although ownership structures in the media field are becoming increasingly multinational, and the market principle serves more and more as a universal regulatory paradigm,[20] the national scale continues to provide an important geographical context for the production of news and for interpreting news in a manner that is meaningful to an audience. In other words, the national scale geographically defines the media field and the associated dialectics of journalistic practice. For example, Bourdieu's English translator, Priscilla Parkhurst Ferguson, emphasized the importance to situate *On television and journalism* in a French context. She had to explain some of the important differences between the American and French journalistic fields to make the book (which deals with a French context) accessible to an American readership (Bourdieu, 1998a: 83–5).[21] Variations between France and the United States have also been observed in the relationships the media maintain to commercial and political fields (Benson, 2005).[22] The national scale seems to be particularly important in the manner in which the media is institutionally (and thus materially) organized and journalism is practised.[23]

The nation is a dialectical construct that not only shapes media practices but is in turn also shaped by the media. As material circumstances are geographically organized at the national scale, the meanings and identities constructed by the media also fit into the national container. In his later work, Rogers Brubaker (2004a: 11) suggests that the nation itself is a 'discursive frame.' This discursive container of the nation makes a pivotal difference in the way the media discusses immigration.

For example, the Canadian media constructed the landing of the 599 refugees from China on Canada's western coast in 1999 as a crime and framed the event in a context of racialized national identity (Hier and Greenberg, 2002; Mahtani and Mountz, 2002; Vukov, 2003). The imagination of Canada as a non-Chinese place certainly contributed to this construction. In other national contexts, with different immigration histories, immigration laws, and policies towards multiculturalism or social cohesion, the debate of similar events would likely have assumed a different character. In Germany, for example, the media tends to frame Turkish foreign residents – rather than Chinese refugees – in racialized terms and as a threat to ethnic national identity (Beck-Gernsheim, 2007; Korteweg and Yurdakul, 2008).[24] Even the discussion of the same international event often takes on distinctive features in different countries. For example, the interpretation of the 2005 riots by second-generation youth in suburban Paris varied between newspapers in Canada, France, Germany, the Netherlands, the United Kingdom, and the United States (Snow et al., 2007). Although the concrete material events and circumstances and their interpretation differ between national contexts, the general dialectical principle of media practice and identity formation applies across nations.

Language provides another important context that characterizes the media field. Bourdieu's work proposes the existence of a 'linguistic habitus' (1991: 37). This habitus also guides how journalists apply language and, subsequently, how the dialectic of media practice unfolds. In addition, language is closely related to the very conception of the national community. For example, in the nineteenth century, the German language served as the defining marker for the construction of a pan-German national identity that could unite many of the fragmented political units of the disintegrating Holy Roman Empire.[25] Language, in this case, played a key role in the creation of the German nation. In Canada, English and French languages are also defining elements of the imagination of national communities. In November 2006, for example, the Canadian prime minister Stephen Harper recognized the French-speaking Québécois 'as a nation within Canada.' The French language serves as a defining characteristic of the Québécois as a nation.[26]

Benedict Anderson (1991) has argued that the invention of the printing press and the emergence of print capitalism had a catalytic impact on the normalization of national languages and the formation of modern nations. Print capitalism and the print media 'gave a new fixity to language' (Anderson, 1991: 44) and thus facilitated the formation of the nation as a language community.[27] From this viewpoint, the field of the media – the print media in particular – has a close historical connection with the national community and the formation of national identity.

The subfield of the newsprint media is an especially suitable site for observing the formation of national identity. The subsequent chapters deal with the role of immigration and immigrants in the dialectic of national identity formation as it unfolds the press. The media typically frames immigration as a matter of belonging to a national community. By presenting images of who belongs in the nation, who does not belong, and who should be allowed to become a member of the national community through immigration and naturalization, the media dialectically constructs meanings of nationhood. The media constructs these meanings through overlapping dialectical practices. On the one hand, it establishes dualisms and juxtaposes contradictory positions. On the other hand, it references reporting in material contexts and constructs corresponding meanings of immigration and national identity. This triple dialectic is the framework that I apply in the empirical analysis of the nation–immigration dialectic in Canadian and German newsprint media.

3 The Immigration Debate in Canada and Germany

Immigration law and immigration debate in Canada and Germany are embedded in particular historical, political, and cultural contexts. In this chapter I discuss these contexts and provide a brief introduction to their relevance to immigration debate. In addition, I provide a general overview of the recent legal reforms of and the media debates on immigration in both countries. With this discussion and overview, I will set the stage for the empirical analyses in parts 2 and 3.

Canada

Immigration and the National Imagination

Canada's identity as a settler society – defined by immigration and the integration of newcomers – has its origin in the country's history. This history includes the French settlement of Acadia, the subsequent arrival of British migrants, westward expansion to the Prairies, and the settlement of the west coast. Although Aboriginal populations played a considerable role in establishing European settlers, they have remained marginalized in the national imagination. Instead, Canada was imagined as a society of European settlement.

A driving force of immigration and settlement policy was the need for demographic growth and the demand for labour to support the ongoing colonization. For example, as early as the seventeenth century, French colonial expansion required significant numbers of immigrants and their labour. Later, Canada's westward expansion would have been impossible without the European immigrants who settled and farmed the Prairies.[1] Non-European immigrants also came to Canada, although they typically served as subordinated workers, such as Chinese immigrants who helped build the Canadian Pacific Railway (Knowles, 1997).

Formal citizenship established the settlers and immigrants on Canadian territory. The Immigration Act of 1910 provided British subjects with Canadian citizenship if they resided in Canada for three years or more. After 1946, with the Canada Citizenship Act, every person born on Canadian soil acquired Canadian citizenship. This principle of citizenship is known as *jus soli*.[2] It ensured that the second generation had a legitimate claim to be in Canada. First-generation immigrants were given the opportunity to naturalize after five years of residence in Canada. Legal practice thus formalized the imagination of Canada as a settler society, in which immigrants from abroad could acquire legitimate claim to Canadian territory. The *jus soli* principle and citizenship through naturalization remain cornerstones of Canadian citizenship today.

The Canadian state has been a global leader in establishing multiculturalism policy (Kelley and Trebilcock, 1998). This policy critically engaged with the European-origin identity of Canada and acknowledged the pluralist character of Canadian society. It recognized not only the diverse cultural identities of immigrant populations but also affirmed the rights of First Nations. In 1971, while Pierre Elliott Trudeau was prime minister, Canada adopted multiculturalism as an official policy. Under the Progressive Conservative government of Brian Mulroney, multiculturalism was incorporated into law, and in 1988 lawmakers passed the Multiculturalism Act. This act has provided a mandate for multicultural programs and initiatives, many of which affect immigrants and their settlement in Canada today. Multiculturalism has also had its critics. For example, some immigrants, such as writer Neil Bissoondath (1994), have publicly criticized multiculturalism policy as socially divisive. Others have argued that multiculturalism fails to unify Canadians under a common national identity (see, e.g., Day, 2000; Harles, 1998).

Immigration policy has also undergone important changes in the post-war period. Revisions to the immigration law in 1967 no longer included racial bias and regional origin as criteria for the selection of immigrants. The new policy triggered a shift in the origin of immigration away from mainly European countries to predominantly Asian countries. The 1976 Immigration Act further liberalized immigration to Canada and laid the foundation for today's immigration policies and practices. The act aligned immigration with economic interest and demographic goals, multiculturalism policy, and international obligations under the 1951 United Nations Convention and the 1967 United Nations Protocol relating to refugees. To meet these interests and goals, the 1976 act recognized different immigrant 'classes' to facilitate family reunification, meet Canada's humanitarian responsibilities, and select needed workers, investors, and business people (Knowles, 2000).

The 'classes' that were established in earlier immigration legislation continue to be the central feature of Canada's current immigration system. The *economic class* includes the so-called points system, which assesses immigrants based on their human capital. This class also enables investors, entrepreneurs, self-employed people, and, since 2008, individuals with Canadian work experience and recent post-secondary graduates from Canadian institutions to immigrate to Canada.[3] The *family class* serves the purpose of reuniting immigrants with their loved ones who still live abroad. The third category refers to *refugees.* Canada fulfils its humanitarian obligations to people in need of protection from prosecution and unfair punishment by offering them permanent residency and the prospect of citizenship. Although the family class included the greatest number of immigrants in the early 1980s, its share of all immigration to Canada declined over time. Instead, Canada's immigration officials increasingly focused on selecting economic-class immigrants.[4] This economic role of immigration features strongly in the imagination of Canada as a highly industrialized nation. Immigrants contribute to the economic development and global competitiveness of the nation.[5]

Immigration Reform

In the mid-1990s an immigration debate began that would eventually lead to a reform of immigration legislation. This debate culminated in the 2002 Immigration and Refugee Protection Act, which replaced the 1976 Immigration Act. Table 3.1 depicts important milestones of this debate. In 1995, the Legislative Review Advisory Group began reviewing the existing immigration legislation. A year later, the group published its report, *Not just numbers: A Canadian framework for future immigration.* This report made 172 recommendations and proposed a new legislative framework for the regulation of immigration. The report was the main trigger of a debate about overhauling the Canadian immigration

Table 3.1 Timeline of immigration reform in Canada

1996	November	Canada's Immigration Legislative Review Advisory Group's releases *Not just numbers: A Canadian framework for future immigration.*
1997	December	Auditor general releases report on immigration policy.
1998	March	UN High Commission for Refugees releases its comment on *Not just numbers.*
1999	January	Publication of *Building on a strong foundation for the 21st century: New directions for immigration and refugee policy and legislation*
2000	April	Tabling and first reading of the Immigration and Refugee Protection Act as Bill C-31; auditor general releases *Citizenship and Immigration Canada: The economic component of the Canadian immigration program.*
	June	Second reading of the act
2001	February	Immigration and Refugee Protection Act reintroduced as Bill C-11.
	May	Standing committee tables report, with proposed changes, for House of Commons after reviewing 150 submissions on the act.
	September	Airplane attacks in the USA (New York, Washington, DC)
	November	Bill C-11 receives royal assent.
	December	Public comment period of proposed regulations under Immigration and Refugee Protection Act begins (ends March 2002); section 145 of the Anti-Terrorism Act is enacted by Parliament (Bill C-36); Canadian and USA governments sign Smart Border Declaration.
2002	March	Release of the Standing Committee on Citizenship and Immigration's report with 76 recommendations for changes and adjustments
	June	Final regulations under the act are published along with government's response to the Standing Committee report; Citizenship and Immigration Canada introduces Permanent Resident Cards in response to the New Security Agenda; the Immigration and Refugee Protection Act comes into force.
	November	Tabling of Bill C-18, amending Citizenship Act
2003	October	Maher Arar returns to Canada.
2004	December	Safe Third Country Agreement with USA, closing the border for most refugees who seek asylum at border ports of entry

system (Wynnyckyj, 1998). It also established major themes that would frame the ensuing debate. It stated that the objectives of the newly proposed framework were

> to facilitate entry for persons who would enhance Canada's cultural and economic well-being, ... address the necessity for protecting our society from those whose entry into Canada could result in harm or danger to others [and] ... reflect Canada's international obligations and the will of the majority of our citizens to provide protection on Canadian territory to persons who truly need it. (Immigration Legislative Review Advisory Group, 1997: 1)

The subsequent debate was fuelled by a series of reports, including one by Canada's auditor general in 1997, which criticized the refugee acceptance process for being slow and open to abuse. The auditor general, Denis Desautels, urged Parliament 'to adopt a comprehensive strategy' to rectify existing problems (Office of the Auditor General of Canada, 1997). Another significant publication was the 1998 'Comments on *Not just numbers*' by the United Nations High Commission for Refugees, which criticized many of the recommendations made in the original 1995 document (United Nations High Commissioner for Refugees, 1998).

The series continued with the Canadian government's publication in early 1999 of *Building on a strong foundation for the 21st century: New directions for immigration and refugee policy and legislation,* which presented the guiding principles for an overhaul of existing immigration legislation. In this document the government reaffirmed its commitment to family reunification, the selection of skilled workers and business people, and the protection of refugees. In addition, it continued to link immigration to multiculturalism, referring to the 'global village' that brings 'the world to Canada and Canada to the world' (Citizenship and Immigration Canada, 1999: 2). Furthermore, the report presented plans to curtail dangers emanating from the entry of 'transnational criminal organizations, ranging from drug cartels to ethnically based criminal gangs' (2).

An important milestone in the immigration debate occurred in April 2000, when the federal government tabled the Immigration and Refugee Protection Act as Bill C-31. In the same month the auditor general released a report entitled *Citizenship and Immigration Canada – The economic component of the Canadian immigration program.*

This report noted that immigrant selection criteria should be improved to increase the benefits of immigration to the Canadian economy. This focus on the economic contribution of immigration coincided with an upswing in the business cycle and an annual unemployment rate that had dropped from 9.6 per cent in 1996 to 6.8 per cent in 2000 (Statistics Canada, 2006). The auditor general's report also stressed potential dangers and harm to Canadian society resulting from inadequate medical assessments and screens of immigrants' criminal records. In a press release, the auditor general, Denis Desautels, stated that 'deficiencies . . . seriously limit Canada's ability to get the economic and social benefits that immigration affords and seriously weaken the level of protection for Canadians' (Office of the Auditor General of Canada, 2000).

The following year was an important one for immigration reform. The federal election of November 2000 disrupted the passage of the Immigration and Refugee Protection Act. However, the Liberal government, which was reinstated in the election,[6] quickly reintroduced the act as Bill C-11 in February 2001. A significant event that occurred while the bill was reviewed in the House of Commons was the 11 September attacks in the United States, which was committed by immigrants and foreign visitors. After this event, international terrorism was discursively linked to immigration. In November of that year, the Immigration and Refugee Protection Act was passed by parliament, allowing for 'secret trials' and the indefinite detention and deportation of foreign visitors and refugee applicants. In a press release of February 2002, the federal ministry Citizenship and Immigration Canada stated that the new immigration law is 'tough for people who pose a threat to public security,' and immigration minister Denis Coderre noted explicitly that he supported 'the immigration and refugee elements of the government's security agenda.'

The Immigration and Refugee Protection Act maintained the basic structure of the three immigration classes.[7] Although the proportionate distribution of immigrants across these classes was already biased towards the economic class,[8] the federal government announced its intention in 2002 to increase the economic benefits of immigration by raising the number of immigrants who enter Canada under the 'skilled worker' category (Citizenship and Immigration Canada, 2002: no pages). This economic agenda was promoted at a time of a relatively low annual unemployment rate of 7.7 per cent (Statistics Canada, 2006), when the labour market was able to absorb skilled immigrants. After regulations were fine-tuned and the recommendations made by the Standing Committee on Citizenship and Immigration were addressed, the Immigration and Refugee Protection Act finally took effect in June 2002. In November 2002, Bill-C18 was tabled, amending the Citizenship Act and allowing Canadian authorities to deny and revoke citizenship on the grounds of national security.

Immigration Debate

Immigration debates in settler societies often revolve around the question of how immigration can benefit society. In such debates, 'the self-interest of the receiving country is taken for granted' (Li, 2003: 7). Immigration debate in Canada exemplifies how this self-interest can translate into positive attitudes towards immigration. A recent public-opinion study describes Canada as an 'outlier' in terms of public optimism towards immigration compared to other industrialized countries, including the United States (Gustin and Ziebarth, 2010: 979). Generally, Canadian public discourse on immigration supports the principles of economic and demographic growth, humanitarianism, and the need for national security, although discussions often emerge on fine-tuning and modifying particular aspects or the overall balance of these principles (Mahtani and Mountz, 2002).

A long-established aspect of immigration debate is the belief that Canada should receive economic benefits from immigration. In the Mulroney era, for example, this aspect entailed that immigration policy incorporate the interests of businesses, corporations, and organized labour (Veugelers, 2000). Anti-immigrant voices have applied similar economic arguments, but they depicted immigrants as competitors in a zero-sum competition for economic resources (Esses et al., 2001). According to such voices, immigrants flood the domestic labour market, undercut domestic wages and labour standards, and cost taxpayers millions of dollars every year in public services (Collacott, 2002; Stoffman, 2002). Following a general trend of the neoliberalization of public policy, the 1990s witnessed a shift in immigration policy towards emphasizing 'the "economic worth" and "self sufficiency" of immigrants' (Abu-Laban, 1998: 205). With the debate that began in 1996 and that led to the reform of the existing Immigration Act, this neoliberal orientation of immigration policy was consolidated.

Of course, the political debate of this period did not present an entirely one-sided picture of immigration as a purely economic matter. As I noted in the previous chapter, public discourses and debates involve multiple perspectives. In immigration debate, the various aspects of immigration are weighted against each other and evaluated based on a range of criteria that relate to party politics, political conviction, and practical considerations.[9] For example, in 2000, Rahmi Jaffer, of the conservative Canadian Alliance Party and a member of parliament, proposed to lift all immigration restrictions to increase the supply of immigrant labour and thereby stimulate business growth. In a dialectical riposte, this proposal was quickly rebuffed by Jaffer's fellow party members because of the apparent contradiction to the cultural, political, and security-related interests and visions of the Alliance Party.

Next to the economic utility of immigration, the 'culture'[10] aspect has played a role in immigration debate. For example, racial stereotyping of non-European immigrants as non-belonging has a history in the media (Mahtani, 2001). Until the 1960s, racialized representations affected the treatment of migrant workers by Canadian immigration officials and influenced migration policies (see, e.g., Satzewich, 1991). Racial and ethnic equality in the labour market had to be legislated by the 1986 Employment Equity Act. Despite anti-discrimination legislation and the official adoption of multiculturalism by the Canadian state, ethnic and racial unease with immigration often surface in contemporary immigration discourse. For example, Peter Li (2001) uncovered racial subtexts in discourses of immigration circulating through government documents, academic scholarship, and public opinion. Conservative voices have expressed 'concerns over increasing social tensions . . . and racial incidents' arising from the immigration of visible minorities (Collacott, 2002: 28).

This negative view of the cultural aspect of immigration, however, is not supported by all evidence. A public poll, for example, has suggested that a large majority of Canadians welcome immigrants of various religious and cultural backgrounds (Jiménez, 2006). The popular endorsement of multiculturalism policies seems to have translated into wider-ranging recognition of 'cultural' diversity and support for non-European immigration (Kelley and Trebilcock, 1998). A recent public-opinion survey confirms that the vast majority of Canadians 'share the opinion that immigration enriches, rather than negatively affects, national culture' (Gustin and Ziebarth, 2010: 980).

It is commonly accepted that the events of 11 September 2001 in the United States significantly changed immigration debate in Canada: security became a core concern of immigration policy. However, similarly to other aspects of immigration debate, security concerns were subject to critique. This critique became particularly vocal during the so-called Arar controversy, which unfolded in 2003. Maher Arar is a Syrian-born Canadian who was detained by US authorities at New York's John F. Kennedy Airport while he was on transit from Switzerland to Canada. After his detention he was deported to Syria. The controversy reached a peak with Arar's return to Canada in October 2003. The disclosure of evidence that he was tortured in a Syrian prison and allegations that the Canadian government cooperated in the unlawful detention and deportation triggered public outrage (Arar, 2006). The Arar controversy drew public attention to the negative impact of Canada's participation in the so-called war on terrorism on the country's self-image as a global human rights leader and a shepherd of humanitarianism. The controversy continued to smoulder even after the government's inquiry into Arar's case was formally completed in the fall of 2006 (Arar Commission, 2006).

An additional event that drew public attention to humanitarian aspects of immigration policy was the announcement of a Safe Third Country Agreement between Canada and the United States in December 2004. This agreement effectively denies entry to most refugees at US-Canada border points. Although this agreement may have eased political tension between the two neighbouring counties, it was also received with scepticism and disapproval by migration and human rights advocates.

Germany

Nationhood and Immigration

Germany's national identity also has deep historical roots. In response to the decline and political fragmentation of the Holy Roman Empire in the eighteenth century, a German-speaking cultural elite, including philosophers, writers, artists, and scholars, began promoting Pan-German nationalism. When Napoleon Bonaparte's armies occupied German-speaking territories in 1806, this emerging German national consciousness rapidly gained popularity. It played the role of a powerful catalyst for political change, leading up to the revolution of 1848 (Sheehan, 1992; Preuss, 2003).

Early on, German national identity was defined through the principle of negation. In particular, German nationalism was constructed as an alternative to French nationhood; it was based on ethnocultural rather than political principles of membership. For example, in the nineteenth century, the German nation builders of the Romantic movement, including Johann Gottfried Herder, Johann Gottlieb Fichte, and Ernst Moritz Arndt, constructed the German nation as a community speaking the same language, descending from a common history, and embracing a shared mythology.[11] They thus defined German national identity in ethnic terms and through the connection between the *Volk*,[12] ancestry, and territory. This identity stood in opposition to the French nation, which embraced an identity as a political community. In light of the absence of a state that included all German-speaking people, the Volk-centred approach of nation building suited the situation. In this way, negation – the first step in the dialectical process of identity formation – has been an important early characteristic of German nation building.[13]

Ethnic non-Germans, in particular immigrants, were excluded from the imagined national community.[14] This exclusionary attitude towards newcomers persisted throughout the Wilhelmine Empire, the Weimar Republic,[15] the Third Reich, and the Federal Republic of Germany[16] (Brubaker, 1992). Correspondingly, citizenship was defined in terms of ancestry, rather than through birthplace or naturalization. In 1913 the *jus sanguinis* principle was scripted into the citizenship law of the Wilhelmine Empire. According to this principle, citizenship was passed on from one generation to the next through blood lineage, rather than place of birth. The *jus sanguinis* principle of citizenship was maintained through the Weimar Republic, continued in Nazi Germany, and was eventually enshrined in article 116 of the constitutional law (*Grundgesetz*) of the Federal Republic of Germany. In agreement with this law, the German political leadership considered Germany a country of non-immigrants throughout most of the post–Second World War period.

The post-war treatment of migrants in Germany relates to the historically ethnic understanding of national identity. Immediately after the war, almost fifteen million ethnic German refugees from Eastern Europe arrived in West Germany (Münz et al., 1999). Although these individuals and families were crossing international borders, they were not considered immigrants but homecoming Germans. For example, the young Federal Republic of Germany described these migrants with the terms 'expelled persons' (*Vertriebene*) and 'persons expelled from home' (*Heimatvertriebene*). These terms associate the migrants with meanings of ethnic and cultural belonging (Wengeler, 1995). Other cross-border migration flows during the post-war period included the movement of ethnic Germans escaping the repressive East German regime (*Übersiedler*) or fleeing Stalinist oppression in Eastern Europe (*Aussiedler*). Again, these immigrants were imagined to belong automatically to the German national community.[17]

A parallel flow of economically motivated immigration consisted of fourteen million ethnic non-German workers, who arrived in Germany under the so-called guest-worker program that existed between 1955 and 1973.[18] Although eleven million of these migrant workers – many of whom came from Turkey, the former Yugoslavia, and Italy – returned to their countries of origin, many others stayed in Germany. After the guest-worker program was discontinued in 1974, this foreign population in Germany continued to grow due to natural increase and family reunification (Bade, 1997; Münz and Ulrich, 2000). Two terms were typically used to describe these migrants: 'guest workers' (*Gastarbeiter*), reflecting the intended role for these workers as temporary labour; and 'foreigners' (*Ausländer*), expressing their cultural and legal non-belonging. After 1970, towards the end of the program, the term 'foreigners' was used more often than 'guest workers,' reflecting a declining appreciation of the economic contribution made by these immigrants and an increasing disapproval of their presence in Germany (Wengeler, 1995).

A third major migration stream involved ethnic non-German asylum seekers and refugees, who have been admitted to Germany on humanitarian grounds. Annual numbers grew from a trickle of below 10,000 in the early 1970s to 438,200 migrants in 1992 (Münz et al., 1999: 58). With the increase in numbers, the negative rhetoric directed towards these migrants also grew more intense. By the end of the 1970s, the public media began using the terms 'economic refugees' (*Wirtschaftsflüchtlinge*) and 'bogus asylum seekers' (*Scheinasylanten*), questioning the migrant's legitimacy as refugees (Wengeler, 1995). To reduce the numbers of asylum seekers, the main parties in the German parliament reached the 'asylum compromise' (*Asylkompromiss*) in 1993. This compromise resulted in a change in German law and the toughening of refugee acceptance standards. Due to these changes, the number of asylum applicants dropped to 98,600 in 1998 (Bade, 1994; Münz et al., 1999: 58).

In the 1990s the image of Germany as an ethnically homogeneous nation was increasingly challenged. For example, the controversial leader of the Social Democratic Party, Oskar Lafontaine,[19] critiqued the existing law for favouring newly arriving ethnic German *Aussiedler* over foreigners who had lived and worked in Germany for generations. A scientific survey confirmed that most indicators of ethnocentric attitudes among Germans towards foreigners declined throughout the 1990s (Terwey, 2003). An opinion poll, however, also revealed that Germans continued to favour immigration by ethnic German *Aussiedler* over non-German migrants (Münz and Ulrich, 1998). Apparently, in the mid-1990s, Lafontaine's ideas reflected general public opinion only in a limited way. Nevertheless, a series of laws restricted the intake of ethnic Germans in the early 1990s.[20]

The political debate of immigration gained momentum in the late 1990s. In preparation for the 1998 federal election, Germany's political parties began developing competing models of immigration. The conservative Christian Social Union held on to immigration prevention and the ethnic principle of German identity. Its 'sister' party, the Christian Democratic Union, also campaigned on the platform that immigration should be restricted. The liberal Free Democratic Party and Social Democratic Party promoted a model of regulated but limited immigration based on economic and labour market needs. The Green Party (*Bündnis 90/die Grünen*) and the Party of Democratic Socialism argued for immigration on humanitarian grounds[21] (Zinterer, 2004: 250–62).

After the election, the Social Democratic Party and the Green Party formed a government coalition. This coalition sought to discontinue the previous sixteen-year period of conservative 'policy on foreigners' (*Ausländerpolitik*). In fact, immigration was explicitly mentioned in the coalition contract between the two parties (SPD & BÜNDNIS 90/DIE GRÜNEN, 1998: paragraph 9.7). The pursuit of a reform of German citizenship law and immigration framework now became official government policy. This shift in policy coincided with a revival of the idea that immigration can be useful to German's economy. Although this economic argument was dormant for almost twenty years, its resurrection illustrates the pervasiveness of the economic perspective in post-war German migration debate (Wengeler, 2006: 16). Matthias Hell (2005: 77–115) observes that this economic argument for immigration was not necessarily associated with a greater acceptance of ethnic diversity among Germans. Rather, the viewpoint that Germany should remain a culturally homogeneous society, that immigration threatens social cohesion, and that Germany could economically benefit from immigration may have coexisted in public discourse during the late 1990s.

Immigration Country Germany?

Against the historical backdrop of ethnic-German national belonging a political debate unfolded that challenged the existing identity of Germany. Table 3.2 presents the highlights of this portentous debate. In the political context of the late 1990s, the long-standing paradigm that Germany is a non-immigrant country began to falter. Contemporary commentators observed that a paradigm change had occurred in German politics around the turn of the millennium. In an article originally published in 2000, migration scholar Klaus Bade suggests that the paradigm that Germany is an immigration country had now gained official recognition (2004: 469). Likewise, in 2002, Karl-Heinz Meier-Braun remarked that politicians across the political spectrum had generally accepted the paradigm change by 2001 (2002: 30).[22]

This newly emerging paradigm of German identity was hotly debated before the 2002 federal election. The Bavarian president, Edmund Stoiber of the Christian Social Union, declared during his campaign for chancellor that 'Germany is even today not an immigrant country' (quoted in Meier-Braun, 2002: 134). While the conservative parties continued to favour the ethnic/cultural principle of nationhood, social-democratic and liberal parties supported an immigration regime based on economic criteria and labour-market need. The Green Party and the Party of Democratic Socialism advocated for immigration guided by humanitarian considerations (Zinterer, 2004: 256).

Whether the German public accepted the paradigm shift from non-immigration country to immigrant nation is a matter of debate. Some commentators suggested that, between 1998 and 2002, such a shift occurred in Germany's civic institutions and the majority of its population (see, e.g., Meier-Braun, 2002; Bade, 2004; Krause, 2004). Data from the European Social Survey show that the acceptance of immigration was higher in 2002 in Germany than in other European countries (Fertig, 2004). Other observers, however, maintained that the paradigm of Germany as an immigration country never shared 'undivided agreement' in politics or public opinion (Renner, 2004: 266).[23]

At the legal and administrative levels, the implementation of the new paradigm was initiated by the reform of Germany's citizenship law in 1999. With this reform, the Social Democratic/Green government introduced territorial *jus soli* elements into the long-standing ancestral *jus sanguinis*-based law.[24] Jürgen Gerdes and Thomas Faist (2006) interpret the new citizenship law as a compromise between two competing models of republican citizenship, and as a reflection of the

Table 3.2 Timeline of the German immigration law

2000	February	The public debate of immigration begins with the announcement of the German Green Card.
	July	Federal minister of the interior Otto Schily orders an independent commission, with Rita Süssmuth as chairperson.
	September	First meeting of the 'Süssmuth commission'
2001	June	The main opposition party (CDU) announces its own immigration program based on the recommendations of the 'Müller' commission.
	July	The Süssmuth commission presents its final report.
	August	The ministry of the interior introduces the proposed 'Law for the Management and Limitation of Immigration' (*Gesetz zur Steuerung und Begrenzung der Zuwanderung*).
	December	The conservatively governed states in the upper house of parliament (*Bundesrat*) oppose the law and demand revisions.
2002	March	The lower and upper houses of parliament pass the law; the opposition parties challenge the procedural correctness of the vote.
	December	The Federal Constitutional Court (*Bundesverfassungsgericht*) nullifies the law due to procedural errors.
2003	May	The law passes the lower house of parliament for the second time.
	June	The upper house of parliament rejects the law.
	September	Formal negotiations between the government coalition and the conservative opposition begin.
	October	A parliamentary committee is established after negotiations gridlock.
2004	March	Terror attacks in Madrid
	May	The Green Party threatens to pull out of negotiations, but party leaders reach a compromise.
	June	The negotiating parties accept the new proposal.
	July	The law passes the upper and lower houses of parliament; the German president signs the law.
2005	January	The immigration law takes effect.

Sources: Storr and Albrecht, 2005; Bundesministerium des Innern, 2005

transformation from an ethnic to a political framework of national belonging. As the next step on the road towards formally becoming an immigration country, Chancellor Gerhard Schröder announced the German Green Card in February of 2000. The Green Card was supposed to attract foreign IT specialists from non–European Union countries and enable them to settle in Germany for up to five years.[25] The Green Card initiative marked the symbolic departure from the non-immigration paradigm and set a course that aligned immigration policy with economic interests.

The Green Card initiative was followed by the more ambitious project of an immigration law. In July 2000, the federal minister of the interior, Otto Schily, appointed Rita Süssmuth, a highly respected opposition politician and former president of the lower house of parliament, to lead an independent commission to develop guiding principles for the proposed law. Members of this commission included twenty-one migration experts representing political parties, academia, industry, labour organizations, churches, and the ethnic community. A year after its initiation, in July 2001, the 'Süssmuth commission' presented its final report, which was supposed to be a blueprint for Germany's first immigration law. In this report, the commission recommended a Canadian-style points system to attract highly skilled immigrants, envisioned comprehensive measures tolegally and socially integrate Germany's foreign residents, and promoted humanitarian immigration. These recommendations expanded on the new citizenship legislation, which took effect in the previous year.

Based on the Süssmuth commission's recommendations, Schily introduced an immigration bill in parliament in August 2001. Although this bill passed both houses, it was struck down by Germany's Federal Constitutional Court (*Bundesverfassungsgericht*) based on a procedural error during the vote in parliament. Subsequent negotiations continued throughout 2003, with a revised version of the law taking effect on 1 January 2005. In the final law, the points system was dropped, humanitarian aspects were scaled back, and immigration was restricted rather than enabled. In the eyes of many pro-immigration advocates, the new law failed to turn Germany into a true immigration country (Bendel, 2004; Krause, 2004).

Despite the initial political momentum in support of immigration, the law that eventually passed failed to achieve its main goals and did not implement many of the Süssmuth commission's original recommendations. Apparently, during the long debate of the law, which stretched over several years, public and political support for the innovative aspects of the proposed law eroded.

Immigration Debate

While the idea for a new immigration law grew out of an emergent paradigm shift towards immigration during the 1990s, the final outcome of the law is a product of the political and public debate that occurred between 2001 and 2004. During this period the pendulum of public and political opinion apparently swung back towards rejecting immigration.

Tanja Zinterer (2004) examined this period, in particular the Süssmuth commission's effort to formalize the paradigm shift from non-immigrant country to immigrant country. The inclusion of politicians and interest groups in the commission's membership was a calculated attempt by the ruling Social Democratic/Green government coalition to legitimate the pro-immigration paradigm among a wide segment of the German population. Zinterer concludes that the government had a window of opportunity to achieve its goals during the initial period of the immigration debate. During this period the German public was receptive to formalizing the new paradigm into law. Even the conservative opposition's counter-commission – the so-called Müller commission – supported the paradigm switch[26] (CDU Deutschland, 2001a, b).

A few years later, however, it became clear that the Süssmuth commission had failed to 'create a lasting social consensus for its policy recommendations' (Zinterer, 2004: 297). The commission had focused on making sensible political recommendations and did not see it as its primary mandate to shape public opinion in such a manner that it would support the image of Germany as an immigration country. By refraining from playing a more active role in the public opinion process, it permitted public sentiments rejecting immigration and multiculturalism to recover.[27] A series of polls commissioned by the European Union confirm this trend: support for multiculturalism increased in the former West Germany between 1997 and 2000, but it had declined again by 2003[28] (EUMC, 2005: 13). The window of opportunity to formally turn Germany into an immigration country had closed.

The long-lasting debate of the immigration law was characterized by strategic manoeuvring and political 'power struggles' (Meier-Braun, 2002: 145). Nevertheless, the course of political discourse could not have been re-charted without convincing arguments. The existing literature describes some of the arguments that circulated in public discourse during the debate of the immigration law. One argument emphasizes the economic benefits of immigration. For example, the influential industrial leader Hans-Olaf Henkel (2003) suggested that the initially proposed immigration law was a political response to the business community's demand for skilled labour. A counter-argument, however, was that immigration constitutes competition for German workers. Another argument, relating to Germany's persisting ethnic-national identity, sees immigration as a threat to the traditional understanding of nationhood. What could not be anticipated by the Süssmuth commission was the increasing association of immigration with international terrorism following the airplane attacks of 11 September 2001 in New York and Washington, the subsequent wars in Afghanistan and Iraq, and the 2004 bombing attacks in Madrid. These events placed immigrants and foreigners under 'general suspicion' (*Generalverdacht*) of criminal activity and terrorism (Bendel, 2004: 206).

Aspects of the Media Debate on Immigration

Canada's reform of its immigration act and Germany's preparation of its first immigration law occurred roughly around the same time. The considerable overlap between the periods enables me to compare the debates on new immigration legislation in both countries.[29] In the remainder of this chapter, I present a preliminary assessment of these debates as they occurred in the Canadian and German newsprint media. For this purpose, I selected a systematic sample of 490 articles from the *Calgary Herald, National Post, Ottawa Citizen, Toronto Star,* and *Vancouver Sun,* and 609 articles from the *Frankfurter Allgemeine Zeitung, Stuttgarter Zeitung, Süddeutsche Zeitung, Tageszeitung,* and *Bild Zeitung,* which covered the immigration reforms of both countries (see appendix for details). At this point, I am offering a general, quantitative overview of the relative importance of various aspects of immigration.[30] In particular, I examine the frequency with which the media applied certain aspects of immigration in their coverage of legal immigration reform in Canada and Germany.

This analysis revealed that the media focused on five aspects with considerable frequency in the debate of immigration. The *economic* aspect of immigration addresses issues of labour migration, the labour market impacts of immigration, and other economic considerations related to immigration and immigration law. For example, in a Canadian context,

British Columbia's (BC) provincial minister responsible for immigration, Murray Coell, supported immigration policy under the condition that 'communities throughout B.C. will benefit from new investment and a more diverse workforce' (Coell, 2004); and former labour minister Joe Fontana said that 'we will have to attract many more immigrants' to increase Canadian economic productivity (Canadian Press, 2004). Economic aspects can be applied in positive and negative ways. For example, statements in the German debate suggest, on the one hand, that 'immigration of highly-qualified people increases the growth potential of the German economy and contributes to the creation of employment' (*Süddeutsche Zeitung,* 2002a) and, on the other hand, that 'we have almost four million statistically assessed unemployed. We cannot fight unemployment by moving additional workers into the country' (*Tageszeitung,* 2001).

Another aspect of the immigration debate relates to *humanitarianism.* Both Canada and Germany have a history of supporting humanitarian migration. The efforts to offer refuge to migrants in need of protection can reflect particular practices of national identity formation, as I have argued in chapter 1. The humanitarian aspect is represented by the following statement: 'Victims of racist violence and traumatized refugees must be allowed to stay immediately' (*Tageszeitung,* 2005). The press often linked immigration to humanitarianism in positive ways, for example, the belief that refugees deserve protection. However, the media also presents a negative view of humanitarian immigration. For example: 'When Ahmed Ressam, an Algerian suspected of plotting a millennial bombing . . ., first came to Canada, he entered using a false passport, admitted being a suspected terrorist and was nevertheless allowed to stay in the country on "compassionate" grounds' (*National Post,* 2000b: A19).

A third aspect associates immigration with *danger.* This aspect emphasizes crime, threats to 'national security,' and social problems. Arguments against immigration often hinge on the perception that some immigrants are destructive to democracy and social order (see, e.g., Collacott, 2002; Stoffman, 2002). For example, a high-level government administrator defended the Immigration Act in the *Calgary Herald* because 'it is removing people who constitute a threat to Canadians who shouldn't be here and don't have a right to be here' (Mertl, 1996: 28). In the same vein, the *Vancouver Sun* reports: 'The immigration department has been flooded with up to 100 media calls a day . . . since the terrorist attacks in New York and Washington almost three weeks ago. The interest stems from signals from the U.S. administration that it believes Canada's immigration and refugee procedures are too lax, increasing the threat of terrorist infiltration over the Canada-U.S. border' (Naumetz, 2001: A9).

The '*culture*' aspect of immigration has also influenced immigration and policy debate. For example, the *Süddeutsche Zeitung* (2002b) reported that 'party leader Friedrich Merz . . . thinks that the law indicates a change towards a multicultural society, which is rejected by the [Christian Democratic] Union.' The 'culture' aspect can appear in positive and negative forms: as a defence or rejection of multiculturalism, or as an expression or rebuff of racism, ethnic discrimination, and Eurocentric hegemony.

A final aspect, which occurred at considerable frequency in the media debates, relates to *political* considerations of immigration. The academic literature has related this aspect, for example, to the activities of the Economic Council of Canada (1991), which explored whether raising immigration levels and the resulting growth of Canada's population and economy would offer significant strategic benefits vis-à-vis the United States and European countries (cited in Li, 2003: 61–2).[31] In the media, the political aspect is represented by statements like 'It is rumored that federal politicians are loath to offend the powerful immigration consultant lobby which has deep roots in various ethnic communities' (Suelman, 1997: A19). In some cases, this aspect associates immigration with negative political consequences to the Canadian state. For example, a front-page article in the *Ottawa Citizen* (2001: A1) reported that the proposed immigration law could erode Canada's sovereignty.

I examined the frequency with which these aspects of immigration occurred in the media debates of immigration legislation in Canada in Germany. Figure 3.1 shows the four most common aspects in the Canadian and German newspapers.[32] The figure illustrates important differences between the two countries in the manner in which the media debated immigration legislation. In the Canadian sample, the most frequent aspect refers to the danger of immigration. A detailed reading of the data showed that in the majority of cases, the danger aspect was used to argue against immigration. The second most frequent aspect associates immigration with humanitarian considerations. In most cases, this aspect presented immigration in a favourable light. In a few cases, however, the humanitarian aspect also argued against immigration. The support for humanitarian immigration confirms my expectation based on the existing literature (see, e.g., Dauvergne, 2005).

Figure 3.1 Distribution of aspects in immigration debate

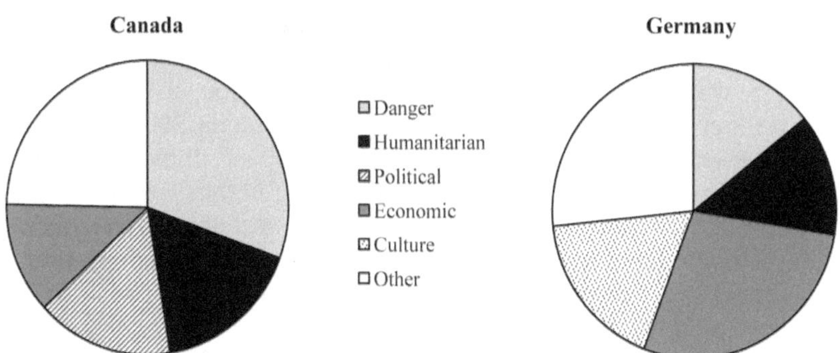

The political aspect ranked third. The relatively frequent occurrence of the political aspect suggests that media debate often discusses the political ramifications of immigration. In the majority of cases, this aspect was neither positive nor negative but neutral towards immigration.[33] Economic considerations define the fourth most common aspect. A considerable number of articles associated immigration with economic benefits. A smaller number of articles alerted readers to the negative economic consequences of immigration.

The German debate differs from the Canadian debate. In the German sample, the economic aspect occurred more frequently than any other aspect. Overall, economic arguments were used mostly in a positive manner. For example, newspapers frequently argued that immigration will bring needed skilled labour to Germany. Occasionally, newspapers also printed negative economic arguments, suggesting, for example, that immigration increases unemployment. The culture aspect was the second most frequent aspect. Interestingly, this aspect was of little relevance in the Canadian debate. In the German sample, the 'culture' aspect is often related to the integration of immigrants and foreigners. The danger and humanitarian aspects are roughly equally represented in the sample.[34] The danger aspect usually argued against immigration. The sequences associated with the humanitarian aspect, by contrast, tended to present pro-migration arguments, for example, for admitting people in need. A considerable proportion of this aspect, however, also expressed negative views of immigration.

The distribution of aspects in the Canadian and German debates permits some initial comparisons. In the Canadian media, the dominance of the danger aspect illustrates the importance of the viewpoint that immigration constitutes a threat to Canada and its population. Given the media's general attention to the airplane attacks on the World Trade Center in New York and the Pentagon in Washington in 2001, and the ensuing 'war on terrorism,' the negative association of immigration with danger does not seem to be surprising (Tsoukala, 2008a, 2008b).[35] The overwhelmingly negative use of this aspect tinted the entire Canadian immigration debate in a negative hue. In the German debate, by contrast, associations between immigration and danger were made with relatively low frequency. Contrary to Canada, where immigration is predominantly framed as a threat, the German media pays greater attention to other aspects.

As I anticipated, the economic aspect was included among the four most frequent aspects in the Canadian debate. However, given the strong economic orientation of Canadian immigration policy, I also expected this aspect to be more prominently represented in the debate and to take first or second rank. Apparently, economic considerations are not the top concern in the media's discussion of immigration. An explanation for the relatively weak representation of the economic aspect may be that media commentators agree on the existing economic orientation of Canadian immigration policy and do not see much need to debate this matter further.

In the German debate, however, economic-based arguments were on top of the agenda. In contrast to Canada, Germany did not have an economically oriented immigration policy. In fact, Germany's new immigration law still prohibits significant economically oriented immigration. Under these circumstances, the media may have perceived a need to bring this matter to public attention and engage in an extensive discussion about the economic merits of immigration.

Notably absent from the top four aspects in the Canadian debate is 'culture.'[36] Although Canada has official multiculturalism legislation and Canadian politicians, government administration, and scholars place great value on the enrichment of Canadian 'culture' through immigration, the newsprint media apparently does not attribute the same importance to this aspect of immigration. The lack of discussion of cultural aspects of immigration may, again, suggest that the media is comfortable with the current relationship between immigration and multiculturalism, and does not perceive this relationship as problematic. While the 'cultural' aspect was not represented among the top four aspects in the Canadian debate, it ranked second in the German debate. This difference may indicate that anxieties about the 'cultural' impacts of immigration are – unlike in Canada – a contested issue in the German media.

Patterns over Time

So far, my preliminary analysis has offered a basic but static overview of the immigration debates in Canada and Germany. It has addressed neither the dynamic nature of these debates nor the impact of particular events. The following analyses therefore examine the immigration debates in their temporal context.

Canada

Media coverage of immigration reform in Canada was inconsistent over time. Figure 3.2 shows the frequency of sampled articles over time. The temporal patterns correspond with important developments in the political conception and implementation of the Immigration and Refugee Protection Act. After the initial review of the 1978 Immigration Act in 1996, the debate subsided to some extent in 1997. The discussion heated up again in 1998 with the release of the United Nations commentary on *Not just numbers.* It subsequently reached an initial peak in 1999, coinciding with the publication of the government's white paper *Building on a strong foundation for the 21st century.* In 2000, media attention declined slightly, although the new legislation was first tabled that year. Immigration debate, however, reached its second and overall peak in 2001, when the legislation was reintroduced and passed by parliament, and when the September 11 attacks on New York and Washington occurred. Thereafter, media attention to the immigration law steadily declined, reaching its low point in 2004.

In the next step of this preliminary analysis, I examined the relative frequency of the danger, humanitarian, political, and economic aspects over time. Based on the existing literature, I expected that media reporting related to the dangers of immigration would correlate closely with the attacks of 11 September 2001. According to this expectation, the relative frequency of the danger aspect would increase in 2001 and subsequent years. Furthermore, I anticipated that the humanitarian, political, and economic aspects would be represented more consistently over time.

Figure 3.2 Frequency of articles over time in Canada

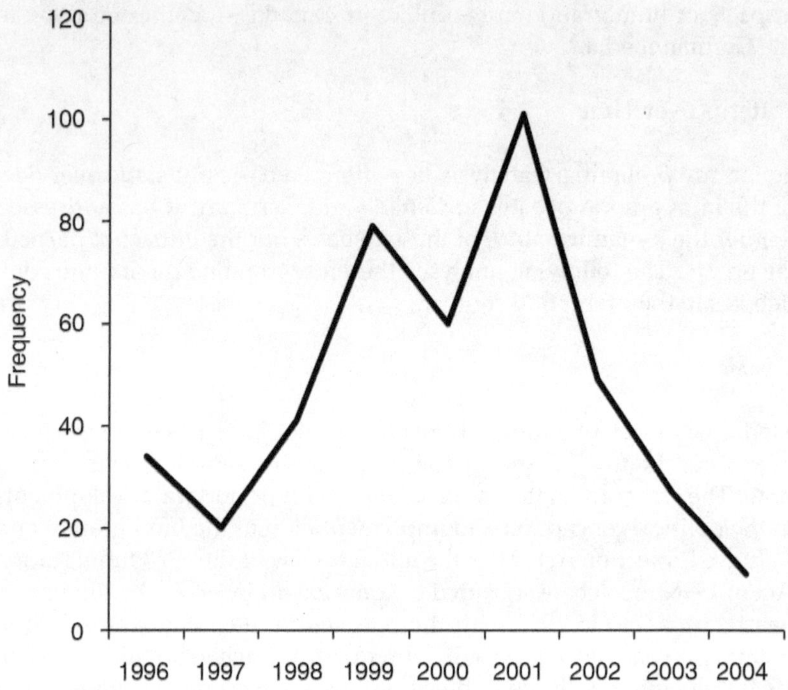

Figure 3.3 depicts how often an aspect occurred in a given year as a percentage of the total coverage in that year. The danger aspect, in particular, did not fluctuate as much as I expected. With the exception of 2001, when it captured roughly one-third of the media debate, the danger aspect represented between one-fifth (19.1 per cent in 2000) and one-fourth (24.3 per cent in 1997) of the debate. Furthermore, a closer reading of the data showed that the negative orientation of the danger aspect did not increase in 2001. Immigration was associated negatively with danger long before the 2001 airplane attacks in the United States. Apparently, danger and fear of immigration were not ad hoc responses to September 11, but rather more consistently and systematically engrained in Canadian immigration discourse. If the airplane attacks in New York and Washington had an effect on the immigration debate in Canada, it was small and short-lived.

The humanitarian aspect, however, fluctuated to a greater degree. In 2003, relatively few articles presented humanitarian arguments. One

Figure 3.3 Relative frequency of aspects over time in Canada

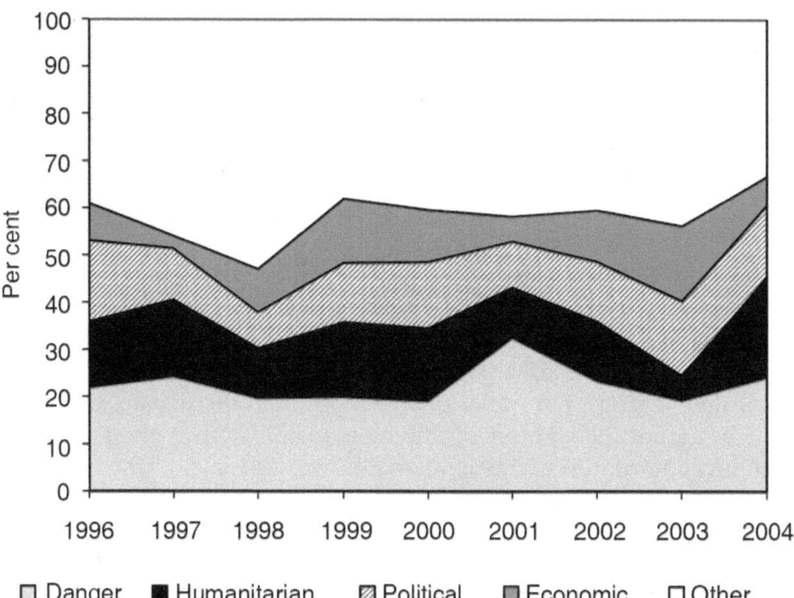

year later, the share of the humanitarian aspect climbed to roughly one-fifth of the media coverage of the debate. Interestingly, when I examined the data more closely, I found that negative arguments related to immigration were relatively rare in 2001, suggesting that the events of September 11 did not cast a negative light on humanitarian immigration. Furthermore, the 'war on terrorism' did not result in a dramatic increase in the negative association between immigration and humanitarianism. In fact, towards the end of the study period, when the Arar controversy occupied the newsrooms, humanitarianism was represented in a more positive light than in previous years. This pattern may suggest that the media was dissatisfied with violations of humanitarian principles. The humanitarian shortcomings of the 'war on terrorism' may have produced a counter-effect of rallying support for humanitarian immigration.

The political aspect also experienced a considerable degree of fluctuation, with a peak in 1996 and a low point in 1998.[37] However, during the height of the immigration debate, between 1999 and 2002, the political aspect remained relatively stable. Apparently, the politics behind immigration legislation were a matter of continuous media interest.

The economic aspect reached its relative high point in 2003 and its low point in 2001. Interestingly, 2001 was also the year when more articles were published than in any other year during the study period (see figure 3.2). Over the course of this year the Immigration and Refugee Protection Act was reintroduced to parliament, debated, and eventually passed into law. During this critical year in the creation of the act, the economic perspective received relatively little attention from the press compared to other perspectives. In absolute terms, however, the economic aspect was a relatively constant feature of immigration debate.

Germany

Similarly to Canada, German media attention to the immigration law also fluctuated over time. Figure 3.4 depicts the temporal patterns of coverage.[38] During the initial twelve months of the debate, the media paid a significant amount of attention to the immigration law. This high level of interest corresponds with the discussion of the law in the federal parliament, which included the controversial vote in the lower house of parliament of 22 March 2002, and the decision by the Federal Constitutional Court to annul the law. Throughout 2003 the volume of articles declined, reaching a low point in the second half of that year. This low point occurred at a time when parliamentary parties were negotiating about the content of the proposed law and reached an apparent impasse. Media interest in the topic increased again thereafter. Coinciding with the bombing attacks in Madrid, media attention to the immigration law peaked in the first half of 2004.[39] At this time, political negotiations and party manoeuvring also intensified, leading up to the final passage of the law by both houses of parliament. In the remainder of the study period, the volume of articles remained at a modest level.[40]

Next, I examined the relative frequency of aspects over time. Figure 3.5 shows the percentages that the economic, danger, culture, and humanitarian aspects captured of the debate at different time intervals. Although the economic aspect fluctuated during the study period, it never declined below 10 per cent. This aspect was relatively frequent in the first eighteen months of the immigration debate. It peaked in the second half of 2003, when the overall debate of the immigration law was relatively quiet (seen figure 3.4). Overall, the economic aspect was a relatively stable ingredient in the immigration debate. A closer examination of the newspaper coverage further reveals that the economic

Figure 3.4 Frequency of German articles over time in Germany

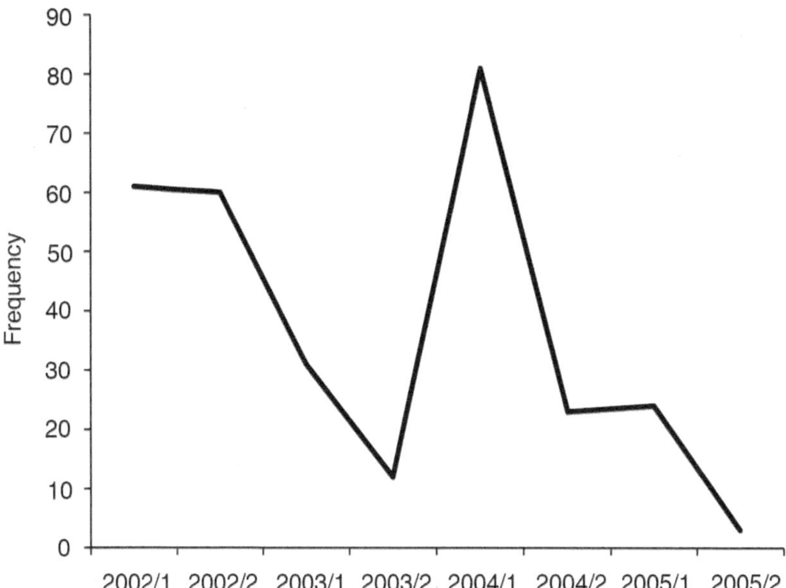

arguments in favour of immigration were used relatively consistently throughout the study period. The economic argument against immigration was less consistent and was clustered in periods between mid-2001 and mid-2002, and between 2003 and mid-2004.

The danger and culture aspects fluctuated to a greater extent than the economic aspect. The danger aspect was the most inconsistent. In 2002 and 2003, relatively few newsprint articles associated immigration with danger. This situation changed dramatically in the first half of 2004, when the danger aspect captured almost 40 per cent of the entire debate. This interval also marked the overall peak in the frequency of articles (see figure 3.4). This remarkable turn towards associating immigration with danger followed the Madrid attacks of 11 March. In chapter 8 I explore the link between the events of Madrid and the representation of immigration to Germans as danger in greater detail.

The 'culture' aspect also fluctuated to a considerable degree. Between mid-2002 and mid-2003, approximately every fourth argument presented in the debate referred to cultural aspects of immigration. Thereafter, the occurrence of the culture aspect declined in relative

Figure 3.5 Relative frequency of aspects over time in Germany

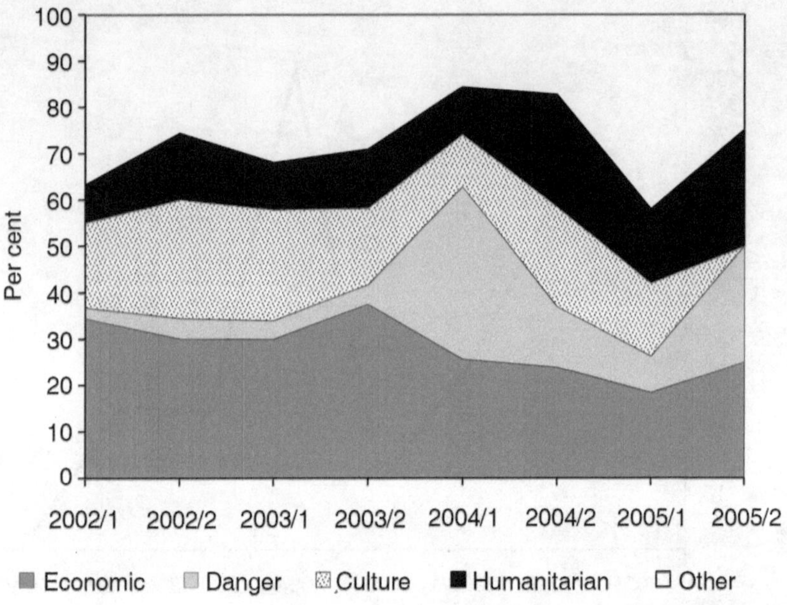

terms. In the hottest period of the immigration debate, the first half of 2004, the 'culture' aspect captured about 10 per cent of the debate. In the final interval of the study period (in which the overall count of articles was very low), this aspect was absent from the sample.

The humanitarian aspect occurred relatively consistently over the period. Despite this relative consistency, the press used humanitarian arguments to a somewhat greater extent in the second half of 2004 and 2005. In light of the existing literature, which in my view tends to neglect the humanitarian consideration of immigration discourse in Germany, I was surprised about the strong and consistent representation of this aspect.

Conclusion

In this chapter, I have offered an overview of immigration debates in Canada and Germany. First, I reviewed the historical contexts of immigration and nationhood as a backdrop for the new immigration legislation in both countries. Second, I presented a preliminary assessment of the media debates of these legislative reforms. This assessment of the media debate of immigration reform in both countries sketches out the character of the debates in the two countries. By mapping different aspects of the debate against the time scale, I also related the debate to particular political and news events. Although I used Canada and Germany as case studies, the analysis has remained inductive and exploratory in nature; that is, I did not presuppose particular identities of settler society or ethnic nation when I sampled or analysed the data.

The focus on various aspects of immigration enabled me to organize the debates according to different perspectives and frameworks of argumentation. This strategy resonates with the dialectical nature of media discourse. It describes the various perspectives that commentators assume in reference to the same issue, that is, immigration legislation, and shows how the various viewpoints and multiple interests coexist. In a way, this analysis of various coexisting aspects illustrates how media debate of immigration simulates a conversation among multiple speakers.

The dynamic patterns of media attention devoted to Canada's immigration reform and Germany's immigration law permits an initial comparison between the two countries. In both countries, media coverage ebbed and flowed with the level of attention devoted to immigration by the national parliaments. However, the media debates were influenced not only by the political processes in the two countries but also by external events that were discursively linked to immigration. Such events included the 'war on terrorism' and the bombing attacks in Madrid. In response to these events, the contents of the debates changed and the relative weight of aspects shifted.

A distinction can be made between aspects which the media mobilized on a sporadic or ad hoc basis and aspects which they used relatively consistently. Interesting national differences exist in this respect. These differences emerged from an exploratory, inductive empirical analysis. An example is the danger aspect. In the Canadian debate, it occurred relatively consistently. The events of 11 September 2001 had only a short-term impact on the relative occurrence of this aspect. This finding raises interesting questions about the relationship between material events and discursive practices. The New York and Washington airplane attacks may not have had the effect on Canadian immigration debate I anticipated. Rather, this finding provokes the thesis that danger is a structural element of immigration debate in Canada. Conversely, in the German debate, the association of danger with immigration increased considerably after the 2004 attacks in Madrid. In the German case, the danger aspect may have served opportunistic politics, which, in the end, appear to have been successful in derailing a proposed law that would have implemented a pro-immigration paradigm.

In addition, different aspects receive different weights in the two national debates. For example, in the German debate, economic issues are the lead topic. This orientation of the debate suggests that the German media concentrates on fundamental effects of immigration, which would be consistent with a society that is just coming to terms with being a nation of immigrants or non-immigrants. Conversely, in the Canadian debate, the economic aspect is not the major issue. It may seem paradoxical that Canadian immigration policy selects most immigrants based on economic criteria, but the press has not put this aspect on top of its agenda. Apparently, the Canadian media accept the economic utility of immigration as a fact, and focuses instead on more contentious issues, such as the danger emanating from immigration.[41] Cultural aspects receive even less attention than economic matters in the Canadian debate, which further indicates that commentators in the Canadian debate have long consented to the cultural changes created by immigration. That the German press pays greater attention to cultural aspects of immigration implies that anxieties about cultural change continue to be an issue in Germany. Rainer Geißler (2003: 23) argued in the midst of the German immigration debate that 'Canadian multiculturalism fits considerably better to the Western (*abendländische*) norms than the German policy on foreigners.' Can the relative decline of the culture aspect in the second half of the debate be interpreted as a departure from the traditional treatment of immigration as a cultural threat and an implicit endorsement of multiculturalism by the German media? Chapter 8 will explore this question.

The preliminary analysis, which I presented above, can be interpreted in light of the dialectical formation of national identity. For example, in an apparent contradiction to Canada's reputation as a country that welcomes its immigrants, the media discusses immigration first and foremost as a danger. From the viewpoint of dialectical national identity formation, this perspective of immigration, however, makes sense. The Canadian media may project an image of difference and danger as a practice of negating the national self. That the danger aspect was relatively consistent throughout the debate may indicate the systematic nature of this practice. The negation, however, may be followed by a subsequent second negation, in which the Other is incorporated into the national imaginary. In the German debate, however, the danger aspect was not represented as consistently. Likely, it was deployed not as a systematic aspect of negation and identity formation, but rather as an ad hoc mechanism to argue against immigration.

Instead, in the German debate, the press used the economic aspect more frequently and with relative consistency. Given the existing literature's emphasis on the relationship between ethnic-national identity and immigration policies, I would have expected the 'culture' aspect to be represented even more prominently in Germany's immigration debate. Perhaps this relatively weak performance of the 'culture' aspect and the strong showing of the economic aspect reflect a paradigm shift away from the closed, ethnic conception of German nationhood towards an identity that emphasizes economic achievement and welfare. Immigration would occupy an important position to contribute to this identity. Such an interpretation would also be consistent with Germany's post-war policies on migration and foreigners that situated economic growth in its centre.

A final interesting result of the analysis in this chapter is the relatively strong representation of humanitarian arguments in the debates of both countries. Catherine Dauvergne (2005) has suggested that liberally minded immigration countries use humanitarian immigration as a tool for nation building. Does the strong performance of the humanitarian aspect in Germany indicate a departure from the nation's traditional self-perceptions as an ethnic society and suggest a convergence with nation-building processes in both Canada and Germany? Investigating such practices of identity formation in further detail will be the task of the following chapters. Parts 2 and 3 will explore the 'context-specific fillings' (Wengeler, 2006: 13) of the aspects, which I have examined in a cursory manner in this chapter.

PART TWO

Immigration Debate in a Settler Society

4 Immigration as Danger

Conventional wisdom holds that the securitization of immigration relates closely to the attacks of 11 September 2001 in the United States and the subsequent 'war on terrorism.'[1] International mobility has been a major concern in the context of these events. Taliban leaders were able to escape US forces by moving across the Afghan-Pakistani border; Al-Qaeda was so evasive because it is a transnationally highly mobile network; and the fund-raisers of 'terrorism' transgressed national boundaries. Most importantly, the attacks on the twin towers of the World Trade Center and the Pentagon were committed by immigrants and visa holders.[2] In particular, media reports portrayed Canada as the 'weak link' enabling the tragedy in New York to occur (Adelman, 2002: 15), and asked whether Canada was 'complicit in allowing a "terrorist" haven to exist with its borders' (Jiwani, 2005: 16). The danger associated with immigration is that any immigrant can *potentially* commit atrocities and murder civilians. Taken-for-granted convention contends that in the unusual times after September 11, immigration policy must protect citizens from serious threats and grave danger.

If the catastrophe of the airplane attacks in New York and Washington fundamentally changed immigration debate, the date of 11 September 2001 should stand as a defining marker after which the media associates immigration with danger, in particular terrorism. In the context of the United States, a report[3] by the 'low immigration' think tank Center for Immigration Studies (2007, no page) asserts that prior to 11 September 2001, 'The lack of rigor in this [immigration-related] journalism has in some way obscured the nature and source of the threat (militant Islam)'[4] (McGowan, 2003: 9). This report suggests that the media neglected its responsibility to scrutinize policymaking and failed to warn the public of the dangers associated with immigration. This inadequate media reporting on the dangers of immigration prior to September 11 supposedly led to lenient immigration policies that permitted the attacks in the United States to happen:[5] 'Politically correct journalism . . . has allowed too many confused and contradictory policies offering weak protection [against dangerous immigrants] to endure' (ibid.). The events of 11 September 2001 apparently changed the nature of media reporting to the satisfaction of the think tank's agenda.[6]

The analysis in chapter 3 confirmed that the debate on immigration reform in Canada focused disproportionately on the dangers associated with immigration. 'Danger' was the most common aspect of the media debate of immigration reform. However, this analysis also illustrated that danger was a relatively consistent aspect of the Canadian immigration debate. The argument that immigrants are dangerous was not an ad hoc response to the events of 11 September 2001, but existed before these events. This finding is important because it suggests that danger is a structural element of Canadian immigration debate. Public and media debates on immigration also mediate anxieties of wider global changes. Accordingly, immigration may be perceived as a danger (Faist, 2002). Is the perception of immigration as dangerous structurally engrained into Canadian immigration debate? Is the dangerous immigrant the non-belonging Other? Do these anxieties about change offer clues and insights into the perception of the national self? With these questions in mind, I examine the contents of the danger aspect in Canadian immigration debate.

'Danger' in the Immigration Debate

In the context of immigration reform, an argument was made that immigration constitutes a threat that requires legislative change. This idea had surfaced at various stages during the debate. It was not something that occurred only after 11 September 2001. For example, after the publication of the government's report *Building on a strong foundation for the 21st century* in January 1999, the press commented on the inability of existing legislation to curb the dangers emanating from immigrants. An article published in the *Vancouver Sun* stated: 'The Immigration Act has tied the hands of frontline immigration officers and allowed criminals, violent and otherwise, to walk our streets. Examples include Hondurans selling drugs on our streets, Asian triad members and smugglers bringing people, crime and drugs, Middle Eastern terrorists who are not wanted back in their home countries' (Dillon, 1999).

A few months later, on 6 April 2000, the day when the government first proposed the Immigration and Refugee Protection Act, an article was published in the *Calgary Herald, National Post,* and *Ottawa Citizen* that represented the proposed bill as an improvement over existing legislation in terms of fighting crime and terrorism.

> Refugees will undergo a criminal and security screening as soon as they file a claim in Canada under terms of a revamped Immigration Act to be unveiled today.
>
> Currently, refugees are checked for criminal and terrorist connections only after their claim has been decided and they have applied for landed status or citizenship. It means they can stay here for years before ever being subject to screening by the RCMP[7] or the Canadian Security and Intelligence Service. (Duffy, 2000a)

Shortly thereafter, an article in the *Vancouver Sun* presented a quote by immigration minister Elinor Caplan of the Liberal Party in which the minister suggests that the proposed reforms will better protect Canada from the dangers emanating from criminals, terrorists, or human rights violators. '"Our priority is the safety and national security interests of Canada," she [Caplan] said in introducing the revamped Immigration Act in the Commons. "We are not going to be a place that welcomes serious criminals, terrorists, war criminals or those who committed crimes against humanity"' (Ward, 2000).

As the debate on immigration reform continued after the 2000 general election, so was the danger aspect represented in the debate. Again referring to immigration minister Caplan, an article in the *National Post* noted that the proposed law would enable the removal of criminal immigrants who pose a danger to Canada.

> Ms. Caplan said ... 'What is being proposed is the ability to remove criminals who are inadmissible and not eligible to stay in Canada,' she said.
>
> ...
>
> Ms. Caplan dismissed the worries [by Commons Immigration Committee chairman Joe Fontana], saying 'Canadians want to know that we have the tools to remove criminals from Canada as quickly as possible and that's what the bill does.' (Fife, 2001)

In the same year, an article in the *Vancouver Sun* portrayed the proposed law as more effective in keeping criminals out of Canada than current immigration legislation:

> Under the current law, 'it takes years to remove serious criminals and those who pose a risk to Canadian society. I believe that is something that is intolerable,' Caplan said.
>
> . . .
>
> Caplan said the challenge of the new bill was to balance 'tough, targeted measures to curb criminal abuse of our immigration and refugee systems,' while at the same time trying to 'open the front door wider to immigrants and refugees who will continue to build our country.' (Mofina, 2001)

In this quote, the minister rhetorically separates criminal immigrants and refugees from those who come to Canada under economic or humanitarian considerations. By distinguishing between different aspects of immigration, the minister is able to focus attention on the particular argument of 'danger' and present policy measures to deal with dangerous immigrants as moderate and commonsensical. This quote illustrates how the danger aspect coexists with other aspects.

The danger aspect was also represented in the immigration debate when the Senate discussed Bill C-11 after it had passed the House of Commons. In the context of this discussion, the *Toronto Star* published an article that emphasized the link between a public sense of safety and the reform of immigration law:

> Caplan said in an interview that critics of the package [i.e., Bill C-11] are out of touch with Canadians, who want a crackdown on serious criminals abusing the immigration process.
>
> 'Liberals are not patsies, we recognize that Canada's safety is a No. 1 priority,' Caplan said. (Thompson, 2001b)

The above quotes from the media illustrate that immigration and the admission of refugees was linked to 'danger' long before 11 September 2001. According to the argument presented in the press and by the quoted politicians – first and foremost immigration minister Elinor Caplan – existing legislation was insufficient to avert danger. The reform of the existing immigration law was supposed to address this problem and prevent 'dangerous' immigrants from entering Canada.

After 11 September 2001, the attacks in New York and Washington became rhetorically entangled with the reform of immigration law and policy. The Canadian government reiterated its efforts to reduce the dangers of terrorism associated with immigration and placed greater emphasis on 'security issues' in matters of immigration and refugee claims (Fleury, 2004, no page).

The entanglement between immigration and the terrorism attacks of September 11 can also be observed in the reporting by Canadian newspapers in the immediate aftermath of the attacks. For example, two days after the attacks, an article in the *Toronto Star* assessed 'the grim aftermath of the deadly, unprecedented attacks on New York and Washington' in the following manner: 'Canada now has no choice but to be an eager partner in what [University of Toronto political scientist John] Kirton predicts will be "a massive program to protect America." Ottawa's goodwill will be demonstrated by speedy passage of a new immigration act that only months ago was labeled draconian' (Travers, 2001).

On the following day, a *Toronto Star* (2001a) editorial remarks: 'Canada's new Immigration Act faces a tougher fight to become law since horrific attacks in the United States threw to the forefront the need for sound anti-terrorism policies, says a Liberal senator.' Eight days after the attacks, the *Calgary Herald* (2001) wrote the following in a special report on 'The War on Terror – Canada's response': 'Some senators want quick passage of Canada's proposed new Immigration Act, but others called Tuesday for sober second thought after last week's carnage in the United States.' Still in the same month as the attacks an article in the *Vancouver Sun* suggested that the US administration 'believes Canada's immigration and refugee procedures are too lax, increasing the threat of terrorist infiltration over the Canada-U.S. border' (Naumetz, 2001).

Despite these reservations that the proposed Immigration and Refugee Protection Act (Bill C-11) was not tough enough on terrorism, lawmakers passed the bill, and it was signed into law by Canada's governor general in November 2001. The legislation included a range of measures to cope with the potential dangers of immigration and terrorist infiltration, including harsher penalties for people smuggling and document forgery, giving immigration officers greater powers to detain foreigners, denying persons who committed serious offences the right of appeal, streamlining the process of issuing so-called security certificates, and lowering the bar for rejecting refugee claims (Adelman, 2002; Fleury, 2004). These 'security' measures implemented with Canada's new immigration law were planned long before 11 September 2001.[8]

In addition, the Canadian government passed a series of 'anti-terrorism' bills, including the Public Safety Act (Bill C-42),[9] which was introduced in parliament in November 2001. An editorial in the *National Post* (2001) linked the proposed Public Safety Act with immigration, and defended it for speeding up the implementation of the Immigration and Refugee Protection Act: 'Most important of all, the new bill [C-42] includes provisions that will make it harder for suspected terrorists who seek to enter Canada as refugees. Under current law, any suspected terrorist – or even a convicted terrorist – who tries to gain admission to Canada can be refused access to the refugee process only through the personal intervention of the Minister of Immigration.'

The dangers emanating from immigration were an important argument in the media's support for the reform of immigration law. Although the attacks in New York and Washington were incorporated into this debate, this narrative had circulated in the media long before 11 September 2001. Refugees have played an important role in this association of migration with danger. More than a decade ago, Reg Whitaker observed that after the end of the Cold War, the 'refugee' has been 'reconstructed in the dominant state discourse as an object of fear' (1998: 414). Refugees were associated with Palestinian 'terrorism' in the 1960s, Sikh 'terrorism' in the 1980s, and Sri Lankan 'terrorism' in the 1990s. In addition, refugees were discursively linked to organized crime, narcotics trafficking, and 'narcoterrroism' – a term that associates the drug trade with the financing of terrorism (ibid.: 425). Below, I examine the particular themes of terrorism, violence, and organized crime within this aspect of danger in the Canadian immigration debate.

Terrorism

The danger of terrorism is an important theme of immigration debate. An opinion poll by the *Globe and Mail* taken shortly after the study period had ended, revealed that 59 per cent of surveyed Canadians believed Canada will experience a terrorism attack in the near future that is carried out by Muslim Canadians (Jimenéz, 2006).[10] In the media debate on immigration reform, this theme was on the agenda before 11 September 2001. For example, a 1997 article in the *Toronto Star* reports that an immigrant 'accused of involvement in last year's bombing of a U.S. military complex in Saudi Arabia has been jailed here after being declared a public danger by the Canadian government' (Thompson, 1997). Similarly, before the September 11 attacks, an article, which ran in the *National Post* under the headline 'Scale up the war against terrorism,' called for an amendment to 'the Immigration Act to give immigration officers greater discretion in detaining arrivals who arouse terrorism-related suspicions' (Landy, 2001). This article argued that immigrant terrorists make Canada unsafe: 'Because terrorists are using Canada for fundraising, for procurement of equipment and identification and travel documents, and as a "safe haven" and "support base" from which to plan and direct terrorist operations elsewhere, the likelihood of Canada itself becoming a target has increased.'

In Spring 2001, an article in the *National Post,* covering the trial of a former Montreal resident who had attempted to smuggle explosives into the United States, remarked that 'in the 15 months since the arrests, Canada has made little progress toward changing its reputation as Club Med for terrorists' (Bell, 2001a). Two month before the September 11 attacks, the same author published another article in the *National Post* that also warned about the threat of terrorism related to immigration law. The article, titled 'No way to fight terrorism,' noted Canada's insufficient legislation for prosecuting terrorists: 'Our laws do not recognize that terrorism is more than a crime – that it is an act of war deserving special treatment. As it stands, Canada's only terrorism law is the Immigration Act. The worst punishment terrorists can suffer is deportation' (Bell, 2001d).

After the attacks in New York and Washington, the media continued to present the theme of terrorism as a danger associated with immigration. For example, a 2004 article on the front page of the *Ottawa Citizen* reported on the use of so-called security certificates to detain terrorism suspects. The article explained that 'defenders of the security certificate process . . . contend it is an immigration safeguard that ensures Canada will never become a haven for terrorists' (Duffy, 2004).

Three cases involving the deportation of terrorism suspects further illustrate that the media's attention to the threat of terrorism emanating from immigration and refugee admission existed before 11 September 2001.[11] The press covered these cases in a typically dialectical fashion, juxtaposing the threat of terrorism to Canadian society with the injustice of detention and deportation experienced by the refugee claimants.

The first case involved the deportation of Mahmoud Es-Sayy Jaballah, who was a refugee and an alleged member of Egyptian al-Jihad, a group linked to the bombings of embassies in Kenya and Tanzania in 1998. A 1999 article in the *Toronto Star* reported that 'the Canadian Security Intelligence Service says Jaballah's activities on behalf of al-Jihad constitute reasonable grounds to believe he . . . has "supported and engaged in terrorism" and continues to "actively support the al-Jihad's terrorist agenda"' (Vincent, 1999). In early 2001, a front-page article in the *Ottawa Citizen* reported on a memo written by CSIS 'alleging Mr. Jaballah's active support of Al Jihad, a division of the notorious Mr. bin Laden's extensive terrorist web' (Bronskill, 2001). In August 2001, two weeks after Jaballah's detention, a front-page article in the *National Post* wrote: 'The arrest comes amid growing concerns Canada is becoming an offshore base for Islamic-inspired terrorists' (Bell, 2001c).

After 11 September 2001, the reporting on Jaballah shifted unexpectedly. In a dialectical twist, the media's attention switched from terrorism threat towards CSIS's methods of investigation. Two weeks after the September 11 attacks, the *Ottawa Citizen* published an article remarking that Jaballah's case 'reveals the convoluted methods of Canada's spy agency' (Dimmock, 2001). Similarly, in December 2001, the *Toronto Star* published an article mocking the procedures of a trial in which secret evidence was denied to Jaballah's defence lawyer and reporting on the 'bizarre legal clash over whether Muslim teacher Mahmoud Jaballah is a threat to national security or not' (Gillespie, 2001). In summer 2002, a front-page article in the *Ottawa Citizen* wrote that Jaballah's lawyer 'described his client's legal battle as "beyond Kafka-esque"' (Kari, 2002) and quoted the Canadian Arab Federation's demand '"to end the persecution" of the Jaballah family.' In 2004, a front-page report in the *Toronto Star* reviewed Jaballah's case and questioned the legitimacy of the charges: 'If one can be judged solely by the company one keeps, Jaballah appears to be guilty' (Shephard, 2004). Aggressive anti-terrorism rhetoric in the context of Jaballah's case was relatively uncommon after 2001.[12]

A second case involved two individuals: Manour Ahani, a former narcotics officer and member of the Iranian Ministry of Intelligence Security, and Manickavasagan Suresh, an alleged fund-raiser for the Liberation Tigers of Tamil Eelam, which was classified as a 'terrorist' organization in the United States. Ahani's case was already featured in the *Ottawa Citizen* in 1998, under the headline 'Iranian "assassin" to be deported' (Bronskill, 1998). In the summer of 1999, when immigration officials prepared his deportation, the *National Post* (1999) reported: 'Mr. Ahani has acknowledged he was a narcotics officer in Iran and received specialized police training in assassination techniques . . . After his release [from Iranian prison], he came to Canada in 1991 and made a successful refugee claim. CSIS began interviewing Mr. Ahani and in June, 1993, declared him a security risk.' This same issue of the *National*

Post featured a front-page article that presented the government's viewpoint on the case:

> The Canadian Security Intelligence Service believes that Mr. Ahani, whose appeal to stay was turned down recently in federal court, is a dangerous trained terrorist who works for a branch of Iran's government that plans and executes terrorist operations. Mr. Ahani's lawyers have fought his removal with a long series of challenges in the federal and Ontario courts.
>
> 'We are now in a legal position to remove Mr. Ahani,' said Huguette Shouldice, a spokeswoman for Citizenship and Immigration Canada. 'We intend to remove him as expeditiously as possible. Canada won't be safe haven for terrorists or criminals.' (Jimenéz, 1999b)

Several articles used the same language and reiterated the fear that Canada would become a 'haven' for terrorism (Bell, 2001b; Chwialkowska, 2001c; Tibbetts, 2001a, 2001b, 2001d.).

In February 2001 the Supreme Court of Canada heard the cases of Ahani and Suresh. In the context of these hearings, an article in the *National Post* linked their cases to the rhetoric of Canada as terrorist haven:

> The case is a crucial test of Canada's only anti-terrorism law, the section of the Immigration Act that allows the government to weed out suspected terrorists posing as refugees.
>
> . . .
>
> 'This case will determine whether Canada will become a haven for terrorists,' lawyers Urszula Kaczmarczyk and Cheryl Mitchell, representing the government, said in their written arguments obtained by the National Post. (Bell, 2001b)

In May 2001 the *National Post* published an article claiming that 'Canada's ability to expel refugees with links to terrorist groups comes under sprawling legal attack . . . by two men fighting deportation' (Chwialkowska, 2001b). An article in the *Vancouver Sun* used the case to portray Canada as a 'base camp' for terrorism: 'The federal government will ask the court to avoid opening Canada's borders to terrorists, particularly since it is already a country of choice, second only to the United States, in being used as a "base camp" for fund-raising' (Tibbetts, 2001a).[13]

Immediately after the attacks of 11 September 2001, the same author wrote two articles that linked the Ahani and Suresh cases with the terrorist attacks in New York and Washington. One article published in the *Ottawa Citizen* and the *Calgary Herald*[14] drew attention to the 'new circumstances' in which the cases should be seen: 'In light of last week's attacks in the United States, [Justice Minister] Ms. McLellan said there are new circumstances that could prompt the court to rethink the case . . . "I think the events of last Tuesday speak very clearly to the very real risk of terrorism to all of us and how very difficult it is to deal with terrorist organizations," said Ms. McLellan' (Tibbetts, 2001c). An article in the *National Post* suggested that the September 11 attacks strengthened the government's case against Ahani and Suresh, 'since judges have likely read about the events in the newspapers' (Chwialkowska, 2001c).

Despite the inclusion of the September 11 attacks into press reporting on the cases of Ahani and Suresh, the coverage after the attacks continued to reflect general ideas and rhetoric similar to those before the attacks. For example, the language of Canada being a 'safe haven' for terrorism was linked to Ahani and Suresh's case not only before but also after 11 September 2001. According to a 2002 report in the *Toronto Star:* 'The court . . . could strike down the law's deportation sections, which Ottawa has argued would create a safe haven for terrorists in Canada' (MacCharles, 2002).

The third case involved Mahmoud Mohammad Issa Mohammad, a former member of the Popular Front for the Liberation of Palestine and participant in an attack on a civilian Israeli airplane in 1968 in Athens, Greece. A 1999 front-page article in the *National Post* reported:

> On Friday, an immigration adjudicator ruled that Mahmoud Mohammad Issa Mohammad is inadmissible under the Immigration Act because of his criminal past, his membership in a terrorist organization, and his terrorist activities.
>
> . . .
>
> 'We're not going to give terrorists protection in Canada no matter how long ago the act was committed,' said Ms. Shouldice [an Immigration Canada spokesperson]. (Jimenéz, 1999b)

Shortly after the 11 September 2001 attacks, the *Ottawa Citizens* ran a story on the case with the sub-headline 'Convicted terrorist remains in Canada legally while case grinds through appeal process' (Cobb, 2001a). Other articles in the *Toronto Star* (2001b) and *Ottawa Citizen* (Cobb, 2001b) also reported on the case in a similar tone as before 11 September 2001. These three examples illustrate that the theme of terrorism already played a strong role in Canadian media debate and the reporting on immigration reform before 2001. The attacks on the World Trade Center and the Pentagon in the United States were incorporated into an already existing narrative of danger.

Violence and Organized Crime

As I mentioned earlier, the idea that danger emanates from immigration involves themes other than terrorism. For example, Ayse Ceyhan and Anastassia Tsoukala (2002: 22) describe how contemporary discourses in 'Western' societies link migration with danger by representing migrants as 'criminals, troublemakers, economic and social defrauders, terrorists, drug traffickers, unassimilable person[s], and so forth.' In Canadian immigration debates similar representations of migrants circulate. A recent opinion survey, for example, showed that 44 per cent of surveyed Canadians thought that the refugee program was doing poorly or very poorly in preventing criminals from entering Canada (Spencer, 2009).[15]

Early in the media debate of immigration reform, an editorial in the *Vancouver Sun* (1996) critiqued existing immigration policies and listed several themes associated with danger. 'Former immigration minister Sergio Marchi granted more than 1,500 special entry permits to rapists, murderers, suspected terrorists and drunk drivers last year.' This editorial continued to identify 'inadmissible classes,' listing persons who pose a 'health risk,' 'persons who have been convicted in Canada of an indictable offence,' persons who 'have been convicted outside Canada of two or more offences,' persons who engage in 'espionage or subversion against democratic government,' and 'persons who . . . will engage in acts of violence that would or might endanger the lives or safety of persons in Canada.'[16] In this section, I discuss the media reporting on the themes of the danger aspect that relate to violent crimes, sexual assault, drug trafficking, corruption, and human smuggling.[17]

An important theme relates to the admission of violent criminals as refugees. In 1999, a front-page article in the *Calgary Herald* reported about the inadequacy of existing immigration law to protect Canadians from criminals:

> Immigrants who commit serious crime should receive automatic deportation orders as soon as they're convicted, says Calgary Reform MP [Member of Parliament] Art Hanger.

> The appeal process open to them once they are released is too lax, said the former policeman, meaning immigrant criminals are walking free when they should be sent back to their country of origin.
>
> ...
>
> 'I'm very concerned about our lax laws,' said Hanger, supporting proposed changes to the Immigration Act that would make it possible to deport people without an appeal hearing after their release. 'Many have served time and then they're still walking the streets of Canada.' (Marshall, 1999b)

In the same year, the *National Post* published an article describing the criminal history – including assault, rape, and drunken driving – of an El Salvadoran refugee who disappeared after immigration officials released him from prison. The article remarked that 'some 5,000 deportees have gone missing because the dummies in Ottawa release them and ask them to return to be deported' (Francis, 1999). More than four and a half years later, in 2003, the *National Post* published an article by the same author with the headline 'Dangerous strangers in our midst.' The article pointed out that '36,000 people have been ordered deported but have gone missing. Among those who have disappeared are dozens of war criminals from 24 countries, according to arrest warrants' (Francis, 2003). The fact that this author was able to present a similar story more than four years apart illustrates the consistency of this theme in the Canadian immigration debate.

Another aspect of the danger is sexual assault committed by immigrants and refugees. At the beginning of the study period, in 1996, an article in the *Calgary Herald* reported on an Alberta woman who was the victim of sexual assault by an Iranian refugee. Under the headline 'Flight of a refugee,' the story retraced the steps of the refugee's escape, which included 'attempted rape of an 18-year-old near Melbourne [Australia]' and 'sexual assault of two Red Deer women and one Edmonton woman,' and ended with his sentencing to four and a half years in prison by an Edmonton court (Mofina, 1996). Two years later, the *Calgary Herald* published an article by the same author using the same case to defend changes in the immigration law. After a detailed description of how the attacker gained the confidence of his victim, intimidated her, and 'raped her anally,' the article concluded that this 'case and others like it also helped change Canada's Immigration Act. Would-be immigrants like [the attacker] can now be turned away if officials believe they committed a crime outside Canada punishable here by a jail term of ten years or more' (Mofina, 1998). Again, the time span over which this case was reported in the media confirms that sexual assault was a continually relevant theme in the debate of immigration reform.

In another case, the *Calgary Herald* reported on 'a permanent resident in Canada since 1983 [who] was convicted in April 1996 of sexually assaulting a minor two years earlier, and of assault in January 1997 . . . "If he's a threat, he should be deported. We're playing Russian Roulette with the lives of other people," said Alberta Wildrose MP Myron Thompson' (Bergen, 1998).

Throughout the immigration debate, the media continued to report on sexual assault cases. For example, in 2003, an article in the *National Post* reported on a refugee from Ethiopia who 'was convicted of assault and sexual interference. His victim was his nine-year-old niece' (Francis, 2003). The article commented on the refugee's legal challenge of his deportation in the following manner: 'Mr. Ali should have been unceremoniously booted out of Canada the minute he had served his sentence . . . Unlike any other developed nation, Canada has no reasonable or efficient means of deporting people, no matter how serious their misdeeds.'

Crime related to drug trafficking is another important theme of danger. A 1998 front-page article in the *Vancouver Sun* reported on the imminent deportation of a Vietnamese drug dealer, juxtaposing his self-representation as a humble worker with his life as a brutal gang leader:

> The 34-year-old Vietnamese man passes himself off as a lowly kitchen worker and clam digger, apologizing in a letter to immigration officials that he 'hadn't speak and understand English.'
>
> But on the street he swaggers and smirks as only a powerful gang leader can. Dressed in tailored suits and casually tossing orders to his underlings, the man who tried to take over the Vancouver and Nanaimo heroin trade ordered beatings and kidnappings and randomly attacked fellow members of the Vietnamese community to establish his power. (Ouston, 1998)

Narcotics trafficking was also the topic of an article on the front page of the *Vancouver Sun* in 2000 that reported: 'In a recent police crackdown in the Lower Mainland, 63 of 157 people wanted by police for drug dealing were refugee claimants' (Skelton, 2000a). In the same year, the *National Post* published an article lamenting that existing immigration legislation did not permit the deportation of a non-status drug dealer:

> The Federal Court of Canada has prevented immigration officials from deporting a convicted Guyanese drug dealer living in Toronto because a

> technicality invalidated the government's opinion that he was a danger to society.
>
> Hewlette Harris, who has lived in Canada with no official status since 1983, was deemed a danger to the public by immigration officials after he was sentenced in 1998 to six years in prison for two offences of trafficking narcotics and for possession of a restricted weapon, court documents show. (O'Reilly, 2000b)

The press also reported on drug trafficking cases in the later phases of the debate on immigration reform. For example, an article in the *Calgary Herald* states: 'A Jordanian man with alleged terrorist connections has been quietly deported to Florida where he faces drug charges' (Bronskill and Mofina, 2002). Although this article ran under the rubric 'The War on Terror,' it acknowledges that the allegation of a terrorist connection 'was never substantiated in any concrete way.'

Other press reports of organized crime focused on smuggling and corruption. For example, in February 2001, the *Vancouver Sun* featured a story on business person Lai Changxing, who is wanted in China on smuggling and corruption charges:

> Chinese authorities allege he masterminded a network responsible for smuggling $10 billion US worth of goods into the country, protected by corrupt officials.
>
> ...
>
> Immigration officials and news reports have portrayed Lai as China's most wanted man, accused of controlling a multi-billion-dollar smuggling operation in the coastal province of Fujian, opposite Taiwan. (Joyce, 2001)

A year and a half later, in 2002, the same case resurfaced in the *Vancouver Sun,* when the paper reported that Lai's legal struggle to remain in Canada had failed. Although the article made an effort to present Lai's perspective on the case, it also noted that 'Lai's company, Yuanhua, smuggled cigarettes, heating and cooking oil, textiles and other raw materials into China through Hong Kong. Using cars and money, officials were bribed . . . to evade hundreds of millions in duties and taxes' (Fong, 2002).

An additional theme of danger is human smuggling. In the context of the 1999 arrival of four boats off Canada's west coast, a series of reports focused on human smuggling in association with immigration. An article in the *Vancouver Sun* quoted the Reform Party's justice critic, John Reynolds: '"These people are criminals. They paid money to be knowingly smuggled in somewhere. And we shouldn't let criminals into this country"' (Skelton, 1999a). Another article in the *Vancouver Sun* reported:

> Immigration Minister Elinor Caplan . . . said Canada will not tolerate criminal actions.
>
> 'I want to make it clear that I deplore the actions of human smugglers,' she told a news conference. 'I am also deeply concerned about the increasing number of people who turn to the criminal element in choosing to enter Canada surreptitiously and illegally.' (Lee, 1999)

In the context of the same events, the *National Post* reported: 'Police have removed and jailed 13 more men from among the Chinese migrants who tried to sneak into Canada last week aboard a broken-down boat, saying they are potential "organizers" and security risks' (Gillis, 1999).[18]

In subsequent years, the media debate of immigration reform continued to involve human smuggling. For example, a November 2001 article in the *Ottawa Citizen* reported on 'the Immigration department's incompetence in deporting outright those unfounded cases refused by the [refugee] board. The result of this double-barrel tragedy is that criminals looking for an easy dollar have created a business specializing in the illegal smuggling of peoples' (Beaulne, 2001). This article was published under the rubric 'The War on Terrorism.' As in the above case of drug trafficking, after 11 September 2001, the 'war on terrorism' captured non-terrorism-related themes of danger associated with immigration. However, the general nature of the ideas and arguments expressed through different themes related to the dangers of immigration remained relatively stable throughout the study period.

Conclusion

The analysis of media reporting on the dangers of immigration offers support for the preliminary finding of the previous chapter that the dramatic events of 11 September 2001 had a relatively small impact on the overall character of the immigration debate. The perceived threat of terrorism existed in immigration discourse before the attacks in the United States. Although the press incorporated the New York and Washington attacks into the existing theme of danger, this incorporation did not fundamentally modify or challenge the underlying ideas of the dangers of terrorism in the immigration debate. After the airplane attacks in New York and Washington, some press reports even began defending terrorism suspects, such as Mahamoud Es-Sayy Jaballah, for being the victim of questionable legal practices.

In addition, the analysis revealed a certain consistency in the reporting of the danger of immigration related to themes other than terrorism, including violent crime, sexual assault, organized crime, and human smuggling. Although the general nature of the arguments and ideas did not change, some themes, such as drug trafficking and human smuggling, were partially integrated under the 'war on terrorism' rubric after the September 11 attacks. While these events and the subsequent war on terrorism may have shaped the rhetoric of the debate, it did not affect the main argument deployed in it.

This finding that media perception of the danger aspect of immigration was relatively consistent before and after the tragedy of 11 September 2001 resonates with other international research on immigration, which suggests that 'the course of recent history had not fundamentally changed' in light of the attacks (*International Migration Review,* 2002: 6). In a Canadian context, Cynthia Wright (2003: 6) has similarly argued that 'well before September 11, the federal government's immigration policy was moving in increasingly regressive directions,' although September 11 transformed some of the parameters of the debate. In addition, the consistent media representation of immigrants as dangerous refutes the claim that the media – at least the Canadian press – was lenient about the potential terrorism dangers of immigration before the September 11 attacks. Rather, by representing refugees and immigrants as lethal terrorists, sexual predators, violent criminals, and crime bosses, the media has perpetuated a powerful politics of fear related to immigration.

The construction of immigrants and refugees as objects of fear is consistent with a wider trend of 'securitization' as a technique of governmentality.[19] This technique relies on the social construction of fear and danger based on past events, and the possibility of these events occurring again in the future (Buzan et al., 1998). Drawing on a Hegelian view of history and polity, Anthony Burke argues that security signifies an 'ideal political, economic and cultural order' that is dialectically dependent on the production of 'images of "insecurity" in order to retain meaning' (2002: 20).[20] This issue of securitization has been increasingly linked to international migration (Bigo, 2002). In an era of heightened fear of foreign terrorism, 'international migration takes on added significance' in public debate because terrorism has been closely linked to migration, as this chapter demonstrates (Kritz, 2002: 33). In this context, refugees seem to be an ideal target for perpetuating fear and for evoking the need for security. Years before the attacks of 11 September 2001, Reg Whitaker (1998: 416) observed that refugees could be attributed 'a kind of irreducible aura of political instability' owing to their origin in oppressive regimes and their entanglement in violence and conflict.

The interpretation of the data that I offer in this chapter supports the thesis I established in chapter 3 that danger is a structural element of the immigration debate. The aspect of danger is not only consistent in frequency throughout the debate of the immigration law, it is also fairly consistent in terms of its contents. According to Thomas Faist (2002), the perception of threat emanating from immigration reflects anxieties about challenges to social cohesion and the loss of an external enemy with the end of the Cold War. The representation of immigrants as danger is part-and-parcel of a process that upholds such images of external enemies.[21] In the language of Hegelian dialectics, refugees and migrants are constructed as the unwanted Others of the nation. They represent characteristics, such as terror, violence, and crime, which are irreconcilable with being Canadian. The significance of the analysis presented in this chapter lies in demonstrating that this construction of the immigrant Other is not a spontaneous response to an unusual set of events, but rather a systematically engrained practice of Canadian immigration discourse.

The immigration dialectic, however, does not end with these images of migrants as Others. In particular, in the context of refugees – who tend to be associated with danger like no other group of migrants – this dialectic assumes greater complexity and significance in respect to the formation of Canadian national identity. In the next chapter, I examine refugees in the context of the humanitarian aspect of immigration.

5 Humanitarian Immigration

Humanitarian immigration is, next to economic and family-oriented immigration, one of three pillars of Canada's immigration system. Refugees, however, make up the smallest of the three immigration 'classes.' In the period of immigration reform, the share of refugees reached its high point in 2004, with 13.9 per cent of all immigration to Canada. Within this period the share fell as low as 11.0 per cent in 2002 (Citizenship and Immigration Canada, 2008). In public opinion, refugee admission is a highly divisive issue. In a poll conducted at the end of the study period, 50 per cent of sampled Canadians agreed and 47 per cent disagreed with the statement that 'Canada ought to be accepting more immigrants from those parts of the world which are experiencing major conflicts' (Yasmeen, 2004: 13). Despite the relatively small proportion of refugees among Canada's total immigrants and the divisive nature of the issue, Canada's refugee category plays an important ethical and political role. Through humanitarian immigration and refugee admission, the Canadian state fulfils its commitment to humanitarianism and constructs an image of Canada as a liberal and compassionate nation.

Technically, refugees are not immigrants. Refugees arrive in Canada for different reasons and under different circumstances than immigrants.[1] In addition, their mobility is controlled under different international and national regulations and legal frameworks. The debate on Canadian immigration reform, however, involved both groups, and the difference between immigrant and refugee was often blurred. As the name indicates, the Immigration and Refugee Protection Act regulates both immigration and refugee admission. Furthermore, Canada differs from many other countries, including Germany, in its treatment of refugees. In Canada, refugees receive permanent residence and the prospect of citizenship once their cases are approved. In this way, the integration of refugees and immigrants into Canadian society formally follows a similar path.[2] The permanency of refugee settlement is reflected in the debate on this group in the context of immigration reform.

Refugee admission is guided by the principles of humanitarianism. The humanitarian aspect of immigration debate consequently deals primarily with refugees. This language, however, may be confusing to readers who are familiar with the terminology used by the Canadian Ministry of Citizenship and Immigration, which oversees immigrant and refugee admission. In the language of Citizenship and Immigration Canada, 'humanitarian' and 'compassionate' cases refer not to refugees, but rather to exceptional cases that fit neither the refugee category nor the economic or family classes.[3] In statistics, humanitarian immigrants are included under the rubric 'other immigrants.' The category 'other immigrants' provided only between 0.1 per cent (2001) and 4.2 per cent (2004) of all accepted permanent residents in the period between 1996 and 2004 (Citizenship and Immigration Canada, 2008). While the humanitarian aspect of the immigration debate also included 'compassionate' cases, the vast majority of the discussion of this aspect involves refugees.

In this chapter, I take a closer look at the humanitarian aspect of the immigration debate. The analysis of chapter 3 showed that humanitarianism is the second most frequently discussed aspect in the debate of immigration reform. Apparently, the press is giving greater weight to matters relating to refugees than the relatively small share of refugees within Canada's total immigration reflects. My exploration in this chapter is driven by the question of why humanitarianism is so prominent in Canadian debate. Something about humanitarian immigration must be important to Canadian society. The interpretation which I offer in this chapter rests on Hegelian dialectics of national identity formation.

This interpretation highlights the importance of Canada's international reputation, the discursive construction of the boundary between deserving and undeserving refugees, and coverage of contested cases of refugee applications and deportations. Furthermore, I link the discussion of humanitarian immigration to the aspect of danger, which was the topic of the previous chapter and which showed that refugees are often associated with danger.

Canada's Reputation

Canada's international reputation is an important element in the self-image of Canadian society. The country has a long and proud history of admitting persons in need of protection. This history includes Canada as the destination of the 'underground railroad,' which promised freedom to fugitive slaves; the settlement of Mennonites and other persecuted religious minority groups in the late nineteenth and twentieth centuries; and the 1986 receipt of the United Nations High Commissioner for Refugees' Nansen medal in recognition of Canada's efforts in refugee protection.[4] Although refugee admission is a contested issue among the Canadian public, once refugees are in the county they serve as an important tool of identity construction. Mary Liston and Joseph Carens recently observed that Canadians on the whole endorsed refugee 'policies, at least after the fact, and the image of Canada as a haven for refugees became part of the public projection of Canada's self-understanding of its place in the world' (2008: 212).

Humanitarianism in the form of refugee admission enables Canadians to express a positive dimension of their national identity. In the words of Catherine Dauvergne: 'Part of our humanitarianism is about . . . applauding ourselves' (2005: 73). In the context of the debate on immigration reform, the media established this link between humanitarian immigration and national identity by making an association between Canada's immigration policy and the country's reputation for compassion and its tradition of generosity. For example, in 1996, at the beginning of the debate on immigration reform, the *Toronto Star* quoted citizenship and immigration minister Lucienne Robillard: '"Canada has a tradition of fair and generous immigration and refugee programs," she said. "The [Immigration Legislative Review] advisory group will provide a series of recommendations to guide and update future immigration and refugee legislation in a way that will maintain this tradition"' (Vienneau, 1996: A2).

The idea that Canada's refugee program shapes Canada's international reputation was expressed throughout the debate on immigration reform. For example, in 2001, when the Immigration and Refugee Protection Act was debated in parliament, an article in the *National Post* paraphrased the chairman of the Commons Immigration Committee, Joe Fontana, who opposed the removal of rights from refugee applicants: 'The bill must be tightened . . . to protect Canada's reputation as a nation open to immigrants and refugees' (Fife, 2001: A7). The same rhetoric about Canada's reputation appeared in an article more than a year later. While the government made adjustments to the act before it took effect in June 2002, the *Toronto Star* opposed the denial of second hearings to rejected asylum seekers and accused immigration minister Denis Coderre of creating 'a lopsided piece of legislation that compromises Canada's reputation as a safe haven for those whose lives are in danger at home' (*Toronto Star,* 2002: A20).

The press often evoked Canada's reputation as a way to construct existing and planned policies and practices towards humanitarian immigration as problematic. For example, when the Canadian government proposed to stop recognizing Somali passports as legal identification, refugee advocates accused the government of racism and of violating Canada's reputation as a champion of human rights. An article in the *Ottawa Citizen* stated:

> 'From the community perspective, this is a very racist piece of legislation and we think it's the way of curbing Somalis from coming into the country,' said Hamdi Mohamed, program manager at the Somali Centre in Ottawa.
>
> . . .
>
> To Ms. Mohamed, the situation 'is disgusting, something that shouldn't be happening in a so-called civilized country that claims to advocate for human rights.' (Pritchett, 1999: B3)

The reference to Canada's reputation is a rhetorical strategy to problematize the retraction of humanitarian assistance to refugees and immigrants. If Canada loses its roles as a humanitarian leader around the world, so the argument goes, the national image will suffer. Avvy Go, director of the Metro Toronto Chinese and Southeast Asian Legal Clinic, wrote an article in the *Toronto Star,* in which she used this strategy to advocate for better treatment of refugee claimants:

> With the election now behind us, the first thing that our new minority government should do is to restore some compassion and basic respect for human dignity back into a system that has once made us all proud to be Canadians.
>
> Then and only then, can we truly live up to our hard-earned reputation as one of the most humanitarian countries in the world. (Go, 2004: A18)

Through improving the country's international image, humanitarian immigration makes an important contribution to Canada's national identity.

Humanitarian immigration, however, can also serve to construct an unfavourable image of Canadian immigration policy. For example, the 'crisis' that was triggered in 1999 when several boats carrying Chinese refugees arrived on Canada's western coast attracted the attention of several studies. In one study, Sean Hier and Joshua Greenberg (2002) suggest that the media represented these Chinese refugees as racialized, illegal, and non-belonging. These representations legitimated the rejection of these migrants as deserving refugees. In another study, Minelle Mahtani and Alison Mountz support the view that media reporting failed to apply humanitarian principles to the treatment of these migrants. 'Canadian immigration officials came under attack for their treatment of the Chinese migrant boat crisis. The media scripted Canadians as irate citizens with a government constructed as "soft": letting people in through the "back door"' (Mahtani and Mountz, 2001: 29). In this case, the humanitarian argument was flipped to construct a negative image of Canada as soft and weak.

In the debate on immigration reform, similar arguments against humanitarian immigration and for the toughening of refugee policies occurred. Interestingly, Canada's international reputation was evoked again – but this time in a negative way. For example, an article in the *National Post* proposed that the arrival of refugees from democracies, such as the United States, Israel, Hong Kong, and European countries, has made 'refugee policy à la Canadien . . . the joke of the globe' and 'an embarrassment to Canadians' (Francis, 1999: C3). Similarly, an article in the *Vancouver Sun* presents the Reform Party's immigration critic Leon Benoit's viewpoint that 'all refugee claimants who arrive in Canada by illegal means should be detained and their cases decided within 30 days. It's the only way, he said, to get rid of Canada's reputation as a "soft touch"' (Duffy, 2000b: A6). In these cases, the reference to Canada's reputation was strategically used to argue against humanitarian assistance to refugees and migrants. An editorial in the *National Post* relates the arrival of unwanted immigrants more directly to Canada's identity by speaking of a challenge to its 'national sense of hospitality': 'By effectively encouraging economic migrants to enter our country illegally, the government only erodes our national sense of hospitality' (*National Post*, 2000a: A17).

Boundary Construction

The refugee selection process distinguishes between the deserving and the undeserving refugee. Although both deserving and undeserving refugees represent the Other, only the deserving refugee is worthy of the nation's compassion. The nation exercises this compassion by granting refugee status (Dauvergne, 2005). The debate of immigration reform reflected this distinction between deserving and undeserving refugees. Regular refugee admission procedures, however, are rarely discussed in the press or public debate. Apparently, conventional practices of refugee selection fail to make the news and contribute only little to the media's construction of Canada's identity.

Rather than focusing on the mundane and everyday practice of refugee selection, the debate on immigration pays much greater attention to the construction of the *boundary* between deserving and undeserving refugees. The representation of Canada as compassionate and caring occurs, in particular, through reporting on borderline cases and contested refugee claims. The construction of this boundary not only is important for identifying worthy recipients of Canadian compassion, but also goes to the very core of the national imagination: it defines who is eligible as a future member of the national community, and who must remain beyond of 'impassable symbolic boundary' (Hall, 1996 [1989]: 445) of Otherness.

A particular area of borderline construction related to humanitarian immigration is that of gender equality and oppression. An article in the *Vancouver Sun* featured a story on the court battle of a South Korean mother and her two daughters seeking refugee status on the grounds of domestic brutality:

> Earlier that morning, the eldest child was vomiting at the prospect of being sent back to face a father who had threatened to kill them for running away, the family said.
>
> Her mother had the look of the condemned.
>
> Lawyer Jim Henshall argued that this woman and her daughters were being sent back to a society where spousal abuse and family violence were tolerated to a degree unknown in Canada, and that their family history of abuse – and belief that a vengeful husband and father was lying in wait – equated to a claim for refugee status. (Ballett, 2004: B2)

The author of another article in the *Vancouver Sun* defended the decision by the Immigration and Refugee Board to grant refugee status on the basis of gender violence. This case involved a Chinese woman who had travelled on one of the boats that arrived on Canada's west coast in 1999.

> She told the board she underwent a forced abortion 13 years ago, when she was seven months pregnant with her third child.
>
> After the abortion, she told the board, she had another child in hiding. When authorities discovered she was pregnant with a fourth child, she was dragged to the hospital for another abortion, which included the fetus being injected with a poison in front of her. Later, she was forcibly sterilized.
>
> The ruling includes an excerpt of the woman's interview with a psychologist in Canada about the second abortion.
>
> 'I thought she [the baby] was alive,' the woman told the psychologist. 'After it was aborted [the nurse] threw it in the corner on the floor . . . I told them: 'It is alive baby, let me have it, raise it.' They said: 'No, because of the injection it's going to die soon' . . . I saw her die and it was very painful. My heart got broken then.'
>
> 'She cried shamelessly when describing her experiences,' Robles wrote. 'She was trembling and her hands were shaking as she testified.' (Skelton, 2000b: A4)

Although the woman neither faced persecution in China nor fit the strict United Nations definition of a refugee, she received refugee status 'because the "atrocious and appalling" treatment she received in China before leaving . . . caused her "continuing psychological and emotional trauma"' (Skelton, 2000b: A4). Although in legal terms the boundary of who is a deserving refugee could be drawn elsewhere, media reporting draws this boundary to include people who experience gender discrimination and violence.

In another case, the policy and program director of the Canadian Council for Refugees, Janet Dench, wrote a commentary in the *Toronto Star* on the government's proposal to establish a new Resettlement from Abroad Class (RAC) catering to people who are not refugees according the United Nations' definition, but are nevertheless in need of protection. Dench used the example of gender to illustrate the need for the proposed class: 'The new class would mean an immigration official need not shut the door on an Afghan woman in a refugee camp in Pakistan simply because she is not singled out for persecution in her home country' (Dench, 1997: A13). Again, by extending refugee status to cases of gender discrimination and violence, reporting in the Canadian media pushes the boundary of who is considered worthy of protection beyond international convention. In this way, the press affirms gender equality as a principle of Canadian identity and paints an image of Canada as compassionate towards women who suffer from the violation of this principle. Through this practice, Canada acquires an identity that situates gender equality at its centre.

Another area of tension between the commitment to humanitarianism and current political practice involves children. The press sees vulnerable children as especially entitled to protection. When a federal court in Vancouver overturned the decision by the Immigration and Refugee Board (IRB) to deport nine Chinese refugee children, the press supported the court's ruling. An article in the *National Post* quoted the judge:

> 'The [children] were members of a "particular social group," [and this] warranted more serious consideration and analysis than was provided by the [IRB],' wrote Justice Frederick Gibson. 'As members of a particular social group so defined, [their lawyers] urged that the children were persecuted by virtue of their being "trafficked" on the basis of arrangements made between their parents and human smugglers . . . I accept without reservation that argument.' (O'Reilly, 2000a: A4)

Another case further illustrates the viewpoint that children are in need of special protection. An article in the *Toronto Star* protested against Citizenship and Immigration Canada's intention to separate three refugee youths and suggested that 'the conditions in which they were living violated their rights under the U.N. Convention on the Rights of a Child' (Lower, 2001: A6). The article highlighted why these youths were particularly deserving of compassion:

> Last year, they say that Unita rebels attacked their hometown of Luanda, Angola's capital. Amid heavy gunfire, the girls say that they fled with their mother and neighbours. They say that the rebels captured them and blindfolded them so that they would not know the location of the camp where they were being taken. The last time the girls saw their mother, they say, was in the seconds before their blindfolds were put on. (Lower, 2001: A6)

In another case, Canada's Supreme Court overturned the deportation order of a Jamaican refugee claimant to accommodate the needs of her four Canadian-born children. An article in the *National Post* celebrated the court's decision:

> The court found that immigration officials were biased against [refugee claimant] Mavis Baker, and 'completely dismissive' of the interests of her

> four Canadian-born children when they turned down her application to stay on humanitarian grounds.
>
> 'Children's rights and attention to their interests are central humanitarian and compassionate values in Canadian society,' wrote Justice Claire L'Heureux-Dubé in the unanimous decision. (Jimenéz, 1999a: A8)

Although this case involved the rights of children who are Canadian citizens,[5] the language of the quoted text illustrates the role of refugee policy and practice in upholding Canadian 'values' and thus constructing Canadian society as caring towards children and youths, and acting in their best interests.

A final example of a contested practice relates to victims of natural disaster. A Turkish Canadian made an emotional plea to the minister of citizenship and immigration in the *Ottawa Citizen* to permit the sponsorship of a distant cousin who had lost his right foot in an earthquake in Turkey, but survived by laying in the rubble 'on top of his father's body, unable to move for 35 hours. His foot was caught under the same block of cement as his father's, but thankfully he was not losing that much blood and he was able to survive... His only wish is to be able to come to Canada to at least escape from the horrible memories of the earthquake for a while' (Avunca, 1999: B5). A reader's letter supported the admission of the earthquake victim and suggested that 'under some circumstances, this law [Immigration Act] should be flexible' (Karaokcu, 1999: B5). Both articles construct the earthquake victim as deserving due to the emotional and psychological hardship he experienced and juxtapose this case with the Chinese refugees who arrived around the same time via boat and who the press portrayed as 'illegal.' This case illustrates the dialectical practice of boundary construction, which involves the strategic juxtaposing of deserving and undeserving examples of refugees.

Undeserving Refugees

National identity is constructed not only through the admission of refugees in need of protection, but also through the rejection of refugee applicants represented as unworthy of inclusion in Canadian society. For example, the press expresses little compassion for refugee applicants who have committed war or hate crimes. An article in the *Vancouver Sun* supports efforts to deport war criminals from Latin America:

> Some in Vancouver's Latino community call them los fantasmas de guerra – the ghosts of war.
>
> The community applauds Canada's stepped-up efforts to expel the ghosts and deport those who have tortured and murdered civilians back home. (Ouston and Jimenéz, 1998a: A1)[6]

Another example is the case of Ernst Zundel,[7] which received a significant amount of attention in the Canadian media. This case was also covered in the context of Canadian immigration reform. Zundel was wanted in his native Germany for hosting an anti-Semitic website that denies the Holocaust, which in Germany is a crime. After leaving Canada for the United States, Zundel returned to Canada and claimed refugee status. An article in the *National Post* reported that 'Mr. Zundel's attempt to claim refugee status has caused outrage across Canada' (Curry and Bell, 2003: A4). A separate article in the *National Post* reiterated the Canadian government's position that 'Holocaust denier Ernst Zundel is a threat to Canada's security because he fosters hatred of Jews, finances hate groups and could incite his followers to violence' (Bell, 2003: C3). These articles establish very clearly that refugee claimants who are obvious racists should not be tolerated in Canadian society.

Violent criminals are also not wanted in Canada. An article in the *National Post* elaborates on the criminal history of Jose Salinas-Mendoza, an El Salvadoran refugee applicant who had 'committed many crimes and was convicted of 12 offences ranging from drunken driving to sexual assault and assault' (Francis, 1999: C3). The article generalized based on this case: 'The only real refugees are those in camps, like the Kosovars, who cannot afford to get here in the first place. The rest are often tricksters, or worse' (Francis, 1999: C3). Although the author obviously overreaches in this generalization, the article clearly expresses that compassion ends at criminal behaviour and violence.

Many articles share the general concerns that 'criminals and queue jumpers are abusing our generosity' (*Toronto Star,* 2000: 1) and that 'people are taking advantage of Canada's good will' (Yaffe, 2000: A15). The term 'bogus refugee' appears in articles throughout the debate on immigration reform; however, it appeared particularly frequently in the weeks before the Liberal government tabled the Immigration and Refugee Protection Act (Bill C-31) in April 2000. The *Vancouver Sun* expressed dissatisfaction with the proposed legislation for failing to 'stop bogus claimants from clogging the system' (*Vancouver Sun,* 2000a: A8). The *National Post* argued: 'In Europe, nearly 90% of those claiming to be refugees are debunked as bogus' and '[If] the West as a whole, and Canada in particular, is to provide a haven to genuine refugees, then we must satisfy ourselves that the refugees meet strict criteria' (*National Post,* 2000a: A17). Drawing parallels to the Canadian refugee system, the *Vancouver Sun* featured an article on Britain, quoting British Conservative party leader William Hague on the suffering of 'genuine refugees . . . because of the massive influx of bogus asylum seekers' (K. Ward, 2000: A14). The term 'bogus' represents a category of refugee applicants who are not only undesired but who also inflict damage by consuming the resources needed to support 'deserving' refugees.

The constructions of undeserving refugees overlap with representations of dangerous refugees and immigrants, which I examined in the previous chapter. These dangerous people are situated on the other side of the boundary that defines the deserving refugee. Dangerous, racist, and violent refugees cannot be invited to join the Canadian community. They are excluded from the national imagination.

This boundary-drawing practice is an important part of national identity formation. On the one hand, all refugees are represented as outsiders that negate the national self – either as victims of violence and oppression, or as criminals or 'tricksters.' The representation of refugees follows the principle of negation of the perceived national self. On the other hand, immigration debate establishes a boundary between deserving and undeserving refugees. In the dialectic of national identity formation, only deserving refugees are welcome to join the national community. Undeserving refugees will remain in their position as Others.

The Dialectic of Media Practice

Although media discourse establishes boundaries separating genuine from 'bogus' refugees, the allocation of refugee applicants to either side of the boundary is not always a straight-forward choice. Sometimes, media opinions differ on whether an applicant is a 'genuine' or 'bogus' refugee. The former scenario entails that a refugees deserve protection; the latter implies the rejection of a refugee claim.

Throughout the debate on immigration reform, the press discussed the deportation of 'terrorist' suspects to places where they could experience torture (for example: Borovoy, 1996; Bronskill, 1997; Thompson, 2001a). Is Canada committed to protecting all refugees from the prospect of torture? Or are 'terrorist' suspects categorically undeserving of

Canadian compassion and protection? The boundary between deserving fugitives of torture and undeserving 'terrorists' itself is undisputed, but the question is which category applies to a particular refugee applicant.

When the Supreme Court heard arguments in 2001 regarding the constitutionality of the anti-terrorist section of the Immigration Act, an article in the *National Post* reported that 'a large number of interveners, including the Canadian Bar Association, the Canadian Council for Refugees and the Canadian Civil Liberties Association, appeared before the court to argue that no one should be deported to possible torture' (Chwialkowska, 2001c: A10). Shortly after this article was published, another article in the *National Post* presented the other side of the argument:

> [Several] court cases have made it clear [that terrorists] . . . entered the country as refugee claimants. This was confirmed at the official level when the RCMP told a conference on Oct. 17 that the modus operandi of all international terrorists coming to Canada was first to claim refugee status and then move on to obtain welfare and medical benefits before turning to crime to boost their income. (Collacott, 2001b: A10)

Interestingly, the opposing interpretations appeared in the same newspaper, the *National Post*, illustrating that dialectical practice is integral to the manner in which this newspaper covers humanitarian immigration.

In order to further show how the media discussed refugee matters in a dialectical fashion, let me revisit the case of Manickavasagam Suresh and Mansour Ahani, which the Supreme Court heard in 2001 and which I introduced in the previous chapter. Suresh was a Sri Lankan refugee and alleged fund-raiser for the Liberation Tigers of Tamil Eelam; Mansour Ahani an Iranian refugee and a former member of the Iranian Ministry of Intelligence and Security. In relation to these court hearings, the media covered the aspect of humanitarian immigration in dialectical opposition to the danger aspect. For example, in May 2001, an article in the *Vancouver Sun* elaborated on the threat of terrorism to Canada: 'Terrorism and terrorist fund-raising are serious threats to Canada's security, particularly as this country is seen as a venue of opportunity for terrorists groups to raise funds, purchase arms and conduct other activities to support their organizations and terrorist activities elsewhere' (Tibbetts, 2001a: A3).

In the same month, an article in the *National Post* saw in Ahani and Suresh a challenge to freedom and democracy:

> The Canadian Charter of Rights and Freedoms allows governments to subject individual rights to limits 'justified in a free and democratic society.'
>
> 'Nothing is more inimical to a free and democratic society than terrorism,' the government will hope to convince the court. (Chwialkowska, 2001b: A8)

The counter-perspective typically presented Suresh and Ahani as deserving fugitives of torture and highlighted Canada's international commitments to humanitarianism. For example, an article that was also published in May 2001 in the *Ottawa Citizen* argued: 'Veteran [Supreme Court] Justice Frank Iacobucci led the pack with his assertion that sending people to countries where they would be tortured would "blow out of the water" international human rights conventions' (Tibbetts, 2001d: 7). Similarly, a report in the *Toronto Star* stated, in January 2002, as the case continued to occupy the media: 'Their [Ahani and Suresh's] lawyer Barbara Jackman says the principle in both cases is Canada's international reputation – "whether Canada is going to meet its commitment to the international community not to put people in a position where they may be tortured"' (MacCharles, 2002: 7).

Another case, which I also addressed in the previous chapter in the context of the danger of immigration, also features this dialectical method of newsprint reporting, weighing the danger of immigration against the valued Canadian principle of humanitarianism and the protection of humans against unjust punishment. This case involves Es-Sayy Jaballah, who was wanted in Egypt for inciting violence. A front-page article in the *Toronto Star* illustrates the conflict between inadmissibility due to alleged involvement in 'terrorism' and the protection of human rights:

> He [Jaballah] came to Canada in 1996 and claimed refugee status. His claim was denied last March and he was arrested. He has been in custody since, and says he would be executed if he returned to his native Egypt.
>
> . . .
>
> CSIS has accused Jaballah of maintaining contact with members of Egyptian al-Jihad, a group believed to be connected to last year's deadly embassy bombings in Kenya and Tanzania, court records show. (Vincent, 1999: A1)

An event that illustrates the contested representations of refugees as either unwanted criminals or victims of human rights abuses involved the deportation of six Somalis from Canada to Mogadishu. An article in the *National Post* defended the protection of human rights by appealing to 'Canadian values and principles' of humanitarianism:

> Some of the deportees had never been to Mogadishu before; many had been raised in North America and were unfamiliar with their native country.
>
> ...
>
> Under the watch of 15 private security officers, the group was flown to Somalia and left in Mogadishu, which many consider to be the world's most dangerous city...
>
> 'We are extremely concerned for these people,' says Mahamoud Hagi-Aden, a Somali-Canadian and a consultant to the Somali Centre for Family Services, based in Ottawa.
>
> ...
>
> Mr. Hagi-Aden suggested that the joint removal was undertaken covertly, in order not to attract attention. 'We work very closely with Immigration Canada, and are usually informed about deportations. In this case, we didn't hear anything. I think it runs contrary to Canadian values and principles.' (Hutchinson, 2002: A1)

The media coverage of these cases illustrates arising contradictions when migrants are pigeonholed into categories of deserving and undeserving refugees.

It would be simplistic, however, to describe the humanitarian aspect of the immigration debate as a binary of danger versus the need for protection. The complexity of media discourse is demonstrated by voices that complicate such a view. For example, newsprint reporting has occasionally highlighted the humanitarian international reputation of Canada beyond the binary representation of Canada as neither compassionate nor 'soft.' An article in the *Ottawa Citizen* quoted Tom Clark, coordinator of the Interchurch Committee for Refugees, who 'suspects Canada is currently "the deportation capital of the world"' (Harvey, 1997: A4). Another article in the *Toronto Star* implies that the number of refugees entering Canada is too small to warrant constructions of Canada as either compassionate or soft on the basis of humanitarian immigration: 'In fact, those presenting their claims for Convention refugee status at Canada's door numbered only 21,803 last year. Out of more than 30 million refugees worldwide, not counting some 15 million 'internally displaced,' a minuscule 0.0007 per cent arrive here as claimants' (Kastner, 1997: L1).

Another example of a challenge to the simple dialectic of the humanitarian aspect is the suggestion that Canada's refugee selection process is not guided by humanitarian principles but rather by self-interest. The same article points out that Canada receives mostly the young, motivated, and affluent: 'And it's not the "masses" who make it to Canada . . . Here, you don't see many old people. Only the well-to-do or the very inventive and very courageous' (Kastner, 1997: L1). Another article in the *Toronto Star* criticizes Canada's pick-and-choose attitude with respect to refugee selection:

> There is a deep-rooted prejudice against refugees who present themselves in Canada and ask for asylum . . . They are viewed as an inconvenience because, by virtue of their presence, we are legally obliged to respect their human rights.
>
> When refugees are overseas, on the other hand, we can pick and choose where and how and when we will bestow our generosity. (Dench, 1997: A13)

These examples illustrate that the narratives contained in the newsprint media's reporting on humanitarian immigration are contested. In fact, many reporters and commentators seek to destabilize conventional media perspectives.

Conclusion

Many newspaper articles I examined suggest that Canadian humanitarian immigration and refugee admission policies convey a positive image of Canada to the international community. Policies towards refugees and people in need create an identity of compassion. This interpretation of the humanitarian aspect of the immigration debate corresponds with existing research on the relationship between humanitarian-motivated immigration and refugee admission and national identity (Dauvergne, 2005). My analysis further suggests that journalists and commentators strategically juxtapose Canada's reputation with current political and administrative practices to construe some policies and practices as problematic – either as falling short of or overshooting Canada's identity as a country of compassion and a champion of human rights.

The media debate on humanitarian immigration revealed a dialectic of national identity formation. The representation of refugees and the circumstances they are enduring negate Canadian national identity. These circumstances are presented as unacceptable to Canada, requiring Canada to provide protection from them. At the basis of this negation rest the material inequalities between the refugees and Canadian society. Thus, the immigration debate reflects a perspective on the dialectical process that was also favoured by Feuerbach, Marx, and Engels and that challenges Hegel's emphasis on the internal reflection of the self. This perspective suggests that the dialectical process has a material basis. In the case of the humanitarian admission of refugees and immigrants to Canada, material inequality defines who is a refugee. Migrants and the conditions that they are escaping serve as objects of negation of national identity. Put simply, refugees come to Canada because it has the liberties, freedoms, and security that the countries of departure do not provide.

To establish where the boundary between deserving and undeserving refugees lies, media reporting focuses on disputed refugee claims and contested humanitarian policies. In particular, women who experience discrimination and violence, children who are separated from or abused by their families, and victims of natural disaster are represented as deserving refugees. These representations create a dialectical image of Canada as a gender-equal society, which protects children and supports victims of random disaster. In these newsprint discussions, violence, abuse, and misfortune constitute the material conditions for the negation of the national self.

The integration of refugees into Canadian society is an important practice of refugee settlement policy in Canada. In fact, after three to four years of permanent residency refugees are encouraged to become Canadian citizens. Implied with citizenship – as the citizenship test suggests – is the assumption that naturalized refugees will embrace 'Canadian' values and norms. In the words of Catherine Dauvergne, refugees and humanitarian migrants 'must be not like us in order to need our protection, but must be able to shed that identity and merge with the nation when required' (2005: 124). The incorporation of the refugee Other into the national self is an important practice of national identity formation. As refugees are absorbed into the national community, the contraction between the Other and the national self is supposed to be resolved. Hegel would call this dialectical practice a second negation, or *sublation*.

The integration of refugees into the nation, that is, the second negation, was rarely addressed in the sampled articles. If this issue was discussed at all, it was mostly done implicitly. For example, in an article in the *National Post*, the expectation that refugees from war-torn Kosovo would become permanent residents and eventually Canadian citizens was only apparent when Canada's refugee policies were compared with those of 'the U.S. [which] is insisting that all 20,000 Kosovars who it is giving temporary sanctuary must be returned to Kosovo when peace is restored,' and when the article quoted foreign affairs minister Lloyd Axworthy's defence of Canada's practice of extending permanent residency as 'part of our refugee commitments' (Fife, 1999: A12).

The newspaper articles also established the limits of Canada's compassion. This limit often conflates with the representation of immigrants as danger. Although the aspect of danger was discussed separately in the previous chapter, it is obviously linked to the humanitarian aspect. The press was outraged, for example, when war criminals, supporters of hate crimes, and violent offenders sought refuge in Canada. Obviously, it does not sanction such behaviour and denies these refugee applicants compassion. The characteristics that these refugees embody have no place in Canadian society. Unlike deserving refugees, the newsprint media does not represent these unwanted applicants as 'both other and not-other' (Dauvergne, 2005: 162). Their representations constitute a negation of the nation, but the second negation – their absorption into the Canadian national community – is prevented. They are excluded from proceeding in the dialectic of humanitarian immigration beyond the first negation.

Interestingly, deserving refugees worthy of inclusion in the national community are represented as passive victims. Conversely, undeserving refugees are portrayed as active agents of violence, crime, and immorality. Apparently, agency in the context of the second negation is reserved for the Canadian nation, which makes a decision on whether to accept refugees and bestow on them permanent residency. The refugees themselves are excluded from this decision and are expected to conform to it. The undeserving refugees, who are represented as possessing agency, are prevented from joining the nation and thus from engaging in the second negation of national identity formation. Furthermore, what defines refugees as undeserving are not material conditions of inequality but violations of normative taboos. A material basis for their inclusion is overshadowed by the path of violence and crime, which these refugees supposedly chose on their own. With the material inequality relativized, the undeserving refugees can be relegated to a permanent status of Otherness.

Even with this second negation, the integration of deserving refugees into Canadian society, the dialectic of national identity formation through immigration does not reach an end point. Rather, contradiction remains a characteristic feature of the immigration debate. The discursive drawing of boundaries that delineate the circumstances that define deserving and undeserving refugees is a separate process from allocating individuals to either side of this boundary. Noteworthy media debates involved the cases of refugees who were accused of supporting terrorism but who would also likely be tortured if deported. As terrorism supporters they are unworthy of incorporation into Canadian society, but as victims of torture they deserve compassion. The media debates of these cases illustrate that the question of admissibility is not a matter of degree of worthiness on a scale of material inequality, but rather a contradiction between conditions of material inequality and the violation of normative taboos. This contradiction, however, has not been resolved – neither in media discourse nor at the levels of policy or law in which this discourse is embedded.

6 Economic Utility

Canadian immigration policies pursue the obvious aim of stimulating economic development and growth. In fact, it can easily be argued that economic considerations are the core material interest and motivation behind Canada's immigration policies. This relationship between immigration and economy is also reflected in public and media debate. Although the media has given greater coverage to other aspects of immigration, such as its danger, it also frequently mentions economic considerations (as illustrated in chapter 3). In both material and discursive contexts, immigration is considered an economic utility.

In this chapter, I investigate the economic aspect of the media debate around Canadian immigration reform. In particular, I explore *how* the media presents immigration as an economic utility and pays special attention to the material context of policy and economic circumstances in which this debate occurred. Thereby, I address two dimensions of the immigration dialectic: first, I examine the material embeddedness of the immigration debate; second, I explore the dialectical nature of journalistic practice related to the economic utility of immigration. In pursuit of the first dimension, I situate immigration debate in a political economy perspective of immigration policy and practice. To fully appreciate this perspective, I begin with a brief discussion of the economic utility of immigration.

Economies of Immigration

Academic debate has long examined the material underpinnings of migration and immigration.[1] The migration of people is often motivated by economic need or want. Many migrants leave places because they suffer economic hardship, ranging from starvation to the lack of career opportunities; and they move to places where they hope to find better economic conditions. While migration practices involve decisions made by individuals, structural circumstances are also important for understanding migration patterns. For many industrial economies, immigration has become a 'structural necessity' (Cohen, 1987: 137). This structural importance of immigration applies to both settler societies and ethnic nations. In previous research I found that immigration regulates the labour markets of both Canada and Germany (Bauder, 2006b).[2] In a Canadian context, other researchers also support this view that the national economy is highly dependent on migrant labour (Basok, 2002; Sharma, 2006). Immigration policies must be understood in the context of such structural economic necessity.

Over the last decade, immigration has become increasingly entangled with neoliberal practice. Economic geographers have examined the relationship between international migration, the regulation of local and regional economies, and 'neoliberal globalization' (Herod, 2000: 1781; also Leitner, 2003). This relationship has been approached from various perspectives. On the one hand, vulnerable migrants – including regular migrants, no-status immigrants, and temporary and seasonal migrants – compete with displaced non-migrant labour in the secondary segment of the labour market, undermining existing labour and wage standards. Throughout industrialized countries, the criminalization of immigrants,[3] their cultural exclusion, and the denial of social and economic rights has produced a highly 'flexible' – that is to say, vulnerable and dependent – labour force (Balibar, 2000; Bourdieu, 2002; Nevins, 2002). The competition between these migrants and non-migrant workers has facilitated the flexibilization of the entire labour market and has undermined the welfare state. On the other hand, international migration can be viewed as an infustion of human capital, a stimulus for creativity, entrepreneurship, and investment (see, e.g., Kloosterman and Rath, 2003; Florida, 2002). Immigration can thus be seen as contributing to economic restructuring from both the bottom and the top of the labour market. From both perspectives, immigration has become an integrated element in industrialized countries' turn away from a strong regulatory and supportive function of the state towards a neoliberal paradigm dominated by small government, market ideology, and the competition principle.

The economic utility of immigration has not been lost on Canadian policymakers. Immigration law and policy in Canada has long been aligned with economic interests (Green and Green, 1999). In Canada's early period of colonization, 'manpower needs' (Knowles, 1997: 6) shaped immigration and settlement policies. This language, of course, is highly misleading, because the needed labour force included women in domestic and other occupations.[4] In the period from 1962 to 1989, Canada's immigration policy underwent several important changes. With the removal of racial bias towards European immigration from official policy and the post-war economic recovery in Europe, the immigration of qualified European labour declined. In response, the 1976 Immigration Act (part 1, section 3h) made explicit reference to the aim of immigration to foster economic development. The new legislation established a carefully crafted points system to attract immigrants who could satisfy the particular demands for labour that existed in a Canadian economy that was still based on import-substitution industrialization and manufacturing (Simmons, 1999b: 43–5). Immigration aimed at regulating the national labour market by attracting needed workers, without undermining the position of the existing Canadian workforce.

Since the late 1980s, Canadian immigration policy has followed a neoliberal agenda, and pursued 'a reduced role of government' and 'increasing national competitiveness in the context of economic globalization' (Simmons, 1999a: 53; see also Arat-Koç, 1999). Correspondingly, the economic class has gained in relative importance for the selection of immigrants permitted entry to Canada. Currently, the majority of immigration falls under this class. Other industrialized countries, including Germany via the Süssmuth commission, have sought to emulate Canada's immigration policy that selects immigrants with a view to making the national economy globally more competitive, while shifting the administrative and settlement costs of immigration to the immigrants.

The neoliberalization of economic-utility-driven Canadian immigration policy can be separated into two phases. The first phase occurred in the years from 1989 to 1994. During this phase, Canadian immigration policy was set on a general neoliberal course. An agenda focusing on competition and small government sought to raise the short-term economic benefits from immigration by selecting immigrants who possessed large amounts of human or monetary capital. At the same time, processing fees and a reduction of government transfer payments to immigrants aimed to recoup some of the costs of administration and settlement. During this phase, Canada's policy of attracting professionals and investors followed the country's self-image as a 'sophisticated niche player in a competitive economy' (Simmons, 1999b: 45–6).

In addition, the resistance against immigration by labour organizations receded. Traditionally, labour unions kept a critical eye on immigration because they saw immigration as raising competition in the national labour market. This resistance declined with the belief that in a climate of 'globalization' an influx of immigrants rich in human and monetary capital would create economic opportunities for all Canadians (Simmons, 1999a; Simmons and Keohane, 1992). During this first phase of neoliberalization, a trend became discernible that suggested that the positions of capital and labour on immigration were converging on the perceived need of Canada to remain globally competitive.

Although immigration policy had generally been reoriented to accommodate the competition principle in this initial phase, by the mid-1990s 'the policy transition was incomplete and was complicated by value conflicts in Canadian society and by new immigration pressures in the international system' (Simmons, 1999a: 54). In light of these complications, the existing neoliberal immigration policy agenda was consolidated in a second phase. This phase coincided with the immigration debate that began in 1996 and continued until 2004.

During this second phase, the 2002 Immigration and Refugee Protection Act (section 3c) reiterated the contribution of immigration to Canada's economic prosperity. The points system was changed to no longer provide points for an applicant's particular occupation but rather to assess the applicant's labour market flexibility based on education, language capacity, experience, and age. A prevailing expectation in Canadian immigration policy debate is that skilled, flexible, and capital-rich immigrants will make the Canadian economy globally competitive. While the concrete economic impact of immigration has proved difficult to assess, the immigration of highly skilled and educated workers has been discursively constructed as an economic opportunity (Li, 2003).[5]

The processes through which immigration policy is formed are complex. In fact, the objectives of Canadian immigration policy are not purely economic, but may be 'much broader and more visionary' (Li, 2003: 79). As I illustrate throughout this book, the immigration dialectic involves multiple aspects. The economic aspect, however, is especially important, as the economic interests of businesses, corporations, and labour deeply penetrate every dimension of society. These interests are also mediated and internalized by the state and the manner in which the state formulates immigration policy (Freeman, 1995; Veugelers, 2000). Furthermore, these economic interests are entangled with cosmopolitan viewpoints that valorize internationalism, multiculturalism, and pro-immigration liberalism (Hardcastle et al., 1994). At the same time, these interests reflect the neoliberal agenda of competition and labour market flexibilization. I would expect these viewpoints also to appear in the media debate of immigration reform.

In the next section, I examine the economic aspect of the immigration debate in relation to the neoliberalization of corresponding immigration policies. The questions which I pursue in this discussion include: how does the media represent the role of economic immigration and immigrants in the period of neoliberal policy consolidation; and how do these representations correspond to the material circumstances of actual immigration policy? I am applying the dialectical principle as a methodology that enables me to interpret the immigration debate as a series of themes within which opposing viewpoints are articulated.

Beyond Dialectics

Before examining the contradictions and opposing arguments related to the economic aspect of the immigration debate, I need to establish the parameters within which this dialectic occurs. In other words, some ideas are so firmly engrained in the collective imagination that they are taken for granted and rarely questioned. Such ideas exist beyond the dialectic of media debate.[6] However, they provide the bedrock upon which the immigration dialectic unfolds.

In the context of the economic aspect of Canadian immigration debate, an underlying idea is that immigration must produce economic benefits for Canada. This idea is a fundamental assumption of the debate. For example, an artice in the *Vancouver Sun* quotes a 1998 report by the legislative review committee on immigration, affirming the report's aim 'that immigrants should contribute to Canada's prosperity' (Coyne, 1998: A19). Similarly, an op-ed in the *National Post*, responding to an article by the newspaper's editor-in-chief, remarks: 'We must ensure that [immigration] levels are established in accordance with the economic and demographic needs of the country and that immigrants are selected on the basis of their ability to contribute to the economy' (Collacott, 2001c: A10). While the author opposes the 'open-door policy' advocated by the original article, he agrees on the principle that immigration should produce 'benefit for the people already here' (ibid.). In a comment on the newly passed Immigration and Refugee Protection Act, the same author criticizes the aspect of the new law enabling family reunification: 'Immigration policies must also take into account the economic interests of the receiving country' (Collacott, 2001a: A12). In a similar vein, the *Toronto Star* quoted the Canadian Chamber of Commerce in the following way: 'Immigrants are critical to the economic viability and success of our nation. Growth is the key to business, and the Canadian economy' (*Toronto Star,* 1999: 1).

The view that immigration should produce economic benefits is also apparent in a *Toronto Star* article that presents a historical perspective on immigration. This article quoted York University political scientist Reg Whitaker as follows: 'In the long term, [immigration] has been the lifeblood of the country, the engine of economic growth' (Schiller, 1999: 1). This front-page article further notes that after the removal of racial bias in Canadian immigration policy in the 1960s, 'it was in Canada's interest to absorb as many immigrants as it could. They are a major contribution to economic growth' (ibid.). An editorial in the *Toronto Star* affirms the importance of eager and hard-working immigrants in the past: 'This country was built by immigrants who, in their day, wouldn't have qualified as the brightest and best. They came because Canada was a land of opportunity and they worked hard to build a new life' (2000: 1). More than one year later, a front-page article in the *Toronto Star* qualifies this perspective, but holds on to the underlying idea that immigration should generate economic growth in Canada:

> [Immigration minister] Caplan said some of the mythology about the hard-working, blue collar immigrants who built this country is a thing of the past . . .
>
> '. . . Right now, we know that the economic competitive advantage for Canada is that we have a knowledge-based economy here. We are looking to bring people here that will integrate and succeed quickly,' she said. (Thompson, 2001c: A1)

Also in reference to a historical context, an editorial in the *National Post* states: 'Immigration can be the lifeblood of a country. For that to be so in Canada's case, however, it must be based on the needs of our economy' (2000a: A17). This editorial compares Canada'a historical aims of stopping US military expansion by welcoming United Empire

Loyalists and settling the prairies by admitting European farmers with today's aims of fostering immigration to produce economic benefit: 'Those were deliberate policies . . . It was Canada's needs that were pre-eminent. Similarly, today, Canada no longer needs large numbers of uneducated migrants who, if they exceed the number of unskilled jobs, are unable to contribute to society. We need skilled, educated entrepreneurs' (ibid.).

The taken-for-granted viewpoint that immigration should produce economic benefits for Canadian society supports my earlier interpretation of the immigration debate. In chapter 3 I suggested that the economic aspect of immigration is not atop the media's agenda in its coverage of immigration reform because the media does not challenge as a contested issue the underlying idea that immigration should produce economic benefits. The economic aspect may be the centrepiece of immigration policy, but for media and public debate it is simply not as interesting as other more contested aspects (in particular, the danger aspect). This interpretation also resonates with another study that found that the economic utility of immigration is widely agreed upon in public discourse (Li, 2003).[7]

Nevertheless, the economic aspect of immigration is not entirely neglected in media debate. In fact, it is the fourth most frequently covered aspect in the immigration debate (chapter 3). Given the assumption that immigration should serve Canadian economic interests, there are still numerous contested questions as to how these economic benefits should be achieved. The agreement on the economic utility of immigration merely sets the stage for a debate on the economic role of immigration that features three distinct themes, each expressing opposing positions.

How to Realize Economic Benefits

The first theme involves the media's discussion of how economic benefits should be realized and how harm to Canadian workers and businesses could be averted. Regarding the question of 'how to realize economic benefits' the media articulates two positions. The first position assumes that Canada competes for labour with other countries and will suffer economically if it fails to attract young skilled immigrants. The second position proposes that immigrants constitute labour competition and could harm the domestic labour force if immigration is not tightly controlled.[8]

Numerous newspaper articles express the idea that Canada is competing internationally for young skilled workers. An article in the *Vancouver Sun* cites the 1998 report of the legislative review committee on immigration that 'Canada is competing with other industrialized countries to attract the best human capital, [and] that we are not always on the winning side of this competition' (Coyne, 1998: A19). An article in the *Toronto Star* quoted immigration minister Elinor Caplan: '"Bringing the best and the brightest is in Canada's interest. We are competing with the rest of the world for those people"' (Thompson, 2001c). Similarly, the *Ottawa Citizen* published an article suggesting that delays in changes to immigration legislation 'are costing Canada the opportunity to draw in top talent' (Baxter, 2002: A6).

Next to human capital, skills, and talent, age is an important factor in maximizing the benefits of immigration to Canada's international competitiveness.[9] An article in the *National Post* furthermore argues that young immigrants will make Canada's economy globally more competitive: 'The relatively young populations of Latin American and Indo-Asia could become comparative advantages while industrialized countries with ageing workers, such as Europe and Japan, will compete with Canada for skilled immigrants' (Chwialkowska, 2001a: A1). This argument is echoed by another article in the same newspaper: 'The global search for skilled labour is heating up as Canada and other industrialized countries, particularly in Western Europe, confront the double-edged sword of slowing birth rates and ageing populations' (Mandel-Campbell, 2002: 1). Immigration of young people is presented as a demographic advantage in the global economic competition among industrialized countries whose natural birth rates are in decline.

Some voices in the press lament that Canada's immigration policies aimed at attracting skilled workers are not aggressive enough. For example, the *National Post* reports:

> But while some countries are easing entry restrictions . . . , Canada is making it harder to immigrate. Changes to the immigration act unveiled this month discriminate against both highly skilled white-collar professionals as well as skilled trades, say critics . . . 'The new rules are going to make Canada a lot less competitive than we are now,' said Mr. Trister [chair of the immigration committee for the Canadian Bar Association]. 'It puts us in a worse position than before, just when other countries are opening up.' (Mandel-Campbell, 2002: 1)

An editorial in the *Vancouver Sun* concurs with this viewpoint. This editorial predicts that 'we can expect stiffer competition [for skilled immigrants] from industrial powers in Europe, the United States and Japan' and in response proposes 'a more hospitable tax environment . . . so we can convince the world's best and brightest to come here rather than go [to] the U.S.' (2000b: A22).

Some voices in the press note the prospect that immigrants might return to their country of origin or move on to third countries. This possibility further intensifies the international competition for immigrant workers. The *Vancouver Sun* published a petition advocating fewer immigration restrictions, stating that immigrants 'will move to greener pastures, taking their brains and profits with them when the occasion arises' (1998: A19). Along similar lines, an article in the *Ottawa Citizen* observes: 'Thirty per cent of immigrants are gone after three years, most of them because Canada does not provide the outlet for their skills' (Martin, 1999: A13).

The opposing position assumes that immigrant workers flood the labour market and thereby diminish the job prospects of non-immigrants or earlier arrivals. For example, an article in the *National Post* suggests that the skilled labour market segment is already saturated:

> It is no secret . . . that many recent immigrants are suffering because they are being encouraged to come here without good prospects of finding suitable employment. The ones affected most severely by this situation are those already here who are struggling to find work in competition with large numbers of new arrivals in a job market where . . . Canada will probably have a surplus of skilled workers in general for the remainder of the present decade. (Collacott, 2003: FP13)

In an opinion piece published in the *Ottawa Citizen*, the president of the Capital Region Guide Association opposes immigration reform because the 'new laws could further strip highly trained Canadian and Ottawa-based tour guides of their jobs . . . The recommended changes to the Immigration Act which would give foreigners more freedom to work in Canada and allow them to do so for longer periods of time, will only lead to further unemployment for Ottawa guides' (Leon, 1998: B5).

Some commentators openly reject the argument that immigrants harm Canadian workers economically because their presence increases competition in the labour market. By making reference to historical injustices, an article in the *Vancouver Sun* conveys that this argument of 'job stealing' is outdated:

> Not long after [1860], British immigrants were complaining bitterly about more recent immigrants from Asia stealing jobs from decent working men and corrupting the city.
>
> . . .
>
> Labor unions that today battle for the rights of minorities were once at the forefront of a bitter struggle to keep Chinese workers out of the coal mines. (Hume, 1997)

The discussion of how the economic benefits of immigration should be realized has a dual character that juxtaposes two opposing positions. This dual character is also apparent in other themes in the debate of the economic role of immigration.

How to Regulate the Labour Market

A second theme involves the economic role of immigration in regulating the labour market. The two opposing positions are as follows: The first position endorses the ideology of the market, suggesting that the mechanism of the market will match immigrants with available jobs. The second position argues that selective immigration should be used to regulate the supply of labour in particular occupations.

Articles that embrace the first position, that is, that endorse market ideology, use particular terminology, such as 'flexible skill sets' (Mandel-Campbell, 2002: 1) or a 'broader view of "human capital"' (Coyne, 1998: A19), to identify the characteristics of desired immigrants. An article in the *Vancouver Sun* supports a report by Citizenship and Immigration Canada proposing to select immigration with 'a wide variety of transferable skills' (Skelton, 1999b: A1). Such terminology is common in connection to free-market ideas of labour market regulation.

Some articles are explicit about the market ideology that this first position represents. For example, one of the aforementioned articles in the *Vancouver Sun* is suspicious of the 'ability of state planners to predict labour market trends' (Coyne, 1998: A19). The author of this article critiques the existing immigrant selection system that assesses applicants based on their occupation. Instead, this author supports admitting immigrants based on flexible skills and 'then let buyers and sellers of labor find each other in the market' (ibid.). According to this viewpoint, immigrant selection based on flexible skills and education is desirable because it avoids 'pigeonholing' (Baxter, 2002: A6) immigrants into occupational categories that are difficult to define. According to this position, immigration plays an important role in the expansion of the entire skilled and educated segment of the Canadian labour force. This expansion ensures continuing economic growth in a global economy in which talent, skills, and flexibility are increasingly valuable. In this context, the media often points out Canada's declining birth rates and aging population. For example, an article in the *National Post* refers to a ticking 'time bomb' that immigration is supposed to help defuse:

> Ottawa has identified a demographic time bomb ticking under the national economy. The growth rate of the Canadian-born work force is expected to hit zero as early as 2011 . . .
>
> Fearing that a shrinking work force will stifle economic activity, Jane Stewart, the Human Resources minister, will introduce measures this fall to help skilled immigrants qualify quickly for jobs in Canada . . .
>
> The economy could suffer unless the labour force continues to grow, economists say. (Chwialkowska, 2001a: A1)

In contrast to the position that the market mechanism should match skilled immigrants with jobs, some articles identify particular occupations in which labour demand should be satisfied through immigrants. The *Toronto Star,* for example, suggests that effective immigration policy needs to ensure that selection is closely linked to labour demand in certain occupations, such as computer programming:

> Canada needs about 20,000 computer programmers now. But the department takes an average of two to two-and-a-half years to process a qualified applicant . . .
>
> That partially explains why so many skilled people have no jobs; by the time they come, the demand is long over. (1999: 1)

This article implies that if immigration policy was implemented properly, the short supply of labour in some occupations would be filled with immigrants in a timely manner. By extension, this article further implies that rather than revising the points system to select flexible immigrants based on general skills and education, the existing system – which at that time assigned points on the basis of an occupational list – should be managed more effectively.

Similarly, a front-page article in the *Vancouver Sun* laments British Columbia's 'critical shortage of nurses' (Lee and McInnes, 2000: A1) and suggests using a special agreement between the federal government and the province to 'import large numbers of qualified foreign workers to solve labour shortages.' The article furthermore argues in favour of a more effective administration of the points system to match immigration with existing labour shortages:

> The General Occupations List used by immigration officials to turn away badly needed doctors and nurses has not been updated in almost four years, federal officials confirmed Tuesday.
>
> Foreign doctors have received similar [rejection] letters, despite severe shortages of medical personnel in hospitals and clinics around the province. (ibid.)

Immigrant workers are also in short supply in other occupations, such as 'high-tech and specialized manufacturing' industries, according to an article in the *National Post* (Mandel-Campbell, 2002: 1).

Another article in the *National Post* criticizes the Canadian government's intention to raise the skill levels of immigrants. According to this article, workers are needed in low-skilled and semi-skilled occupations. The article paraphrases the comments of a lawyer representing the immigration section of the Canadian Bar Association, who

> believes the proposal [of revising the points system] would put up impossible barriers to less-educated, but still-needed, workers like truck drivers and tool and die makers.
>
> The Canadian Trucking Association confirmed yesterday there's an increasingly serious shortage of qualified drivers, more than 2,000 in Quebec alone . . .
>
> The association has recently approached federal immigration officials to discuss how it can attract foreign drivers. (Duffy, 1999: A11)

Along the same lines, an opinion article in the *Toronto Star* reports on a skilled bricklayer, Michael, from Malta, who was discouraged by immigration officials from immigrating to Canada although he had already secured three job offers from Canadian employers:

> Michael was not asked about whether his trade was in demand, or even if he already had a job offer, but whether he spoke English or French fluently and whether he had a university or at least college degree.
>
> . . .

> [This] story illustrates the challenges that the residential construction industry within the Greater Toronto Area is facing – a chronic shortage of skilled trades . . . Historically the need for skilled labour in our industry has been met through immigration.
>
> . . .
>
> Immigration when tied to skilled trade shortages is a positive force for our economy that must be supported. (Libfeld, 2002: M19)

The laissez-faire self-regulation of the labour market and the managed regulation of immigration into particular occupations represent opposing ideological positions of labour market regulation. The press is obviously aware of these positions and includes them in their reporting on the economic aspect of immigration reform.

Victim and Perpetrator

Media discourse covers a third theme that identifies the victims and the perpetrators related to the economic aspect of immigration. As with the previous themes, newspaper reporting presents two opposing positions. According to one position, immigrants are the victims of exploitation and deskilling inflicted by Canadian immigration policies and labour market regulations. The other position reverses these roles of victim and perpetrator, and argues that immigrants threaten the economic well-being of Canadians. Although both positions imply different causal processes, I discuss these positions in the context of a single theme because they deploy a similar discursive mechanism of constructing a victim and a perpetrator. In other words, this theme follows a particular logic of cause and effect. The opposing positions, however, reverse the direction of this logic.

The first position, which identifies immigrants as victims, is represented by an article with the headline 'Illegals used as cheap labour' in the *National Post.* This article reports on the migrants who arrived in 1999 on British Columbia's shores via boat. It describes these migrants as 'fortune-seekers from China's Fujian' province whose vulnerability and desperation define their situation as workers:

> They work for low wages to send money to their families in China.
>
> 'They take jobs that you and I would not take,' Joanne Lau, a Metro Toronto South East Asian Legal Clinic lawyer, says. (Tanner, 1999: A6)

In reference to the same event, another article in the *National Post* quotes former University of Toronto history professor Mike Szonyi: 'There is a huge demand for unregulated cheap labour in North America . . . The only way to stop the smugglers is to stop the demand' (Jimenéz, 2000a: B1). This demand-side argument puts the blame for the migrant's exploitation on Canadian regulators who fail to curb informal employment.

The victimization of immigrants also resonates with the reporting of the non-recognition of foreign credentials and the devaluation of immigrants' skills. A series of articles in the *Vancouver Sun* addressed this issue and consulted experts on the matter. One article quotes Toronto immigration lawyer Peter Rekai: '"If you were a bank manager in Istanbul, you're not going to be a bank manager in Toronto . . . A lot of these people are selling stereos at Future Shop"' (Skelton, 1999b: A1). Another article in this series quotes Leah Diana, a spokeswoman for the Filipino Nurses Support Network: '"There are thousands of Filipino women working as domestic workers who are trained in their home country as nurses . . . But they are trapped in this cycle of being domestic workers because Immigration won't recognize their credentials"' (Lee and McInnes, 2000: A1). In a similar vein, Simon Fraser University economics professor Don DeVoretz stated: '"The problem with [government policy seeking to attract educated immigrant] is they're ending up as taxi drivers"' (Skelton, 1999a: A1). An editorial written by the staff of the *Vancouver Sun* identifies the Canadian government and professional regulatory bodies as the perpetrators and asks when the government will 'stop professional bodies – doctors, nurses, engineers, teachers, accountants among others – from erecting unnecessary barriers that hinder qualified people from working in their fields' (2000b: A22).

The counter-position, that immigrants threaten the economic well-being of Canadian society, is represented in a series of articles in the *National Post.*[10] One article opens with Milton Friedman's well-known statement: 'It's just obvious that you can't have free immigration and a welfare state' (Francis, 2002: FP3). The *Post* article elaborates:

> An unprecedented three million people have been allowed into this country since 1986 and two million were not screened under the economic or educational point system. That's why too many newcomers are a net burden on our economy.
>
> . . .
>
> Welfare is only part of the cost. Newcomers impose untold medical, legal, educational and housing costs. (ibid.)

Other commentators concur with the position that immigration causes economic harm to Canada. An article in the *National Post* suggests that immigrants who are not selected under economic considerations are economically underperforming and a burden to Canada's welfare system:

> The priority we have given to welcoming extended family members has resulted in a dramatic fall in the economic performance of immigrants over the past two decades . . .
>
> . . . Among the various categories of immigrants, family-class members alone show an increase in the use of welfare the longer they stay in Canada. (Collacott, 2001a: A12)

In the same vein, a *National Post* editorial compares the failures of European immigration policies to the potential impact of immigration in Canada: 'Europe has learned what Canada soon will: Poor, uneducated labourers are not the solution to a staggering welfare state' (2000a: A17).

Some reporting links the viewpoint that immigrants threaten the welfare state to the notion that educated and flexible immigrants offer greater benefits to Canada. For example, an article in the *National Post* remarks that 'immigrants with university degrees pay more income tax and rely less on welfare than less-educated newcomers' (Duffy, 1999: A11). Similarly, an article in the *Toronto Star* acknowledges that the immigration 'minister's insistence on attracting the "best and brightest" immigrants . . . will be popular with taxpayers who want newcomers who don't put any strain on the public purse' (2000: 1). Such a perspective joins the theme of victims and perpetrators with the earlier theme of how to regulate labour markets. In particular, it connects the position that wrongly selected immigrants are perpetrators who cause economic harm with the position that only skilled immigrants who are flexible and adaptable are able to perform in an economy that is regulated by the market principle.

Conclusion

The economic aspect of immigration debate reflected an overarching perspective that immigration should bring economic benefits to Canada and its population. The perspective that immigration should generally be restricted to protect the Canadian economy and labour market was absent in this debate. This singular perspective on the economic aspect of immigration indicates that there is wide agreement on the principle that immigration should be accompanied by economic gain for Canada. That this issue is not contested goes a long way in explaining why the economic aspect receives relatively little attention in the press compared to the danger and humanitarian aspects.

Such agreement on the issue that immigration should be economically beneficial to the Canadian national community fits well with the country's identity as a settler nation. This identity does not confront any dialectical opposition. An important part of Canadian identity is the recognition that previous generations of immigrants 'built' the country through their hard labour, their work in the resource industry, and their human capital, which has contributed to making Canada a highly industrialized nation. Currently, their economic contribution and the prospect of economic prosperity are still seen as an important reason why immigrants choose, and are permitted, to come to Canada. In the debate of immigration reform, this idea of the economic relevance of immigration to Canada is represented as a guiding principle for future immigration policy. Despite the relatively infrequent media reporting on the economic aspect of immigration, this aspect of the media debate is important because it relates to a key feature of existing Canadian immigration policy. The majority of immigrants to Canada are selected based on the economic principle, which the economic-class category and especially the points system are designed to implement.

The discussions which have addressed the economic aspect of immigration could be subdivided into different themes. Within these themes the discussion has reflected a dialectic of opposing positions. These insights contribute further to the picture that has emerged from the previous chapters: the immigration debate juxtaposes various positions, and often expresses contradictory dualisms of 'pro and con,' 'for and against,' or 'us and them.'

At first sight, the various themes and the various opposing positions make the economic aspect of immigration debate appear very fragmented. However, two overarching and connecting narratives wave through the debate. A closer look at the debate shows that the various themes and oppositional positions can be reconfigured along the lines of two clashing, but internally coherent, ideological paradigms. The first narrative follows a *neoliberal* paradigm, which endorses the competition principle and market ideology. This paradigm also seeks to reduce costs to the Canadian public associated with immigration. The second narrative involves a *regulatory* paradigm that focuses on the rejection of the competition principle, favours occupational regulation, and expresses solidarity with immigrants.

The neoliberal narrative is represented by the position that Canada competes internationally for young skilled labour. This narrative endorses the competition principle and proposes that a proactive and aggressive immigration policy to compete successfully for international labour enables Canada to realize the economic benefits of immigration. The neoliberal narrative also embraces the ideology of the market as the ideal matching mechanism of immigrant labour with jobs. Immigrants should have flexible skill sets that enable them to be matched with the jobs the market provides. An additional position of this neoliberal narrative is that immigrants threaten the welfare state. Although neoliberal policies usually seek to demolish rather defend welfare systems, this position is consistent with other neoliberal labour strategies, such as rendering immigrants vulnerable and exploitable. When migrants are seen as a threat to the welfare state, the neoliberal response is not to stop needed immigrant labour, but rather to select immigrants who will be less likely to enter the welfare system and deny welfare rights and unemployment benefits to newly arriving immigrants (Simmons, 1999a).

The regulatory narrative suggests that immigrants constitute labour competition for non-migrant workers. In contrast to the neoliberal narrative, it sees competition as destructive. Competition between immigrants and non-immigrants will lead to unemployment and lower wages for all. The role of the state is therefore to protect the national labour market through policies that control immigration. Only for occupations in which labour is in short demand should the supply of labour be increased through selective immigration. The rejection of the competition principle also resonates with the viewpoint that immigrants are victims of deskilling and exploitation in the labour market. If immigrants work for low wages, in unfavourable working conditions, and below their skill levels, then they undermine the wage and labour standards in the entire labour market.

The economic aspect of immigration debate is materially embedded in a historical context that is defined by the neoliberalization of immigration policy. The immigration debate, however, is not as strictly biased towards the neoliberal paradigm as the immigration policies that were actually implemented by the migration reform. Rather, in the media debate, the neoliberal and regulatory narratives coexist. While public policy on economic immigration has pursued primarily a neoliberal agenda, the representations of the economic case of immigration that circulated through the press were more balanced.

In a way, the two paradigms of the media debate of the economic aspect of immigration reflect different historical models of Canadian immigration policy. The neoliberal paradigm reflects the policies that were implemented in the immigration reform and the Immigration and Refugee Protection Act of 2002. The regulatory model, by contrast, was more prominent in the past. For example, for most of the twentieth century, immigration levels were coordinated with the business cycle; they were increased during economic boom periods and decreased in the recessions of the 1930s, 1970s, and early 1980s. In addition, the initial points system assessed immigration applications based on a detailed list of occupations in which labour was in demand. This regulatory model, however, has been increasingly replaced by a neoliberal model which focuses on attracting immigrants with 'flexible' skill sets who compete across the entire job market.

Despite the shift from regulatory to neoliberal immigration policies, media discourse has juxtaposed both models. The media neither blindly follows the neoliberal paradigm nor does it cover immigration in a one-sided manner that suits the neoliberal agenda of policymaking. Rather, the influence of a neoliberal agenda on media discourse is balanced with interests that favour a more stringently regulated labour market. This disconnection between immigration debate and policy raises important questions about the dialectical relation between media representations and the material practices of immigration. I can offer two interpretations for the divergence between media representations and material policy.

The first interpretation is that the balance in media reporting has not translated into immigration policy. Policy has shifted disproportionately towards the neoliberal paradigm because media debate is detached from the political process through which immigration policy and law are formed. On the one hand, media debate may simply lag behind in the manner in which it incorporates the language and concepts normalized by neoliberal practice. On the other hand, the disconnection between media debate and public policy is not unusual with respect to immigration. The analysis that I have presented in this chapter may suggest that lawmakers have implemented the neoliberal paradigm, following structural imperatives while they simply reject the regulatory paradigm that has equally circulated through the press. This first interpretation denies the media a strong role in the process of formulating immigration policy.

A second interpretation looks beyond the period of immigration reform and considers developments that occurred after the initiation and implementation the Immigration and Refugee Protection Act. This second interpretation suggests that the media debate of immigration reform anticipated a policy shift that occurred years later. In August 2008, the minister of citizenship and immigration of that time, Diane Finley, announced the Canadian Experience Class, which allows temporary workers who are already in Canada and foreign students with degrees in professional, technical, and managerial fields from Canadian institutions to immigrate. The Economic Experience Class marks a policy shift towards the immigration of workers who have already found a niche in the Canadian labour market and indirectly targets occupations in which immigrants are obviously in demand. Furthermore, shortly after announcing the Canadian Experience Class, in November 2008, the Canadian government published a list of thirty-eight occupations as an eligibility criterion for applicants to participate in the points system. To some degree, the introduction of this list marks a return to the regulatory paradigm, which selects immigrants to work in particular occupations in which labour is in demand. In addition, Citizenship and Immigration Canada has dramatically increased the number of temporary foreign workers permitted entry into Canada,[11] which has further enabled coordinating migration with the cyclical demands of the labour market.

Both interpretations imply that media debate is more consistent than actual policy. While policy may switch directions from the regulatory to the neoliberal and other paradigms, the media has kept the various perspectives on its radar screen. The dialectical principle is firmly engrained in the Canadian media when it reports on immigration.

PART THREE

Immigration Debate in an Ethnic Nation

7 Nation of *Wirtschaftswunder*?

In the context of Germany's immigration law, the media discussed economic matters more often than any other topic. The manner in which the media discusses the economic utility of immigration in Germany bears similarities to Canada. Most important, the economic aspect of the debate is dialectically embedded in particular material and legal contexts. On the one hand, Germany, like Canada, has been affected by the trend of neoliberalization associated with globalization. On the other hand, the material context in which immigration debate is embedded has deep historical and geographical roots. Therefore, important differences exist in terms of the content and character of the economic aspect of immigration debate between Canada and Germany, and the neoliberal paradigm manifests itself in a nationally contingent way.

As in the previous chapter, I focus on several dimensions of the immigration dialectic. First, I explore the relation between linguistic and material practice. Second, I focus on the journalistic practice of presenting information through juxtaposition and contradiction. Third, I investigate how the economic aspect of immigration debate relates to German national identity. To set the stage for this interpretation, I discuss the material relationship between economy and immigration in the German context.

Neoliberalism and the Economic Utility of Immigration

In the German context, existing scholarship typically approaches immigration from two angles. The first angle sees Germany as an ethnic nation. The image that emerges from this perspective presents Germany as a country that is defined through common ancestry, shared language, and a collective bond with German territory. Exclusionary policies and attitudes towards immigration and immigrants can be explained by the necessary inability of immigrants who do not have German ancestors, are not native German speakers, and come from a 'foreign' country to belong to the German nation. Germany's long-standing and only recently softened *jus sanguinis* citizenship legislation reflects this perspective.[1] According to this ethnic perspective, immigration threatens the imagined ethno-cultural homogeneity of the nation, which explains anti-immigration attitudes among portions of the German public and restrictive immigration policies (Oberndörfer, 1992; Heckmann, 1992; Münz et al., 1999). The migrants' role as cultural outsiders has economic consequences: they are culturally excluded from equal economic participation, experience higher unemployment rates, and work disproportionately in the secondary segment of the labour market (Bauder, 2006b).

This perspective on the immigrant as culturally non-belonging must be juxtaposed with a second viewpoint that stresses the economic role of immigration. As in the case of Canada, Germany and its national economy have been structurally dependent on immigration for much of the post–Second World War period. This economic importance of international migration has not been lost on lawmakers and the media. In previous chapters, I showed that in a settler society like Canada, immigration law serves the economic objectives of the existing population. Similar to the tools in a toolbox, which a mechanic uses to repair various broken items, government can select and apply a range of immigration-related policies to fix various problems, including filling labour shortages and attracting investment capital (Ley, 2003; Piore, 1979).

To a certain degree, European and North American migration policies are converging in this context. In light of global neoliberal restructuring and the associated 'integration of economies [and] alignment of rules' (Pellerin, 1999: 999), settler societies and traditional non-immigration countries are pursuing similar economic objectives with their immigration policies. For example, the global competition for human capital has motivated policymakers in North America and Europe to attract highly skilled migrant labour. At the same time, however, varying institutional systems and ideas of the role of immigration have maintained decisive national and regional differences regarding the relationship between immigration and national economies. For example, an important factor that distinguishes Germany from Canada is its distinct model of corporate governance and its system of labour relations. In addition, Germany's historical identity as an ethnic nation raises important questions about the economic role of immigration in the context of neoliberal economic restructuring.

In German immigration discourse, the view that immigration is an economic tool has been particularly important. In fact, my use of the term 'economic utility,' which I also applied in the previous chapter to the Canadian context, was inspired by a study by linguist Martin Wengeler (2003; also Wengeler, 2006). In this study, Wengeler used the term economic utility (*wirtschaftlicher Nutzen*) to describe the aspect that occurred most frequently in German media discourse of immigration during the 1960s and 1970s.[2] My analysis in chapter 3 confirms this dominance of the economic aspect in the recent media debate of Germany's immigration law. Apparently, the perspective of immigration as a matter of economic utility has been a staple of post-war media discourse in Germany. In the recent debate of the new German immigration law, the link between immigration and neoliberalism is particularly prominent because this debate coincides with a period when neoliberal ideas became firmly entrenched in the German economy and polity.

Germany's policies towards immigration (*Zuwanderungspolitik*) and foreign residents (*Ausländerpolitik*) have historically pursued economic objectives (Herbert, 2001).[3] Before the First World War, the policies of the Wilhelmine Empire already catered to business interests and attempted to fill labour shortages by enabling the recruitment of cheap and seasonal foreign labour from Eastern Europe (Bade, 2004). In the inter-war period, migration policy continued to serve as a regulatory labour market tool. In the Weimar Republic, policies towards transnational migration were linked to the business cycle and fluctuations in the demand for domestic labour. Many of the foreign workers who were recruited on temporary contracts accrued social rights and thus became permanent immigrants to Germany (Oltmer, 2005: 344–61).

After the Second World War and the catastrophe of the Nazi regime, which propagated a grossly misguided interpretation of German nationhood, the ethnic identity of the German nation was discredited. With the resulting mistrust of the ethnic principle of German nationhood, economic considerations became even more important to Germany's policies towards international migration. The unexpected strength of the recovery of the West German post-war economy and the ensuing period of unprecedented economic prosperity provided a new focal point for German national identity. The term *Wirtschaftswunder,* or economic miracle, has been widely used to describe this era, symbolizing Germany's rearticulation of national identity away from an ethnic understanding of nationhood towards an economic identity. The German historian Wolfgang Mommsen (1990, cited in Bosswick, 2008) suggests that a revised national identity in West Germany hinged to a large degree on the post-war economic success. According to his fellow historian and migration scholar Klaus Bade (2004: 443–8), the semantic of the ethno-cultural nation was devalued and replaced with an identity of Germany as the nation of the *Wirtschaftswunder* and advanced welfare state. I included this term in the title of this chapter because the chapter addresses the question whether immigration is still debated in the context of a national identity that is expressed through economic criteria.

In the context of the post-war economic recovery, foreign and immigrant workers were needed to fill the demand for labour created by the booming economy. Germany's post-war policies towards migration were also labour market policies. The guest worker program exemplifies the role of migration as a source for labour. This program was initiated in 1955 to attract temporary workers from a range of Mediterranean counties. The program was terminated in 1974, at the beginning of the global economic crisis, when foreign workers were no longer needed due to the declining demand for labour.[4]

During the 1980s a shift occurred in German politics away from representing migration as a tool of labour market regulation towards considering migration as a challenge to civic order and social cohesion. This shift was symbolized by the gradual reassignment of responsibility for the policy towards foreign residents (*Ausländerpolitik*) from the Ministry of Labour (*Bundesarbeitsministerum*) to the Ministry of the Interior (*Bundesinnenministerium*) (Meier-Braun, 2002). In the public debate on immigration during this period, the economic aspect of immigration declined in significance (Wengeler, 2003: 446–8).[5] Nevertheless, the continuing presence of foreigners who originally came to Germany as workers 'left its mark in the collective memory of Germans . . . [who] treat policies toward foreigners often from the economic point of view' (Hell, 2005: 88).

Even as the economic-utility perspective received less attention in public and media debates, economic considerations were likely a factor in the discussion of other aspects of immigration, such as refugee and asylum policies. For example, some commentators interpret the rejection among Germans of immigrants and foreigners in the 1990s as a result of 'DM nationalism.' This term refers to the former German currency the German mark, or *Deutsche Mark* (DM).[6] According to this argument, refugees were seen as a threat to Germany's accomplished welfare system and economic prosperity because many of them were not issued work permits and therefore depended on transfer payments from the state. Conversely, others foreigners, who were allowed to work, were labelled job-stealers and were not included in the German national imaginary[7] (Knischewski, 1996: 145). The notion of DM nationalism suggests that national identity is centred on monetary value and this identity frames immigration. It raises the question whether immigration debate continues to reflect dialectically an economy-centred national identity.

Around the turn of the millennium, the perspective that immigration should serve as a source of needed labour revived. Contrary to the 1960s and early 1970s, when the guest worker program recruited low-skilled workers for the manufacturing sector, the more recent efforts focused on attracting highly skilled workers. In the wider context of a series of neoliberal economic reforms,[8] the Schröder government announced the German Green Card in February 2000. Matthias Hell (2005: 115–41) suggests that the announcement of the Green Card and the efforts to recruit highly educated foreign workers helped rescript the image of the foreigner from unskilled labourer to information-technology specialist needed in the New Economy. Political resistance against such immigration was relatively small. The idea that immigration is necessary to remain globally competitive became the 'common thread' that weaved through all major German parties' position on immigration (ibid.: 130).

The Süssmuth commission continued to frame immigration as an economic opportunity. In its final report, the commission proposed an immigration law that emphasized utilitarian, labour-market-oriented migration. In particular, it recommended a Canadian-style points system, whereby immigrants would be selected based on their human capital and potential to contribute to a knowledge-based economy. In addition, the commission sought to align immigration policy with both short-term labour needs and long-term demographic developments. Based on the recommendations of the Süssmuth commission, the Federal Ministry of the Interior crafted the initial proposal for immigration law in the summer of 2001. Hans-Olaf Henkel (2003: 124), the vice-president of the Federal Union of German Industry (*Bundesverband der Deutschen Industrie*), suggested that the proposed law was a 'political solution' that responded to the request by leading business organizations for more immigration to satisfy the domestic demand for skilled labour. Henkel referred to a study according to which 57 per cent of businesses attempted unsuccessfully to fill vacancies, despite high unemployment rates in Germany. He also lamented the aging of the German population, which he associated with a diminishing willingness among Germans to take economic risks and establish innovative businesses. Apparently, the business community saw the proposed immigration law as an opportunity to facilitate labour market flexibilization and encourage high-risk entrepreneurship.

However, as I described in chapter 3, the proactive economic-utility approach to immigration that was proposed in 2001 did not materialize in the law that eventually took effect in 2005. After a voting scandal in the upper house of parliament, the subsequent nullification of the law by the Federal Constitutional Court, and the attacks of Madrid in March 2004, minister of the interior Otto Schily reached a compromise with opposition politicians in May 2004 which stripped the final law of many of the features designed to enable the immigration of skilled and educated immigrant workers. The points system was the most significant casualty in this context.

The analysis in chapter 3 showed that the media discussed the economic aspect of immigration not only with greater frequency than any other aspect, but also with relative consistency between 2001 and 2005. This frequency and consistency suggests that economic objectives featured very prominently in the media debate of immigration while politicians remodelled the proposed immigration law from one that enables to one that blocks labour immigration. Observers note that in public and policy debate during this period, the economic benefit of attracting immigrants was increasingly juxtaposed with the need to protect domestic workers from foreign competition (Zinterer, 2004; Bendel, 2004). Over time, the enthusiasm about attempting to attract highly-skilled immigrants diminished, with declining economic growth, the bust in the information-technology sector, and rising unemployment rates (Hell, 2005: 142–64). Polling results from the European Social Survey show that in 2002 the German population was more willing than that of other European countries to send long-term unemployed immigrants back to their countries of origin. At the same time, the poll suggests that Germans still considered occupational qualifications to be important traits of potential new immigrants (Fertig, 2004). In the sections below, I examine in greater detail the contents of the economic aspect of immigration debate.

Positions of Economic Utility

The analysis showed that the media discusses the economic aspect of immigration in a typically dialectical manner. Generally, the media assumes two positions with respect to the economic utility of immigration. The first position presents the economic aspect of immigration in a positive way and advocates *for* immigration. The second position represents the economic aspect negatively and argues *against* immigration. These two positions reflect public opinion. In 2003, 28 per cent of the formerly West German and 22 per cent of the formerly East German population agreed or strongly agreed with the viewpoint that immigrants are good for the economy (Simon and Sikich, 2007: 958). Conversely, 39 per cent of West Germans and 58 per cent of East Germans believed that 'immigrants take away jobs from people who were born in' Germany (ibid.: 959).[9]

In the media, the weight between these positions was reversed. The positive perspective on the economic role of immigration occurred more frequently than the negative perspective.[10] In addition, the positive perspective on the economic-utility argument appeared relatively consistently throughout the immigration debate. The negative perspective, by contrast, occurred relatively inconsistently.[11]

In the analysis below, I follow the dialectical character of the debate. I have organized the sections based on whether the media uses the economic aspect to argue in support of or against immigration. First, I discuss the positive position that presents 'immigration as an economic necessity.' Since this positive position dominated the economic aspect of immigration debate (in terms of both the frequency and volume of the material), I am able to highlight detailed characteristics of this position. Second, I elaborate on the negative perspective of the economic aspect, which presents 'immigration as an economic liability.'

Immigration as Economic Necessity

When the economic aspect is associated positively with immigration, the central theme is that the skills of immigrant workers are necessary for the well-being of key industrial sectors. To convey this message in an authoritative way, the newspapers often quote business leaders and entrepreneurs. For example, in mid-2001, when the immigration law was still on the drawing board, the *Frankfurter Allgemeine Zeitung* presented the experience of Klaus Schwägerl, president of the Frankfurt-based consulting company Contavia, to illustrate the inadequacy of the Green Card and to emphasize the need for an immigration law:

> Instead of bringing programmers with a work permit into the country . . . , Contavia uses large corporations as its role model and, in the future, will hire IT-specialists in Indonesia. The company thus belongs to the first family businesses executing its projects in this way, says Schwägerl. He appeals to the federal government to use the planned immigration law to drastically reduce the employment barriers for foreign workers in Germany. (Bröll, 2001b: 19)

The theme that an immigration law must succeed the Green Card program occurred consistently throughout the study period. Almost two years later, for example, the *Stuttgarter Zeitung* presents a similar case:

> 'We can only hope that the immigration law gets underway soon,' said the spokesperson for the Chamber of Industry and Commerce (*Industrie- und Handelskammer*) of the Stuttgart Region. Otherwise, the discontinuation of the Green Card will create problems in the already weakened [IT] sector. 'Then, many months will pass again, before foreign colleagues can be hired,' fears Eva Canisius of the Stuttgart software firm Trados, which just a few days ago hired an Indian worker using the Green Card. (Lachenmann, 2003: 25)

In another example, the *Süddeutsche Zeitung* paraphrases a respected industrial leader to give credibility to the claim of the economic necessity of immigration:

> The President of the Federal Association of German Industry (*Bundesverband der deutschen Industrie*), Rogowski, points to the durability of the problem . . . As soon as the business cycle starts again (and especially in the long-term, when the demographic development affects the labour market), will growth opportunities be wasted if the demand for skilled workers is not sufficiently met. (Beise, 2004: 19)

By quoting and paraphrasing well-known industrial leaders, newspapers also give credibility to warnings about the consequences of *not* having an immigration law that would enable immigrants to enter the German labour market. In 2001, the *Frankfurter Allgemeine Zeitung* quoted the president of the Association of the German Chambers of Industry and Commerce (*Deutscher Industrie- und Handelskammertag*), Ludwig Georg Braun, to communicate that a delay of the business-oriented immigration law would make Germany less attractive for foreign investment: '"Already today, foreign investors bypass Germany as an industrial location (*Standort Deutschland*), not only because of the [stringent labour regulations], but because they are afraid of not finding enough qualified labour," said Braun' (Stüwe, 2001: 18). The consistency of this theme can be illustrated with a similar newspaper excerpt that relies on the same person for information but was published almost eighteen months later, after the initial proposal of the immigration law failed in court and the immigration debate had entered a different stage. The *Tageszeitung* wrote: 'The President of the Conference of the German Chambers of Industry and Commerce, Ludwig Georg Braun, demanded an agreement in the immigration quarrel. "The law must come – in the interest of Germany as an industrial location," said Braun' (Rath and Husic, 2003: 6).

Many other authorities on economic matters were quoted or paraphrased to attest to the need of immigration for economic reasons. These authorities include, in the *Frankfurter Allgemeine Zeitung*, Volker Fasbender, the managing director of the Federation of Hessian Employers Associations (*Vereinigung hessischer Unternehmerverbände*) (Heptner, 2002: 56); in the *Süddeutsche Zeitung*, Dieter Hundt, president of the Confederation of German Employers' Associations (*Arbeitgeberpräsident*) (Rubner, 2002: 2); in the *Tageszeitung*, Hans-Jörg Schmidt-Trenz, the managing director of the Chamber of Commerce of Hamburg (*Handelskammer Hamburg*) (Weikert, 2004a: 26); and, in the *Stuttgarter Zeitung*, Andreas Richter, managing director of the Chamber of Industry and Commerce of the Stuttgart Region (Höfle, 2004: 23).

A considerable number of the articles, which associated immigration positively with economic utility, contained photographs.[12] Many of these photographs were of aforementioned industrial leaders or entrepreneurs, rather than immigrant workers. That the newsprint media frequently presents opinions and images of business personalities suggests that the positive position of the economic-utility aspect of immigration represents primarily the viewpoint of industry and business. When politicians reiterate this theme, newspapers typically represent these politicians in a pro-business light. Labour leaders are rarely featured as economic experts on the theme of immigration.[13]

When immigration debate represented immigration as a stimulus to business and industrial growth, an implicit assumption was that non-immigrants will benefit from a more competitive economy. I could not find any explicit explanation in the sampled newspaper articles of *how exactly* the economic benefit of immigration would be transferred from industry and business to the general public. Rather, I uncovered two narratives that rationalize immigration in light of economic 'globalization.' The first narrative suggests that knowledge-based economies compete globally for human capital in the form of educated, skilled, and mobile workers. With the increased national competitiveness everybody supposedly benefits. The second narrative proposes that globalization necessitates the liberalization of labour markets. I will discuss both of these narratives below.

The phrase 'best heads' (*besten Köpfe*) symbolizes the skilled labour for which national economies supposedly compete with each other. This phrase is the equivalent to 'the best and brightest,' which appears in the Canadian debate. An article in the *Frankfurter Allgemeine Zeitung* exemplifies how this phrase is used in the German debate: 'Already, Germany trails behind in the world-wide competition for the best heads. If the [Federal] Republic [of Germany] does not manage to pass a modern immigration law in this parliamentary term [*Legislaturperiode*], then the competition is finally lost' (*Frankfurter Allgemeine Zeitung,* 2002b: 2). Many articles explicitly mention Germany's competitor countries for the best heads. In particular, traditional settler societies, such as Australia, Canada, and the United States, are named. Federal minister of the interior Schily declared in an interview with the *Frankfurter Allgemeine Zeitung:* 'Studies show that the greatest economic power of the world, the United States of America, achieved its position because it was the most successful in the competition for the best heads. If we want to remain internationally competitive, and we confront an intensive global competition, then we must realize the opportunities which qualified immigration offers' (Carstens, 2004: 4). Another example is a *Frankfurter Allgemeine Zeitung* article that criticizes German legislation for stifling self-employment among skilled foreigners, while Great Britain welcomes immigrant entrepreneurship. The newspaper reports about the software developer Daniel Wamara, who entered Germany with a Green Card but became unemployed after a slowdown in the information-technology sector:

> His plan: to develop booking-systems for hotels and airlines, as a business owner. 'I have made the necessary customer contacts in my initial job,' he says. But he was not permitted . . .
>
> What is not allowed work here, is simple in other places. Wamara's nephew is also a software developer. He did not go to Germany but to Great Britain. And founded a software company. The visit with the authorities took 15 minutes, says Wamara. So far, the nephew hired three co-workers, all Britons. Worldwide, the competition for highly qualified labour increased over the last ten years. Thus, the United States, Canada and Australia increased their immigration quota correspondingly. (Schmidt, 2004: 42)

While the previous three quotes were taken from the business-friendly *Frankfurter Allgemeine Zeitung*, other newspapers also presented the narrative of global competition for the best heads. For example, an article in the *Süddeutsche Zeitung* reports on a worker who left for Austria after working in a German hospital for six years:

> Her last position was deputy ward director [*stellvertretende Stationsleiterin*]. 'A very competent woman,' praises her former boss Werner Holzner. The Caritas [a Catholic Church–affiliated welfare NGO] would have liked to continue to employ the Bosnian citizen, but she had to leave in 1998 despite all efforts by the employer. Now they would like to have the woman back, but she has already found work in Austria. 'They were smarter than us,' says Holzner. (Maier-Albang and Näger, 2001: 49)

As illustrated in previous examples, the Green Card is portrayed as a step in the right direction towards enabling the immigration of skilled labour. However, it is also represented as insufficient and inadequate to attract the best heads. For example, an article in the *Frankfurter Allgemeine Zeitung* argues:

> Even as employees, highly qualified specialists are not welcome forever. Their visa is valid for a maximum of five years. If a break-through does not occur in the negotiations for an immigration law, then the first [specialists] will need to leave in the coming years. The Green Card[14] holders remain in limbo. The first ones are emigrating already. Foreign countries enjoy the smart heads (*klugen Köpfe*). (Schmidt, 2004: 42)

The story of the first Green Card recipient, Hariato Wijaya, circulated through all the sampled newspapers at various points throughout the immigration debate. The media celebrated the delivery of the first German Green Card as a symbolic turning point towards economic-utility-driven immigration to Germany. The excitement about this event still resonated in the articles collected during the study period, which started a considerable time after the Green Card program began. A year after Wijaya received his Green Card, the *Frankfurter Allgemeine Zeitung* recalled the event in the following way:

> Harianto Wijaya became a media star literally from one day to the next. On July 31 a year ago, in the light of dozens of cameras, the Indonesian citizen accepted the first Green Card in Germany and managed to be featured on the front pages of the daily newspapers. 'I am happy to have the Green Card,' he said over and over again into the microphones. In this respect, nothing changed within a year: 'I am even happier because I have learned so much in Germany,' he says today. (Bröll, 2001a: 13)

Three years after the above article was published, there was still no immigration law in place that would facilitate the long-term immigration of skilled labour. In light of the expiry date of the Green Card, Mr Wijaya decided to leave Germany and immigrate to the United States. All the newspapers I examined published articles commenting on this decision and reaffirmed the need for skilled immigration. For example, the *Frankfurter Allgemeine Zeitung* reports in an article titled 'Germany kicks out smart heads': 'Some are turning their back to Germany already. On July 21, 2000, Harianto Wijara held still happily the first Green Card in his hands. He helped build up the Aachen company Aixcom. But before he will be deported next year, he intends to go abroad voluntarily. "I am indeed disappointed in German politics," he said' (Schmidt, 2004: 42). The *Tageszeitung* regrets the loss of human capital and tax funds:

> Wijaya was the born applicant – he completed his computer-science studies in only nine semesters with the dream mark of 1.0. Thanks to the Green Card he could accept a highly-paid job with the software company Aixcom in Aachen. The mobile communication company was as happy about it as its new employee. 'He fits to us like the plug into the electrical outlet,' marveled managing director Martin Steppler.

> ... At the end of the year, Wijaya now wants to apply for his next Green Card: in the USA. There the Green Card is unlimited. His taxes will then flow into the American state coffer. (Spannbauer, 2003: 8).

The editor of the *Süddeutsche Zeitung*, Heribert Prantl, applies sarcasm to lament that the Green Card was not succeeded by an immigration law that would have enabled Mr Wijaya to stay in Germany: 'The first Green Card that was issued in Germany in July, 2000, can be admired behind glass in the House of History (*Haus der Geschichte*) in Bonn. Its former owner, the 29-year-old Indonesian Harianto Wijaya, donated the card to the museum, so to speak as a memento (Prantl, 2004c: 4).

The second narrative rationalizes the pro-immigration position by suggesting that global competition must be met with the opening of the domestic labour market and the replenishment of the domestic labour force with immigrant workers. With the exception of *Bild Zeitung*, all sampled newspapers quoted business leaders and politicians that articulated this idea. For example, the opinions of business institutions and their leaders were used to convey that a globally networked economy and immigration are interrelated topics. The *Tageszeitung* reports: 'The Bremen Chamber of Commerce agrees [that the City-State of Bremen should support the proposed immigration law] ... The current legal situation has a repelling effect on highly qualified workers and investors from third countries. The law is of "overarching interest" for the export-dependent economy of Bremen' (Schöneberg, 2002: 25). Similarly, the *Stuttgarter Zeitung* presents an expert opinion on the link between immigration and globalization: 'Ludwig Georg Braun, President of the Conference of the German Chambers of Industry and Commerce, demands a quick departure from the "outdated recruitment stop."[15] It cannot be that the international labour market for experts and managers only operates in one direction – and that is out of Germany' (Rubner, 2002: 2).

Newspapers reported about German politicians who were endorsing this narrative. The *Süddeutsche Zeitung* paraphrased minister of the interior Otto Schily in the following way: 'In light of globalization, Germany must be prepared to open "its gates" (*Fenster und Türen*)' (Grassmann, 2003b: 5). In another example, the *Stuttgarter Zeitung* quotes justice minister of the State of Baden-Württemberg Ulrich Goll: 'With the presentation of his annual report Goll required a "flexible instrument" for the demand-driven immigration to single economic sectors ... An opening of the export-oriented south-west is necessary.

"We cannot tighten everything [for immigrants] and, at the same time, trade with the world," said Goll' (Durchdenwald, 2002: no page).

The above excerpts suggest that global trade must go hand in hand with increased immigration. Globalization supposedly requires not only the liberalization of trade with goods but also the mobility of labour. An article in the *Frankfurter Allgemeine Zeitung* argues that the law to which the government and opposition parties finally agreed in 2004 fails to enhance the mobility of international workers who want to work in Germany. This article compares the law to socialist planning principles:

> The process for the selection of immigrants, to which the parties agreed in the immigration compromise (*Zuwanderungskompromiß*), harbours characteristics of a socialist planned economy. Such absurdities are the result, when immigration politics are shaped from the economic view solely by the fear that immigrants take away jobs from Germans. (Welter, 2004: 34)

The message conveyed in this narrative is that the economy would benefit from the influx of internationally mobile labour. The narrative follows the logic of the market, according to which the labour market should not be distorted by restrictive immigration regulations. In pursuit of this logic, some voices in centrist newspapers proposed that labour immigration should not be limited to the high-skill segment. For example, a themed section of the *Süddeutsche Zeitung* contained articles reporting about sectors in Munich's economy that were in dire need of immigrant labour:

> Chronic labour shortages exist here [in Munich]. 25,000 open positions are registered at the Office of Employment (*Arbeitsamt*) alone. The actual number of required workers is much higher ... Urgently needed also are specialists in nursing, in the trades, in the restaurant industry. Employers now hope that the new immigration law offers a solution to their problems: new workers should come as quickly and unbureaucratically as possible, and they should be able to stay as long as possible. (*Süddeutsche Zeitung*, 2001: 49)

A companion article in the same themed section details labour shortages in nursing, janitorial services, the trades, and the restaurant industry. The following excerpt from this article suggest that immigration is necessary to regulate the supply of labour in the restaurant industry:

> The customers would be there, but the workers are missing. For Bavaria, the [Bavarian Association of Hotels and Restaurants] assumes that there are 20,000 to 30,000 open positions in the hotel and restaurant sector; the restaurant managers of downtown Munich alone, estimates spokesperson Karl Langegger, could hire immediately 'several hundred waiters and waitresses, kitchen and bar staff.' And Gerda Sperger, manager of the Hofbräuhaus, calculates that she still needs 'more than 20 people in the service area and an additional twelve chefs and kitchen helpers.' (Maier-Albang, and Näger, 2001: 49)

The same article presents another example from the janitorial sector:

> Mike Rado officially seeks 15 people for his [building-cleaning] company. However, he could hire roughly 30 tomorrow, and in the mid-term he would even hire 200. The boss of the 250-employee company even has to decline contracts due to labour shortage . . . He cannot pay [his employees] luxury wages . . . Eight years ago, he could charge 65 marks for an on-call worker, who waits with a pager in a convention hall until somewhere something drops or spills and cleans it up. Today this service is only worth 29 marks[16] to the client. The standard hourly wage (*Tarifstundenlohn*) lies at 16.35 marks . . . 'The new immigration law would be a dream,' says Rado. 'I don't care where people come from . . . What's important are performance and quality.' (ibid., 2001: 49)

In this case, the lower costs of migrant labour and the ability to provide services more cheaply justify immigration. The role of immigration in facilitating the decline of wages is not only acknowledged but is made a virtue, which reflects a common rhetorical strategy associated with neoliberalism (Fairclough, 2000: 148). A similar sentiment is echoed in some articles, in which politicians advocate for the immigration of low- and semi-skilled labour to fill positions that are below the wage expectations of non-immigrant workers. For example, an article in the *Frankfurter Allgemeine Zeitung* reports:

> Gerhardt [chair of the liberal party in the Bundestag, FDP] warned the Union [Christian Democratic Union and Christian Social Union] and SPD [Social-Democratic Party] that they should resist the temptation to begin a race about blocking immigrating workers who do not belong to the most highly qualified but who are nevertheless needed in the labour market. This includes workers in nursing and the restaurant industry. Gerhardt

> said he still supports giving domestic unemployed workers first access to unoccupied positions. However, if positions remain unfilled for years, then labour demand must be satisfied from abroad. (Leithäuser, 2001a: 2)

Some media voices imply that immigration would be unnecessary if the protection and rights of domestic labour were reduced. Compared to some other industrialized countries, German law specifies generous protection against layoffs, requires high corporate non-wage contributions to employees' pension, unemployment, and medical plans, and articulates a system of codetermination (*Mitbestimmung*) that gives employees the right to representation on corporate boards. Since the late 1990s, this German model has been challenged by industry and business. At the same time, union membership has dwindled and the German state has abandoned its neutrality and 'more recently tended to give more support to the employers, apparently prioritizing their interests above those of the workers' (Bathelt and Gertler, 2005: 5). The idea is that the structure and rigidity of the German business model is an impediment to success under global economic competition. An alternative to importing low-wage labour through immigration is therefore to create greater flexibility in the domestic labour market. In an interview with the *Frankfurter Allgemeine Zeitung,* Hessian minister of the interior Volker Bouffier expresses this view, using the code-phrase to 'pry open . . . encrusted (*verkrustet*)' labour market structures:

> We are sending the fifty-two-year-olds as unemployable (*unvermittelbar*) into unemployment and simultaneously discuss bringing people from other countries here. I cannot accept that I am told that we cannot fill the job and therefore we need immigration. Sure, we must also pry open the encrusted structure of the labour market. (Euler and Schwan, 2002: R1)

The last two newspaper excerpts represent two sides of the same coin. Either immigration is permitted to provide low-wage labour, or domestic workers need to lower their labour and wage expectations, in which case immigration would no longer be necessary. Both perspectives reflect elements of a wider neoliberal project, whereby immigration – or the *prospect* of increased immigration – is a contributing factor to labour market flexibilization.[17]

Immigration as Economic Liability

The position that immigration should be blocked because it would raise unemployment among the non-immigrant population appeared at various points throughout the immigration debate. Articles published in centrist newspapers initially attributed this viewpoint to conservative politicians. An example is the above-quoted interview with the conservative politician and Hessian minister of interior Volker Bouffier. He told the *Frankfurter Allgemeine Zeitung*:

> Businesses spoke of a need for 100,000 [foreign skilled workers]. In the entire Federal Republic [of Germany] we had difficulty getting 8,000 [with the Green Card], mostly distributed to four states – Bavaria, Baden-Württemberg, Hesse, and North Rhine-Westphalia. In regard to skilled workers, we must answer the question whether we can afford an army of unemployed and get people from abroad, or do we want to attempt to bring the unemployed into employment through education, through qualification but also through changes, for example, in the employability criteria (*Zumutbarkeitskriterien*). I plead clearly for the second. (Euler and Schwan, 2002: R1)

Interestingly, usually business-friendly conservative politicians argued against a labour immigration scheme that was strongly supported by business leaders. Apparently, the immigration of needed labour is in conflict with the policy objective of reducing public spending and the size of government. The neoliberal logic of small government is associated with a low tolerance for assistance from the state and vilifies vulnerable recipients of welfare and unemployment transfers. Permanent immigrants who will receive similar social and economic rights and entitlements as citizens are treated as future welfare recipients and vilified in a corresponding manner.

The rhetoric of 'immigration into the welfare system' illustrates this point. It occurred often in conjunction with reporting on the potential rise of unemployment due to immigration.[18] For example, in early 2002, the *Frankfurter Allgemeine Zeitung* reported on the reasons for blocking the immigration law by the conservative parties the Christian Democratic Union and the Christian Social Union: 'The Brandenburg minister of interior [Jörg Schönbohm of the Christian Democratic Union] spoke elaborately about the widespread unemployment among foreigners and about the immigration "in particular into the welfare system"' (Gaus and Herrmann, 2002: 10). This rhetoric appears again at the end of 2002, just before a period when reporting on the negative labour market impacts of immigration temporarily increased. The *Stuttgarter Zeitung*, for example, quotes the premier of Hesse, Roland Koch, of the Christian Democratic Union: 'Immigration is only permissible when jobs can be documented for the arrivals. "Immigration into the welfare system" must end' (Braun and Halbig, 2002: 3).

Around the same time, a debate emerged over whether the German Green Card program should be renewed in light of the absence of an immigration law. Press reports pointed out that the Green Card had failed to create the expected positive impact on the German economy. Instead, some Green Card holders became unemployed. An article in the *Süddeutsche Zeitung* explains:

> A study by the Institute for Labour Market and Employment Research [*Institut für Arbeitsmarkt- und Berufsforschung*], which belongs to the Federal Labour Office [*Bundesanstalt für Arbeit*], indicated that many of the attracted skilled workers have long become unemployed. According to the statistics of the study, every seventh Green Card holder in the Munich area has lost his or her job. But this is only the 'lower threshold.' No statistic captures the magnitude of the national quota. (Jacobi, 2003: 1)

A day later, the *Frankfurter Allgemeine Zeitung* reports about the same study: 'Without a doubt . . . the Green Card holders are not spared by the crisis in the IT sector and the poor situation of the labour market. As the Institute for Labour Market and Employment Research recently discovered, seven per cent of the foreign specialists with a Green Card had to register as unemployed' (Bröll, 2003: 12).

In later phases of the immigration debate, media reporting also associated the main governing party, the Social-Democratic Party of Germany, with the position that unemployment and labour immigration are irreconcilable. For example, the *Frankfurter Allgemeine Zeitung* reported in 2004: 'With 4.6 million unemployed, even the SPD could not find an acceptable reason to let the negotiations fail on this point' (Dietrich, 2004: 1), that is, to insist on the points system to select skilled workers.

While the protection of the domestic labour market from immigration was endorsed by conservative and eventually centre-left politicians, it encountered some resistance in the left-wing press. For example, an article in the *Tageszeitung* questions the validity of linking immigration with unemployment:

> Stoiber [chairman of the conservative Christian Social Union] himself rejected again the request of businesses that the Union support the law because industry needs foreign labour. With 4.3 million unemployed, immigration

> cannot be expanded, said Stoiber in Wildbad Kreuth. Does he simply not care that the boss of the Federal Agency for Employment (*Bundesanstalt für Arbeit*) says the opposite? (Wallraff, 2002: 7)

A year later, the same author wrote an opinion piece, calling the view that immigrants take away jobs from non-immigrants 'irrational': 'Neither of the two mainstream parties (*Volksparteien*) has an interest in a humane and future-oriented immigration policy. Especially not with almost five million unemployed. The irrational fear of foreign competition is at least as common among potential SPD voters as among the clients of the [Christian Democratic and Christian Social] Union' (Wallraff, 2003: 12). This left-wing critique links back to the positive position of the economic aspect and the view that the knowledge-driven economy needs immigration and skilled foreign labour, which I illustrated in the previous section. In the final section of this chapter, I interpret the two positions in light of dialectical media practice, German national identity, and the wider material contexts in which immigration debate is situated.

Conclusion

The economic aspect of the immigration debate in Germany follows a dialectical pattern that juxtaposes two opposing positions. The first and more frequently taken position argues that immigration is necessary to replenish the labour market and make the German workforce more competitive. The second and weaker position proposed to block immigration and protect non-immigrant labour. These two positions coexisted throughout the debate. Similarities exist between Germany and Canada in that the media presents the immigration debate in a dialectical manner.

Similarities between both countries also exist with respect to the contents of the immigration debates. The neoliberal paradigm – represented by the logic of the market and the narrative of competition – was present in the debates in both countries. In some instances, the language is strikingly similar, for example, in expressing the idea that global competition mandates attracting the 'the best and brightest' or 'the best heads.' Another similarity is that the press challenged the neoliberal paradigm. An important difference between Canada and Germany, however, lies in *how* it was challenged. In Canada, the media presented arguments to tightly regulate immigration according to occupational demand.

Immigration, in this context, would be a way to regulate the domestic labour market. In Germany, by contrast, the media presented the argument that the greatest benefit for German workers could be achieved by blocking immigration altogether. While in Germany the media could envision an economy that thrives without immigrant labour and skills, in Canada this idea of a domestic labour market cut off from new immigration seemed unthinkable.

The position that Germany requires skilled immigration to maintain economic growth can be interpreted in the context of German national identity. Throughout the immigration debate, the media linked this position with the particular labour needs of the knowledge-based economy.[19] For example, the articles cited numerous successful business leaders and economic authorities to convey the point that key sectors of the knowledge economy, such as the information technology industry, require the 'best heads' in the form of skilled immigrants. In addition, the press extensively used the case of Indonesian software developer, and recipient of the first Green Card, Harianto Wijaya to communicate to its readers that Germany's knowledge economy will suffer if Germany is not able to keep such skilled labour in the country by offering migrants the prospect of permanent settlement.[20] The need to replenish the labour market with highly skilled workers resonates with the representation of immigrants in settler societies as bringing new momentum to a stalling community. In the German case, new immigrant labour would bring such a new momentum. When immigration debate projects a new identity of Germany as an immigrant nation, this identity is rooted in the material need for immigrants as knowledge professionals. In this case, national identity seeks to legitimate structural economic demands.

The transformation of the image of the immigrant from disposable unskilled labourer to uniquely qualified information-technology professional, reflects the progression of Germany's economy from the coal-and-steal-based manufacturing of the era of the *Wirtschaftswunder* towards high-technology and knowledge-based production. As Germany's post-war identity as an economic powerhouse has been shaken by declining growth rates and a sense of falling behind other G8 countries that have long since implemented neoliberal reforms, immigration was supposed to blow new life into a stagnating economic model. The highly-skilled immigrants were not represented as the Other, but rather as the rescuers of economic prosperity and the leaders into a new economic era. Immigration is supposed to revive the *Wirtschaftswunder* – albeit not in the context of a strong welfare state, but rather of a strong neoliberal economy with a slim state.

Despite this persistent and strong media support for labour immigration, the final immigration law that took effect on 1 January 2005 did not permit any significant permanent immigration of skilled or unskilled workers who are not already European Union citizens. In fact, the main immigrant labour recruitment tool, the points system, was dropped from the law. The new law only allowed for very restricted labour immigration of highly qualified scientists and post-secondary educators, experienced managers, and leading professionals. In addition, it enabled the immigration of entrepreneurs who invest at least € 1 million in the German economy and create ten new jobs (Bundesministerium des Innern, 2004: §§19, 21). Only a very small number of immigrants met these requirements. For example, in 2007, a total 466 skilled workers immigrated to Germany (Focus Migration, 2008: 1). In response to such numbers, the German government slightly relaxed the restrictions to skilled immigration in the years after the immigration law look effect. For example, it reduced the required income threshold for skilled immigrants and made immigration easier for academics from Eastern Europe and for foreign graduates of German institutes of higher education (*Bundesgesetzblatt*, 2008; Deutscher Bundestag, 2008). Nevertheless, the volume of future immigration to Germany can be expected to remain very small.[21]

The discrepancy between the media's call for skilled immigration and the actual law that effectively prohibits such immigration raises similar questions as the Canadian study revealed about an apparent disconnect between media representations and material processes in the immigration dialectic. Did the otherwise powerful voice of the media fail to influence the political process and shape the immigration law? Was immigration discourse really disconnected from the material relations of neoliberalism in Germany? Certainly, non-economic aspects, such as the perception that immigration threatens Germany's social cohesion and the concern of meeting Germany's legal and moral obligations towards humanitarianism, also influenced the debate, as I will show in the following chapters. In addition, at several points during immigration debate, centrist newspapers presented immigration as a liability in a period of high unemployment. This negative representation of immigration was fed by fears that immigrants would either steal the jobs of German workers or that they would become unemployed and thus a burden to the welfare system. What diminishes the explanatory value of the non-economic aspects and rising unemployment is that these anti-immigration arguments were published less frequently and less consistently than the argument that immigration is an economic necessity.

The apparent contraction between media discourse and actual immigration law seems to resolve in light of another neoliberal practice: small government and a reduced welfare state. The mainstream media couched the blockade of labour immigration that was implemented with the law in a language of fighting unemployment and preventing 'immigration into the German welfare system.' Small government and diminished state responsibilities towards unemployed workers are as much a part of the neoliberal regulatory project as flexible labour markets. Thus, media debate of the economic aspect of immigration can be interpreted as following a consistent neoliberal ideology. In fact, complementary labour market legislation aiming to flexibilize the domestic labour market was implemented simultaneously with the debate of the immigration law. Central to this legislation are the so-called Hartz reforms, named after Volkswagen board member Peter Hartz, whom Chancellor Gerhard Schröder appointed chair of a commission on labour market reform in 2002. The recommendations of the Hartz commission were implemented in four steps and included the reduction of unemployment benefits, expectations of the unemployed to be mobile within Germany, training initiatives (Hartz I), tax-reduced part-time jobs, subsidies for small-business start-ups (Hartz II), the reorganization of the Office of Employment (Hartz III), the amalgamation of employment insurance and social security insurance, and so-called 1-Euro jobs available to recipients of unemployment benefits (Hartz IV).

An additional potential explanation for the restrictive immigration law is the expansion of the European Union in Eastern Europe and the Mediterranean. The enlargement took effect in May 2004, around the time when the German government reached its compromise on the immigration law, and shortly before the final law was passed. Although temporary regulations restricted the mobility of labour from the new member states to Germany for a maximum of seven years,[22] an increase in labour migration to Germany could be expected thereafter (Münz and Tamas, 2006). The restriction of immigration of non–European Union citizens through the immigration law could have been motivated by the expectation that the new European Union member states would be a future source of flexible labour for the German economy. Somewhat surprisingly, my empirical analysis of media debate did not reveal any substantial reference to intra-European labour mobility in the context of immigration reform. Because media debate framed immigration reform as an issue related to migration originating from outside the European Union and as separate from the topic of labour migration among European Union members, this debate apparently missed any material connection between migration within the European Union and migration between Germany and non–European Union countries. Nevertheless, although my analysis did not produce conclusive evidence for this interpretation, the argument is feasible.

The labour market reforms and European Union enlargement present material circumstances that cast an interesting light on immigration debate in Germany. Both the media position of immigration as an economic necessity and the political processes that culminated in the immigration law pursued a neoliberal agenda. While the sampled newsprint articles linked neither Hartz reforms nor European Union enlargement explicitly with the immigration law, the restrictive attitude towards immigration that was eventually scripted into law implies that German workers (or foreign permanent residents who are already in the country) will not only need to acquire the skills of immigrants but must also become as flexible and as accepting of low wages, job insecurity, and a less generous social security net as immigrants would be. According to this interpretation, the message of the new immigration law is that the labour market gaps that cannot be filled by German workers or other European Union citizens should be addressed through domestic labour market reforms. In other words, additional immigrant labour will not be needed if German workers perform the task under similar circumstances. While in traditional immigration countries, including Canada, vulnerable recent-immigrant workers serve as a tool of neoliberal labour market regulation, in Germany, the new immigration law asks non-immigrants, rather than new immigrants, to perform the roles of flexible labour. In addition to pitting existing labour migrants (former guest workers, *Spätaussiedler,* and EU citizens) against non-migrant labour, a complementary strategy focuses on diminished expectations of the welfare state, more flexible working conditions, and lower wages for non-migrant workers. These two neoliberal strategies interlock in Germany to facilitate the flexibilization of the national labour market, the reduction of wage expectations, and the weakening of the welfare state. From this perspective, the German immigration law is compatible with the wider neoliberal project.

Ironically, however, the image of the high-wage- and high-technology-based knowledge economy that requires the best foreign heads is reflected neither in the material outcomes of labour market reforms nor in immigation reform. The national identity of Germany as a high-technology and knowledge-based nation, which circulated through the media, seems to be disconnected from the material practices of 'flexibilizing' and 'deregulating' the domestic labour market and of blocking labour immigration. In the context of the third dialectical dimension of national identity formation, this disconnection raises doubts about the contribution that newly arriving immigrant labour makes to contemporary German national identity.

8 From Immigration to Integration

In an era of 'securitization,' representations of immigrants as a danger are often blended with cultural markers, such as religion and language. Although I treated the aspects of 'culture' and danger as separate analytical categories in chapter 3, the contents of both aspects are in fact closely related to each other. In many cases it would be difficult to clearly distinguish between the cultural and dangerous aspects of immigration. I therefore decided to discuss both aspects in the same chapter.

When one examines the aspects of danger and 'culture' jointly, an interesting dialectical pattern emerges that characterizes Germany's immigration debate. This interpretation of the immigration debate reflects a Hegelian dialectical movement whereby an initial position and its negation are followed by a second negation that produces a new and integrating third position. This dialectical movement, however, differs in contents from the sequence of immigrant Othering and immigrant integration (sublation) that could be observed in the Canadian media debate. In a simplified way, this dialectic of the German debate can be summarized as follows: the initial position that triggered the immigration debate and initiated legal reform acknowledged that immigrants have been physically present in Germany for decades and generations; Germany has therefore become an immigrant nation. However, following external events, such as the bombing attacks in Madrid in 2004, a reversal of this position took place. Immigration is no longer conceived as desirable. Instead, immigrants are constructed as the quintessential Others vis-à-vis German national identity. This second postion represents Germany as an ethnic nation. The mediation between these two opposing positions occurs when the debate shifts away from immigration and the selection of new immigrants towards the integration of those migrants who already reside in Germany but who are still considered foreigners.

As I will show, this dialectic of the immigration debate is not as clear-cut as this simplified summary suggests. Rather, various positions temporally overlap. For example, calls for immigrant integration were made all along, including during the period when the idea of Germany as an immigration country emerged and later during the backlash from the Madrid bombings. Similarly, the construction of immigrants as Others has a long history in Germany and is not restricted to the later stages of the debate surrounding the immigration law. In addition, there is no uniform voice in the media debate. Rather, multiple and contradictory viewpoints typically exist at any point in time. The complexity of the immigration debate, however, does not nullify but rather affirms the dialectical principle. Complexity and contradiction are important forces in the progression of the immigration debate.

Despite this complexity, an interesting correspondence exists between the dialectical pattern I described above and the political events that occurred en route to the German immigration law. Before the 1990s, a wide political consensus existed that Germany is a non-immigration country (Hell, 2005). With the emerging recognition by civic and political leaders that Germany is de facto an immigration country, the Schröder government initiated the German Green Card, which is widely regarded as a first step towards implementing the idea that Germany is an immigration country. Shortly thereafter, the Süssmuth commission was established with the mandate to make recommendations for an immigration law and formally enshrine this idea in Germany's legislation. Similarly to Canada and other settler societies, Germany would get a legal framework that regulates immigration.

The law, however, was successfully challenged in federal court. When the debate over immigration reopened, the dominant position in federal politics had shifted away from the idea that Germany is an immigration country. Immigration was now considered undesirable. The revised version of the immigration law that was passed by parliament no longer contained the points system, which was supposed to be the main instrument for immigrant selection. Rather than enabling regulated immigration, the new law became a tool to prevent immigration from outside the European Union. At the same time, the law provides integration assistance to foreigners in the form of language and orientation courses. The law even specifies that participation in these courses can be mandated (Bundesministerium der Justiz, 2004, §44a). Instead of regulating *immigration*, the law now focuses on the *integration* of immigrants and foreigners. By 2007, the governing Christian Democratic Union declared in its major policy statement that 'Germany is an integration country' (CDU Deutschland, 2007: 95).

Germany as an Immigration Country

The notion that Germany is an immigration country took decades to become established in political and public debate. Statements in the late 1970s, such as the declaration by the otherwise conservative Baden-Württemberg president Lothar Spät that 'we are an immigration country,' or the demand by North Rhine–Westphalia's president Heinz Kühn for the recognition of 'de facto immigration' in Germany in the same year (quoted in Meier-Braun, 2002: 46), were exceptions and did not trigger sustained political discussion; neither did these statements translate into corresponding policies and legislation. Similarly, the prominent Christian Democratic Union politician Heiner Geißler presented the idea of Germany as an immigration country against the criticism of his own party in the late 1980s (Wengeler, 1995: 724–32).

In the 1990s this situation began to change. In 1991, the conservative Christian Democratic Union hinted at the coming transformation. At its annual national assembly, the CDU replaced in the so-called Dresden Manifesto the intended sentence 'Germany is no immigration country' with 'Germany is a world-open (*weltoffenes*) country' (Bade, 2004: 423). The transformation accelerated in 1998 with the election of the Social Democratic Party and Green Party government coalition that replaced the conservative government of the previous sixteen years. By 1999, the federal administration declared in an official document that 'Germany has long become an immigration country' (quoted in Meier-Braun, 2002: 98). Public opinion polls supported such political declarations. For example, 76 per cent of Germans were convinced by the year 2000 that Germany had become an immigration country. Only 11 per cent denied this claim (Köcher, 2000). Although the notion of Germany as an immigration country did not remain unchallenged, it presented an important and novel position in the immigration debate.

The media reflected this transformation that occurred in the political field. In August 2001, the influential editor of the *Süddeutsche Zeitung*, Heribert Prantl, wrote an editorial praising the government for its initiative to pursue an immigration policy that treats foreigners as future citizens (2001c: 4). He remarked about the initial proposal of the immigration law: 'It is practical and feasible. It is not an uninviting but rather a welcoming law. It is no longer a police law (*Polizeirecht*) but a civil right (*Bürgerrecht*) for foreigners and future new citizens. It discontinues the labour-market oriented recruitment policy of the past and marks the beginning of a true immigration policy.' Prantl applauds the minster of the interior, Otto Schily, for 'what he has said when he opened a conference of the Friedrich Ebert Foundation in Bonn: "It is bad advice to place a country or a people under quarantine." This sentence can now stand as preamble to the new law.'

A few months later, in light of emerging political resistance to the proposed immigration law, the author of a letter to the editor affirmed the position that Germany is an immigration country: 'Germany has become an immigration country, as all relevant social groups attest. Classical immigration countries of Western brand, such as the USA, Canada or Australia, have centuries of experience in the solution of this task and very clear and efficient immigration laws. Why not use these as a model?' (A. Thomas, 2002: 18). That Germany should be open to immigration and pursue an immigration policy similar to traditional settler societies had become an established position in the media in the early phases of the debate of the German immigration law.

The seeds of dialectical negation, however, had already sprouted in the very beginning of the immigration debate. In the 1990s, conservative politicians resisted the emerging position that Germany is an immigration country. Instead, they continued to favour the traditional position of ethnic nationhood. The prominent politician of the Bavarian Christian Social Union, Peter Gauweiler, for example, distinguished the line of his party, which governed the state of Bavaria, from that of the federal government by declaring that 'Bavaria is not an immigration country' (quoted in Meier-Braun, 2002: 91). In 2002, Gauweiler's party colleague and chancellor-candidate, Edmund Stoiber, followed suit at the federal level and proclaimed during his federal election campaign that Germany still is not an immigration country (ibid.: 134). Similar opinions were expressed by politicians, journalists, and letter writers throughout the period in which the immigration law was publicly debated. Although the position that Germany is an immigration country dominated early debate, the opposing positions of Germany as a non-immigrant nation had also existed since the debate's inception.

In December of 2001, Heribert Prantl was still optimistic that a new immigration law would treat immigrants as future citizens rather than potential danger. Nevertheless, Prantl acknowledges the spreading view of immigration as a concrete danger:

> First of all, the immigration law, in the version that was negotiated between Red and Green [i.e., the coalition partners of the Social Democratic Party and the Green Party], is introduced into parliament this week. This version is the historical step towards a law that sees in the immigrant not a potential enemy but a potential new citizen . . . The second large piece of legislation, which already lies before parliament for its final reading, the Anti-Terrorism law that is, treats foreigners already in a manner in which large parts of the [oppositional Christian Democratic and Christian Social] Union wish for the immigration law to be the case: as concrete danger, not as enrichment. (Prantl, 2001b: 1)

These clouds of change that appeared on the horizon in 2001 would define the political climate of the immigration debate in the years to come.

Germany as a Non-Immigration Country

In the political field, the initial stage of the immigration debate tended to favour the position that Germany is an immigration country. Around the year 2002, the political debate shifted: Germany was portrayed as a nation of non-immigrants. This shift in the political field was reflected in public opinion. Already in 2000, when the majority of the German population recognized Germany as an immigration country, 71 per cent of the population also had doubts about immigration (Köcher, 2000). In 2002, before the initial immigration law was nullified by the court, 50 per cent of polled Germans were against immigration and 49 per cent had reservations about the immigration law (Institut für Demoskopie Allensbach, 2002).

In 2002, a reporter for the *Stuttgarter Zeitung* observed the shift from immigration country to non-immigration country by quoting an migration expert, who said, 'The political symbol, that Germany is an immigration country, is called into question again' (Höfle, 2002: 21). By 2003, the same newspaper reported that Marieluise Beck of the Green Party recognized that 'a "socially shifted climate" renders an immigration law difficult to achieve' (Braun, 2003: 2). The shift was completed in 2004, when Heribert Prantl described the final version of the immigration law as follows: 'The project that was supposed to turn Germany into a modern immigration country has become an immigration barrier' (2004a: 2).

This shift towards representations of Germany as a non-immigration country raises the question of whether Germany had returned to an ethnic model of nationhood, a model with deep historical and political roots. The nation builders of the nineteenth century had promoted a unifying ethno-national identity that integrated geographically dispersed populations into a territorially cohesive German state that included all Germans (Brubaker, 1992: 12). This ethnic conception of national belonging continued to define citizenship in the Federal Republic of Germany. Although German law was amended in 1999 to facilitate the naturalization of immigrants of non-German origin, the 'traditional relic' (Oberndörfer, 1992: 70) of the origin-based conception of the German nation has not disappeared. The German term *Volk* expresses this ethnic understanding of nationhood.

Until the initiation of the immigration debate by a newly elected Social-Democratic/Green government coalition, the ethnic principle was rarely questioned. The results of an ALLBUS poll conducted in 1996 indicate how entrenched the ethnic principle was in the German national imagination. According to the poll, almost one in four (23 per cent) Germans believed that foreigners who live in Germany should not marry Germans (Münz and Ulrich, 1998). By the same token, Germans who have lived abroad for generations were still considered members of the national community. The results of the 2002 European Social Survey revealed that Germans are more open to the immigration of ethnic Germans, or *Spätaussiedler,* from Eastern Europe and the former Soviet Union than to immigration of other ethnic groups (Fertig, 2004: 7).

In 2002, media reporting increasingly expressed anxiety associated with immigration that challenges the ethnic integrity of Germany. Bavaria's representative in the upper house of parliament, Reinhold Bocklet, warned in the *Süddeutsche Zeitung* of the consequences of not restricting immigration: 'In ten to twenty years [there could be] a different *Volk* [in Germany] than there is now' (Grassmann and Höll, 2002: 1). In a commentary entitled 'Voting means to select,' the Bavarian politician Peter Gauweiler, who wrote regular columns for *Bild,* suggests that most German citizens reject immigration because it challenges national identity: 'The polls agree that citizens of almost all political orientations are of the opinion that we already have not too few but too many foreigners. The associated endangerments of the cultural and social inner structure of our county are not barroom talk (*Stammtischgerede*) but obvious' (Gauweiler, 2002: 2). The revival of the position that Germany is a non-immigration country, however, was not simply an argument about the purity of ethnicity or ancestry. Rather, the combination of the aspects of danger and 'culture' served as the harbinger of this position's revival.

The link between 'culture' and danger was partially achieved through the issue of 'security.' European and North American governments placed 'security' on top of their political agendas after 11 September 2001, and the ensuing international war on terrorism. This securitization agenda assumed that a fundamental threat to the state and the nation emanated from outside the country, in particular from the countries with large Muslim populations. The public and policy debates in Germany followed this international trend of securitization. Polls conducted before and after the 2001 events in New York and Washington, and the beginning of the war on terrorism, show that in 1995 about 40 per cent of the population saw the German Muslim population as a threat; by 2006, this figure had risen to 55 per cent (*Spiegel Online*, 2006). Another poll indicated that 46 per cent of Germans feared terrorism attacks in Germany, and 42 per cent agreed that they are afraid that terrorists are among the Muslims in Germany (Südwestrundfunk, 2006). The perceived threat originates, in particular, from the countries outside Europe – precisely those from which the proposed immigration law was supposed to enable emigration to Germany. The conflation of this threat with religious fundamentalism led to the association of the aspects of danger and 'culture.'

German parliamentary debate illustrates this association. When the lower house of the German parliament, the Bundestag, debated immigration, speakers often related the topic of immigration to the Islamic faith. In fact, between 2002 and 2006 Bundestag debates associated immigration far more frequently with Muslim populations than with any other ethnic or origin group. In addition, speakers often connected the immigration of Muslims to the topics of terrorism and state security, and saw Muslim immigration as an assault on Germany's democratic institutions and the constitutionally protected equality of women and men. In the context of these debates, Islam was construed as incompatible with Germany's secular democracy. The immigration of Muslims was subsequently portrayed as a fundamental threat to the German constitutional state. Furthermore, these parliamentary debates dialectically constructed a Christian-liberal national identity as a negation of the Islamic religion and the Muslim immigrant Other. Such an interpretation of parliamentary debate has raised the question of whether the ethnic German identity of the past, and the constitutional identity that some scholars have attributed to post-war West Germany,[1] is complemented by a religious dimension of German nationhood (Bauder and Semmelroggen, 2009).[2]

Similar images of Muslim immigrants that link cultural aspects with danger appear in the media. Elisabeth Beck-Gernsheim observes that the German media depicts Islam as a 'symbol of fanaticism and terrorist threat' (2007: 74). A special issue of the highly regarded German weekly magazine *Der Spiegel* (2008) on 'Islam in Germany' illustrates how the issues of immigration, Islam, and danger interlock. This issue contains three sections under the headings 'Identity and Integration,' featuring articles on immigrant representation and integration, 'Religion and Tradition,' implying that there are differences between Islam and the German social norms, and 'Tolerance and Terror,' establishing the connection to danger emanating from Muslim immigration. The three sections link the religion of Islam not only with cultural aspects of identity and tradition but also with terrorism.

The discursive association of danger and 'culture' is an important practice in constructing Germany as a non-immigration country. This link permits representing immigrants as quintessential Others vis-à-vis German society. Only if immigrants shake off their distinguishing cultural markers and embrace the dominant cultural norms of the liberal German nation will they cease to constitute a threat. The point, however, is that the assimilation of immigrants to these norms is inconceivable. Therefore, the only conceivable way to cope with this treat is to prevent immigration.

The inconceivability of the integration of new immigrants into German society reflects a common discursive strategy of distinction. As I noted in chapter 1, an important practice in the Othering of social groups is the construction of 'impassable symbolic boundaries' (Hall, 1996 [1989]: 445) that fix binary identities. As in the case of Canadian identity formation in the context of humanitarian immigration (chapter 5), German national identity represents the Other as a homogeneous group that stands on the opposite side of the symbolic fence that defines the nation. In other words, the dialectic of national identity formation involves a 'mono-national' and 'mono-cultural' view of immigrants (Elisabeth Beck-Gernsheim, 2007: 205).

According to Beck-Gernsheim, the German media has projected precisely such an image of Islam as a 'homogeneous block' (2007: 74). It has failed to distinguish between nationalities, class, ethnicity, or religious divisions within the Muslim population.[3] In the context of German immigration debate, the homogeneous image of the Muslim immigrant dominates and has rendered non-Muslim immigrants and immigration from non-Muslim regions invisible. Navid Kermani suggests that 'the entire integration debate (of immigrants) has today become a debate about Islam – as if the immigrants were nothing but Muslims' (2008: 15).

Although the image of a homogeneous immigrant population had initially faded with the emergence of the position that Germany is an immigration country, it gained strength again later in the immigration debate. Matthias Hell saw this change occurring at the end of the 'immigration-political honeymoon' (*zuwanderungspolitischer Frühling*) in 2001: 'In light of the threatening perception of foreign cultures, the homogeneity arrangement [*Homogenitätsdispositiv*] moved again into the centre of the debate, and immigration restriction and immigrant assimilation become the main aim of migration politics' (2005: 173).

The case of Metin Kaplan exemplifies the image the media constructed of Muslim immigration. Kaplan is the son of Cemaleddin Kaplan, the founder and emir of Hilafet Devleti, a Cologne-based movement that strove towards a social order following the principles of the Qur'an. After his father's death in 1995, Metin assumed leadership of the movement and declared himself caliph. In 2000, a court sentenced Kaplan to four years in prison for instigating the murder of a rival cleric. A year later, the federal minster of the interior, Otto Schili, declared the movement illegal due to its 'extremist and anti-constitutional (*verfassungsfeindlich*) activities' and the threat it posed to Germany's democratic order (Bundesministerium des Innern, 2001a). After Kaplan's conviction, the government pursued his deportation to Turkey, where he was wanted for planning violent attacks against the Turkish state. Only one day after his deportation was approved on 11 October 2004, Kaplan was deported to Turkey, where a court convicted him to life in prison.

Media reporting on Kaplan's case coincided with the later phases of the debate on the immigration law. In particular, reports on Kaplan's immanent deportation occurred in the wake of the Madrid bombings of 11 March 2004. In chapter 3 I presented data suggesting that the bombing attacks in Madrid were followed by a surge in the danger aspect in newspaper reporting on immigration. Kaplan's deportation was the subject of heated discussion during precisely that time. In addition, around the same time, in the summer of 2004, the main political parties had just reached a compromise on the immigration law, which entailed that the law would effectively prevent the entry of significant numbers of newcomers to Germany. During the phase of the debate when Kaplan's case occupied the newsrooms, the position that Germany is a non-immigration country had solidified.

During this time, the media presented Kaplan as an unwanted foreigner and an immanent threat to Germany's political order and 'culture.' Moreover, Kaplan's case was generalized, suggesting that this threat emanates from immigration as a whole. An article in the *Tageszeitung* illustrates how politicians presented Kaplan as a danger that relates directly to the question of immigration and corresponding legislation: '[Bavarian president Edmund] Stoiber established . . . a link between the immigration law, which in its main features was just negotiated between the federal government and the conservative opposition, and the case of Kaplan. He would sign the immigration law only if people like Kaplan are given short shrift' (Nowak, 2004: 14). The same article acknowledges that Kaplan's case has been abused for the purpose of political manoeuvring and fear mongering. It continues:

> Only few media disclosed to their readers that the case of Kaplan actually was only an orchestration (*Inszenierung*) whereby some media and politicians fed each other lines. Despite all media speculation . . . Kaplan stayed neither in the underground nor abroad. He did not even break the law [after his release from prison] . . .
>
> Yet, the Pentecost performance (*Pfingsttheater*) around the comedian of Cologne has already reached its goal in Germany. The immigration law shall be tightened even further. Not the critics of refugee and human rights initiatives, but conservative Politicians and their sympathizers currently dominate the discussion.

The conflation of Kaplan's case with the topic of immigration illustrates another dialectic in the manner in which the media reports on immigration. On the one hand, the media exposed the struggle of the German authorities to deport Kaplan as an 'orchestration' by some politicians to influence the immigration debate and to achieve restrictive immigration legislation. The *Stuttgarter Zeitung*, for example, paraphrased

Kerim Arpad of the European Association of Turkish Academics as saying: 'It is clear that hate preachers (*Hassprediger*), such as Metin Kaplan, must be deported – however, it is regrettable that it delays the entire [immigration] law' (Höfle, 2004: 23). Similarly, the *Tageszeitung* reports that even Kaplan's fierce opponent the 'Minister of the Interior, Schily, objects to using the case of Kaplan as an occasion to make changes to the immigration compromise' (2 June 2004: 7), which Germany's major political parties reached in late May. Already in March 2004, the outspoken Heribert Prantl warned that 'it is immanent that the immigration law becomes a foreigner-police law (*Ausländerpolizeigesetz*)' (2004c: 4) and spoke of a 'partial abandonment of the principle of the rule of law (*Rechtsstaatsprinzip*), the Guantanamoization (*Guantanamoisierung*) of the alien law (*Ausländerrecht*).'[4]

On the other hand, many voices in the media embraced precisely this association. The link between Kaplan's case and the immigration law reflects a general climate of mistrust towards immigrants that developed after 11 September 2001. Following the attacks on New York and Washington, the conservative opposition party, the Christian Democratic Union, categorically rejected Otto Schily's proposed immigration law and instead linked immigration with the issue of national security (Zinterer, 2004: 303–9). Matthias Hell argues that the 'security' narrative that framed parts of the immigration debate after September 11 presented an image of the immigrant as a 'sleeper' (2005: 151). After the Madrid attacks on 11 March 2004, interior minister Otto Schily adopted the conservative position and linked the fight against terrorism more closely with the issue of immigration. Immigrants became generally suspicious (Bendel, 2004: 206).

When the case of Metin Kaplan hit the news, the fear of immigration had grown to such a degree that a prominent politician of the ruling Social Democratic Party stressed in the *Tageszeitung* that, 'without security rules, the [proposed immigration] law is not acceptable because of the strong feelings of threat (*Bedrohungsempfinden*) among the people' (Weikert, 2004b: 22). This perception of an immanent threat triggered sometimes extreme reactions to Kaplan's case. Bavarian minister of the interior Günther Beckstein and his Lower Saxony counterpart Uwe Schünemann demanded that the immigration law permit the use of electronic shackles, consisting of a micro-chip attached to the ankle, to monitor the movements of Kaplan and other immigrants deemed suspicious (Deutsche Presse Agentur, 2004b: 4). Kaplan was seen as an immanent threat that must be tightly controlled through shackles as long as he could not be deported from German soil. Many conservative opposition politicians subsequently demanded revisions to the immigration law and the inclusion of security measures to better monitor and control the immigrant population. In the eyes of many political and media commentators, the case of Metin Kaplan rendered not only Muslim immigration but all immigration to Germany problematic.[5]

Although Metin Kaplan was often portrayed as a threat to Germany's political order and national security, his case was also linked to the language component of 'culture.' For example, the minister of culture of the region of Baden-Württemberg, Christian Democratic Union politician Annette Schavan,[6] seriously suggested prohibiting the use of the Arabic language for prayers in mosques and instead legislating the use of German: 'We must not continue to permit that in mosques [Islam] is preached in languages which are not understood outside of the Islamic community' (Deutsche Presse Agentur, 2004a). The Arabic language had become a symbol of cultural difference that – unlike other foreign languages – is associated with terrorism and religious extremism. Similarly to the case of Metin Kaplan, the Arab language symbolized a fundamental challenge to Germany's political order and the safety of the German population, and must therefore be tightly controlled, or better yet banned altogether from German society.

Although immigration debate in Germany has been dynamic and has incorporated various aspects and positions, the idea that immigrants should adopt the cultural conventions and ethnic norms of the German population has been present throughout the post-war period. This idea may temporarily have been pushed back in the early phases of the immigration debate. However, it recovered and decisively shaped the later stages of the debate. It remained integral to the third position of the immigration debate, which focussed on the integration of immigrants into German society.

Germany as an Integration Country

The immigration law which parliament passed in 2004 effectively blocked new immigration to Germany from outside the European Union. A report by the Federal Office for Migration and Refugees confirms that net migration to Germany – the balance between the in-migration and out-migration of foreigners – has been negative since the new law took effect (Bundesamt für Migration und Flüchtlinge, 2010: 5–7).[7] Despite this decline, the proportion of foreigners among Germany's resident population remained high, standing at 8.8 per cent in 2008. Approximately 65 per cent of these foreigners carried passports from non–European Union counties, the majority from Turkey (ibid.: 9–10).

The fact that millions of immigrants continue to be present in Germany validated the position that Germany is a country of immigrants. A third position addressed the apparent contradiction that Germany is both an immigration and non-immigration country. This third position focuses on the integration of immigrants already in Germany. It embraces Germany both as a non-immigrant country that rejects new immigrants and an immigration country that supports the inclusion of its immigrants already on German soil. In the context of a series of integration summits organized by the Federal Ministry of the Interior, the president of the Turkish community in Germany, Kenan Kolat, was thus able to declare the dawn of a 'new era,' in which the 'grand delusion' (*Lebenslüge*) that Germany is no immigration country has been overcome (*Stuttgarter Zeitung*, 2006: 1).

Although the issue of integration has been a part of the debate of the new immigration law all along, discussions of new immigration, rather than integration, dominated the initial phase of the public debate. In 2001, euphoric declarations that Germany is an immigration country provided the backdrop for a vibrant discussion of how to regulate new immigration to Germany (Meier-Braun, 2002; Zinterer, 2004; Krause, 2004). However, between 2001 and 2004, Germany's *immigration* debate morphed into an *integration* debate. In 2003, the conservative politician Wolfgang Bosbach declared that Germany is not a classical immigration country and that 'not immigration but more integration is the order of the day' (Grassmann, 2003b: 3). By 2004 most measures to facilitate significant numbers of new immigrants had been dropped from the proposed law and the issue of new immigration disappeared from public view. Instead, the integration of foreigners already in Germany took centre stage.

The third position of the integration of immigrants incorporates important elements from the first and second positions. For example, the position of integration involves the idea that immigrants constitute a potential threat. This aspect of integration was already articulated before integration became the main topic of the debate. In 2002, Heribert Prantl wrote an editorial challenging politicians to treat integration as a matter of national security:

> The [Christian Democratic and Christian Social] Union should actually be competing with the other parties for the better integration concepts

> because integration is also an element of preventive security politics. After all, in security politics, [Bavarian president] Stoiber, [Bavarian minister of the interior] Beckstein and their associates do not want to be outperformed by anyone. (2002: 8)

Days later, the conservative immigration critic and president of the state of Saarland, Peter Müller, and Bavaria's minister of the interior, Günther Beckstein, introduced a new program aimed at revising the immigration law. The *Tageszeitung* reported that this program reiterated the position long advocated by the conservative parties that immigrants must integrate by 'accepting "Western civilization"' (Goddar, 2002: 3). Beckstein added: 'People who name their child Osama bin Laden or dress it up as a suicide assassin demonstrate that they do not recognize [Western civilization]' (ibid.). The idea that integration reduces the threat immigration poses continued in later discussions. For example, in July 2005, the *Süddeutsche Zeitung* wrote in response to the bombing attacks on London's subway: 'The London attacks show that "integration will be a central theme of the future,"' said conservative candidate for German chancellor Angela Merkel. '"Every immigrant must commit to the values and the constitution of the Federal Republic of Germany"' (2005: 6).

I have illustrated above that the aspects of danger and 'culture' are often connected in the media's depictions of Muslim immigrants as Others. This connection is reproduced in the discussions of integration. For example, if the religion of immigrants is perceived to pose a threat to security, then integration supposedly removes this threat by addressing the issue of religion. What is different in the discussion of integration is that the aspect of 'culture' is not necessarily linked to the aspect of danger. Rather, the perceived 'culture' of immigrants is itself an important topic of debate.

The cultural mismatch between immigrants and German society has been a long established idea. Research by Martin Wengeler (2006) revealed anxieties, expressed in the German press throughout the postwar period, that immigrants are unwilling to integrate into German society. For example, in the 1960s and 1970s, the media lamented the formation of the 'slums' and 'ghettos' in which foreigners lived. In the more recent debate of the immigration law, this topic resurfaced with the rhetoric of a 'parallel society' (*Parallelgesellschaft*), in which immigrant communities exist without significant contact with German civic society.[8] Politicians, churches, NGOs, and journalists alike used this phrase to critique the assumed unwillingness of immigrants to integrate. The general secretary of the Christian Social Union, Jörg Schönbohm, claimed that 'integration has generally not worked. Parallel societies have emerged' (Wallraff, 2001: 4). In the same vein, Bremen's senator for the interior argued for a 'duty of integration' among immigrants, 'otherwise a parallel society of foreigners who live here is immanent' (Schöneberg, 2002: 21). Likewise, Catholic bishop and former member of the Süssmuth commission Josef Voß 'warned of the emergence of a parallel society in Germany' (Deckers, 2003: 4); and journalist Jeannette Goddar writes, in the context of integration courses mandated by the proposed immigration law, about a Turkish immigrant who 'lives in an almost purely Turkish neighbourhood in the [Berlin] borough of Neukölln,' and that 'many of her fellow [Turkish] country men and women have lived much longer in the large cities of the [Federal] Republic [of German] . . . and still have almost no contact with the German [social] environment' (2001: V7). Implicit in the rhetoric of the parallel society is the notion that immigrants who do not continuously interact with German non-immigrant society will not assimilate German cultural norms and values.

The rhetoric of the parallel society is directed mainly at Germany's Turkish community.[9] The 'dysfunctional' cultural traits that can supposedly be observed among this community include gender relations. The woman covered by a headscarf has become a media 'spectacle' (Ewing, 2008: 1), symbolizing the oppression of women in Muslim immigrant communities.[10] Several of the German newspaper articles that I examined for this analysis were accompanied by images of covered women, usually shopping or occupying public spaces. An explicit connection between these images and the contents of the articles, dealing with the issues of Otherness and integration, was not always given. Apparently, to the average reader of these newspapers, the image of the headscarf visualizes cultural difference in a way that does not require explanation. According to Katherine Pratt Ewing (2008), the symbol of the headscarf not only represents Turkish women as backward and non-belonging, but also implicates Turkish men as oppressors and objects of abjection. The gender relations of the Turkish community are perceived to be irreconcilable with the imaginary of the German nation.

At this stage, the Turkish community serves as a negation of the German national identity. Based on a detailed examination on the role of Turkish men and women in the German imagination, Ewing concludes that the stigmatization Turkish immigrants 'opens a space in the

German national imaginary for a positive cultural identity as German that nevertheless remains implicit' (Ewing, 2008: 224). The integration narrative, however, moves this dialectic beyond the first negation. The Turkish parallel society is invited to join the German nation, provided that it adapts some aspects of its 'culture.'[11] In this way, integration addresses the contradiction between the non-belonging of Turkish immigrants and their continuing presence in Germany.

An important cultural practice to which immigrants are supposed to adjust regards the relation between women and men. According to polls, more than nine out of ten Germans associate Islam with the discrimination of women (Südwestrundfunk, 2006). The assumption of gender oppression among Muslim immigrants can be interpreted as a way of expressing unease with the religion of Islam. The German constitution protects freedom of religion and guarantees gender equality. Drawing attention to the gender inequalities related to religious practice permits the critique of Islam in a politically correct manner that does not criticize Islam directly.[12] For example, the Christian Democratic Party declared in its policy statement of 2007 that the right to cultural difference is subordinate to the 'principle of equality of women and men. Everyone must agree about this, immigrants and hosts' (CDU Deutschland, 2007: 95–6). Although religion is not explicitly mentioned, this policy clearly targets Islam. Such representations of Islam have been common in parliamentary debates, where members of parliament have accused the immigrant community of forced marriage, polygamy, and male violence (Bauder and Semmelroggen, 2009: 13–14). Sometimes, however, the unease with Islam is expressed in a more direct manner. For example, the report by the so-called Müller commission – established by the conservative Christian Democratic Union as a counter taskforce to the government's Süssmuth commission – emphasizes the Christian roots of the German nation to define the conservative position on immigration (CDU Deutschland, 2001a). In 2004, Edmund Stoiber, the leader of the Christian Social Union stressed the 'Christian orientation of our country' (*Spiegel Online*, 2004). The religion of immigrants apparently challenges the German national identity. Elisabeth Beck-Gernsheim speaks of religion as an 'anchor' of identity that situates the foreigner in opposition to an imagined Christian national community (2007: 32–4).

In an effort to reconcile the Otherness of Islam with the need to integrate, without violating the principle of religious freedom, the Müller commission argued that it is 'self-evident that Muslims in Germany are permitted to preserve, affirm and practice their faith' (CDU Deutschland,

2001a: 84). However, since 'the relation between Christianity and Islam is often still affected by stereotypes and mutual ignorance,' the report advocates for a 'Christian-Muslim dialogue' involving comprehensive talks and information sharing. Furthermore, the report suggests that an 'enlightened Islam' would not be a barrier to integration. Similar to the Roman Catholic and Lutheran denominations of the Christian religion, Islam should be taught in school in the German language and under the supervision of German school boards. The Müller commission's policy statement reflects the attempt to make Islam compatible with a society and constitution that is imagined to rest on a Christian foundation.

Another cultural feature and focal point of the discussion of integration is language. To many commentators, successful integration entails that newcomers adopt the German language. German chancellor Angela Merkel remarked in July 2006 at a widely publicized integration summit, organized by the federal commissioner of integration (*Integrationsbeauftragte*) Maria Böhmer, that the most important mechanism of integration is the German language. Before the summit, the federal cabinet introduced plans to support German-language programs for children in kindergarten, while federal minister of the interior Wolfgang Schäuble stressed that successful integration entails that children learn German before first grade (Wöhrle, 2006). According to polls, Germans find it more important that immigrants speak the host country's language than citizens of most other European countries (Citrin and Sides, 2008: 39–40).[13] In the media, the demand for language acquisition among immigrant groups has been voiced before. Five years before the integration summit, Berlin's senator responsible for education, Klaus Böger, told the *Tageszeitung* that 'the German language is the key to integration' (Am Orde, 2002: 21). A year later, Albert Schmid, president of the Federal Bureau for Migration and Refugees (BAMF), told the *Süddeutsche Zeitung* that 'integration is mainly related to language . . . not only, but mainly' (Prantl, 2002: 8). The newsprint media is full of similar examples that associate successful integration with German-language acquisition.

In the political field, Germany's new immigration law demanded that immigrants learn German with the provision of up to 600 hours of language courses. These courses can be mandated, if deemed necessary. The expectation that immigrants learn German is a central idea of the slogan 'demand and support' ('Fördern und Fordern'), which the Merkel government has advocated in the context of immigrant integration, and which suggests that those immigrants 'who repeatedly refuse to integrate must expect sanctions' (CDU Deutschland, 2007: 95–6). The Christian Democratic Union's policy statement explicitly states: 'Knowledge of German is the key to integration. Clear and comprehensible demands present for us not barriers but the foundation for social integration. Our principle is demand and support' (ibid.: 96).

The requirement that immigrants speak the German language can be interpreted as an effort to stimulate their active participation in Germany's democracy. The German political scientist Dieter Oberndörfer defends this perspective when he argues that 'language serves communication; its value should not be inflated into the mythical-religious' (1992: 99). North Rhine–Westphalia's minister of the interior, Fritz Behrens, therefore praised the mandatory language courses to be included in Germany's new immigration law for their role in promoting 'equal opportunity and the participation in social life' (Jasper, 2004: 2).

In addition to this role, however, language also serves as a key element of Germany's cultural identity. Benedict Anderson (1991) illustrated the historical importance of language in the construction of national identities. In the construction of German national identity, language has played a particularly important role. The German nation builders of the Romantic period, including Arndt, Fichte, and Herder, stressed the bond of the shared German language. The perception of foreign languages as anti-German persisted throughout the Wilhelmine empire[14] and Germany's modern history. Up until the late 1990s, the wide political consensus that Germany is a non-immigration country continued to be associated with the collective imaginary of Germany as a homogeneous linguistic community. This legacy of the German language as a key signifier of national belonging continues to shape the contemporary integration debate.

For example, in an apparent effort to ensure the cultural integration of immigrants and their families, conservative politicians proposed to reduce the age at which foreign children can come to Germany to reunite with their immigrant parents. In 2001, the president of Baden-Württemberg, Erin Teufel, suggested reducing the upper age limit for family reunification to six, 'better still three years' (Durchdenwald, 2001: no page). The idea that language can only be properly learned as a toddler illustrates that Teufel associates the value of speaking German not with its being a mere tool for formal communication – millions of adolescent and adult students are successfully learning foreign languages – but rather with a cultural identity that is cultivated early in life and that signifies national belonging.

Similar arguments have occasionally been made with respect to other cultural markers. The most infamous example is the suggestion by Bavaria's minister of the interior Günther Beckstein (1999) that immigrants should adopt a German *Leitkultur,* which can loosely be translated as 'lead culture' or 'dominant culture.' A year later, this suggestion was picked up by Beckstein's party colleague Friedrich Merz (Ewing, 2008: 212). In the later phases of the debate of the immigration law, when terrorism and national security received heightened attention, the state of Brandenburg's interior minister, Jörg Schönbohm, used the same terminology, arguing that 'those who come to us must assume the German Leitkultur' (*Spiegel Online,* 2004). Although the term was coined by political science professor Bassam Tibi in an effort to propose a multicultural framework for Europe based on individual rights, secularism, and tolerance, the interpretation of the term by Beckstein, Merz, and Schönbohm implied ethnic and cultural meanings (Ewing, 2008: 214). The Leitkultur notion, however, failed to focus the integration debate on the issue of cultural assimilation because the similarity to terminology used by the Nazi regime triggered a public outcry.

Nevertheless, the foiled Leitkultur campaign and the discussions surrounding religion and language illustrate that the responsibility for integration is placed disproportionately on the shoulders of the immigrant. A 1996 scientific poll indicated that 60 per cent of the sampled Germans support the statement that 'foreigners should assimilate their lifestyle to a greater degree to German circumstances' (Münz and Ulrich, 1998: 1). Media voices expressed similar opinions. For example, the *Frankfurter Allgemeine Zeitung* reported in 2002: 'The (Christian Democratic and Christian Social) Union, however, wants "to develop a comprehensive integration concept" for all foreigners, based on the principle "demand and support" (*Fordern und Fördern*). Those who are "not willing to integrate must not receive permanent residence"' (Inacker, 2002: 1). The German term *Bringschuld* reflects this responsibility to integrate on the side of immigrants. This term describes an inherent debt owed by newcomers to the existing national community. Supposedly, immigrants automatically accrue this debt when they enter and settle in Germany. The idea of immigrants arriving in Germany with a debt that should be settled in the form of making active efforts towards integration appears in the later phases of the debate of the immigration law. In 2004, the *Frankfurter Allgemeine Zeitung* reports: 'Integration cannot only entail making an offer [to foreigners] but should also be enshrined in the law as the *Bringschuld* of the foreigners who live here. This is the shared view of all parties' (Dietrich, 2004: 1).

This duty to integrate, which the immigrant supposedly owes to the established national community, illustrates the logic of the third position in the dialectic of German immigration debate. It ensures that immigrants can remain in Germany, that they possess the possibility of shedding their identities as Others, but that they do not have the right to transform the meaning of German nationhood.

Conclusion

The analysis of the 'culture' and danger aspects of the debate on the immigration law revealed a set of overlapping and nested dialectics. The first dialectic was the main theme of this chapter. It described the development of the debate from Germany as an immigration country to non-immigration country and finally to integration country. In a typical dialectical movement, the contradictory first and second positions were subsumed within a third position.

A second dialectic occurred between substance and subject. As I illustrated in chapter 2, the critical discourse scholarship has long established the link between discourse and material practice. Norman Fairclough, for example, notes 'the dependence of texts upon society and history' (1992b: 195).[15] In the context of the German immigration debate, material events affected the debate on immigration and subsequently the imagination of the nation. For example, the war on terrorism and the attacks on Madrid affected the way immigrants were represented in Germany. The association of immigrants with Muslim extremism and their representation as a danger portrayed immigration as the ultimate negation of the German nation. In the wake of the Madrid events, the first, pro-immigration, position weakened and the second, anti-immigration, position gained strength. Similarly, the continued material presence of immigrants in Germany pushed the debate towards the third position, which emphasized the integration of immigrants already in the country. Material events and circumstances thus played an important role in moving the debate along the path of negation and sublation. This interpretation affirms the material basis of the immigration debate. In turn, the integration position of the debate has manifested itself materially in the immigration law and continues to shape policy today.[16]

A third dialectic reflects the practice of incorporating conflicting viewpoints in media discussion and public debate. This chapter has illustrated the point that this practice takes multiple forms. For example, the three positions of the first dialectic were, temporally, not neatly separated from each other, but overlapped. While the position that Germany is an immigration country may have dominated in the initial stage of the debate, media voices had already inserted the other two positions into the debate at this stage. Contradiction has been a characteristic of the debate since its very beginning. In another example, the media, on the one hand, constructed an association between the case of Metin Kaplan and the Muslim immigrant community in general. On the other hand, writers acknowledged that this association was a strategic 'orchestration' for the purpose of political manipulation. In a similar vein, liberal arguments about language as means of communication appear next to cultural arguments about language as a symbolic marker of identity.

The negation of the nation by the immigrant Other provokes an interesting comparison between the German and Canadian contexts. In the German context, this negation was apparent in the second position, which constructed Muslim immigrants as a homogeneous population that is dangerous and does not belong. The practice of Othering was also visible in the third position, which argued that once immigrants are identified as Others they have an obligation, or inherent duty, to integrate by adjusting aspects of their 'culture.' This third position may at first glance remind us of the idea of sublation as it could be observed in the Canadian context. However, in the Canadian debate, newly arriving immigrants – rather than an established parallel society – become an integral part of the nation. In addition, in Canada, immigrant integration is often understood as a two-way street (Biles et al., 2008).[17] Even if, in practice, the relation between immigrants and non-immigrants remains unequal, there is an acknowledgment in the Canadian debate that the established community has responsibilities. Conversely, in Germany, the onus for integration rests disproportionately with immigrants, who supposedly possess an inherent debt or *Bringschuld.* Instead of sublating immigrant and national identities into something new, integration in Germany is understood as a one-way street where the immigrant has a duty to adapt. In the next chapter, I will examine this truncated dialectic in the context of humanitarian immigration.

9 Refugees and Asylum Seekers

In Germany, the humanitarian aspect of the immigration debate involves asylum seekers and refugees.[1] It excludes ethnic German returnees (*Vertriebene, Heimatvertriebene, Aussiedler,* and *Spätaussiedler*), former guest workers and their families, migrants with European citizenship, and temporary migrant workers. Chapter 3 illustrated that the humanitarian aspect was a considerable and relatively consistent factor in the immigration debate. In this chapter, I examine this humanitarian aspect in relation to Germany's national identity formation.

To recap, humanitarian immigration can reveal interesting practices associated with national identity formation. Although images of refugees and asylum seekers are often based on gross stereotypes,[2] these images can function as powerful negations of the national self. In other words, the negative representations of the places that refugees and asylums seekers flee help to construct the receiving country's own national territory in oppositional, positive terms. This negation establishes what the nation is not. When refugees and asylum seekers are invited to settle permanently in the country of refuge, the dialectical process does not end with this simple negation. Rather, refugees who become immigrants shed the image of the Other, acquire an identity of belonging and thereby become an integral part of the nation. This second negation of absorbing the Other into the nation reflects the *sublation* of two opposing positions into a single, more complete national identity.

Catherine Dauvergne observed precisely such practices of national identity formation in the context of humanitarian immigration and refugee law and policy in Australia and Canada. On the one hand, she observes, 'migration law provides a rich site in which to search for images of national identity, and in which national identity can be reinvented, reconstructed, reimagined' (2005: 9). Migration law negotiates the boundaries of national identity by defining the characteristics of refugees and people in humanitarian need and by identifying the places where these characteristics occur. 'Migration law is directed outward, at those beyond the nation's borders. In labelling and controlling these others, it builds a reflected image of the nation and those who are insiders' (ibid.: 30). On the other hand, the settler nation also welcomes these Others as new members of the national community. Thus, in a dialectical twist, the nation internalizes these images of the refugee Other and incorporates them into the national imagination. My analysis of the Canadian immigration debate in chapter 5 confirmed the negation of the nation through the representation of refugees. This analysis, however, also suggested that the formation of national identity through refugee integration is implied and taken for granted; the media rarely address the second negation relating to the integration of refugees into the national community in an explicit way.

My interpretation of the German immigration debate outlines similarities to, but also important differences from, the Canadian debate. On the one hand, it suggests that the German debate of humanitarian immigration, similarly to the Canadian debate, portrays the places that refugees and asylum seekers have escaped as deficient. These negative images of other places construct counter-images of the German state as the protector of human rights and enactor of international law. On the other hand, my interpretation also proposes that the dialectical process of identity formation ends prematurely. It remains at a state where the boundary between the self and Other continues to be solid and never dissolves. German media discourse of humanitarian immigration does not consider the absorption of refugees and asylum seekers into the imagined national community. The media does not present attitudes towards humanitarian immigration and associated refugee and asylum policy that would be expected from an immigration country. Nevertheless, through the principle of negation rather than integration, the humanitarian aspect of immigration serves as a powerful mechanism of national identity formation.

The humanitarian aspect of the immigration debate also relates to other dimensions of the immigration dialectic. In addition to practices of identity formation, I examine the dialectic of media practice in the representation of humanitarianism. Furthermore, any interpretation of the humanitarian aspect of the immigration debate must be interpreted in relation to its particular material context. In the next section, I introduce this context.

Humanitarian Migration in Germany

Humanitarian migration has administratively and legally been separated from citizenship, labour migration, and the return migration of ethnic Germans from Eastern Europe and the former Soviet Union.[3] With this practice, Germany follows international legal practices and policy conventions, which typically distinguish between refugees and immigrants (Karatani, 2005).

In the case of Germany, the right to refuge is even a constitutional right. According to article 16 of the German constitutional law (*Grundgesetz*), 'Political prosecuted persons enjoy the right to asylum.' This right was particularly important when the constitution took effect in 1949, a time when the atrocities committed by the Nazi regime overshadowed German national identity. The drafters of the constitution recognized that many people were politically prosecuted, imprisoned, and often murdered in the Third Reich; most of those who found refugee abroad were able to escape this dire fate. By enshrining the right to asylum in its constitution, the new Federal Republic of Germany therefore symbolized its readiness to provide refuge to politically prosecuted people. Asylum legislation was a way of coping with the past and became a form of identity politics in the early Federal Republic.

Despite this early commitment to refugee protection and the provision of asylum, relatively few individuals and families initially applied for asylum in Germany. Between 1953 and 1978 a total of 178,000 asylum seekers arrived in Germany. Although the numbers increased thereafter, they generally remained below 100,000 annually until 1987 (with the exception of 1980, when 107,818 asylum seekers arrived). From 1988 on, with the opening of Eastern European borders and the upsurge of violence in the Balkans, the numbers skyrocketed. In 1990, 193,063 applications for asylum were submitted. The surge in applications peaked in 1992 with 438,191 applicants (Bundesamt für Migration und Flüchtlinge, 2008: 9).

In light of increasing racism, right-wing extremism, and a series of arson attacks on asylum reception centres in 1991 and 1992, the German parliament conceded to anti-immigrant sentiments by modifying article 16 of the German constitution and limiting the circumstances and countries of origin[4] to which the right to asylum applies. In addition, restrictions to the practice of asylum recognition reduced the success rate of applications. By 2001, when the debate of the immigration law began, the annual number of asylum applications had diminished to 88,287. At the end of the immigration debate, the numbers of asylum applications had declined further to 35,607 (Bundesamt für Migration und Flüchtlinge, 2009: 9).[5] In addition, the chances for success in the application process were minute. In 2001, only 5.3 per cent of the asylum applications were recognized under article 16. In 2004, it was even fewer, 1.5 per cent – although many more applicants were permitted to stay provisionally in Germany (Bundesamt für Migration und Flüchtlinge, 2005: 42).

The trend has been criticized by church-based charities, welfare organizations, human rights activists, and the political left. Throughout the post-war period these groups have supported the acceptance of migration based on humanitarian need (Wengeler, 2006). In the late 1999s and during the immigration debate, they condemned the restrictions of asylum and refugee policy.

During the time when the numbers of humanitarian migrants to Germany dwindled, an identity shift, which triggered the immigration debate, began to occur. In the 1990s the idea of Germany being an immigration country grew in popularity. The simultaneous drop in successful asylum applications and the increasing recognition that Germany is an immigration country are likely related. The decline in undesired humanitarian immigration probably facilitated a debate over what constituted desired immigration, which was supposed to be enabled by an immigration law that would regulate the proactive selection of immigrants.[6] According to this scenario, refugees and asylum seekers are not conceived as future Germans. In other words, humanitarian immigration is not represented as an opportunity to shape and replenish the nation. Instead, refugees and asylum seekers are imagined as permanently separate from the German nation.

In addition, the immigration debate took place at a time when Germany was still struggling with a post–Cold War identity as a unified nation. For example, with the move of government functions from Bonn to Berlin,[7] the newly elected Social Democratic/Green government coalition began using the term 'Berlin Republic' to signify not only a new policy direction but also a new national identity. During the Cold War, refugee and asylum policy has also served as a way to passively engage the 'East Block.' In the Berlin Republic, this policy may have lost its geopolitical appeal; it was no longer able to define the West German community as 'good' vis-à-vis the enemy in the East. An interesting question relates to the role of humanitarian immigration in the construction of national identity at a time when political elites sought to shake off Germany's cold-war image and reinvented the nation's identity as the Berlin Republic.

Obligations of Humanitarianism

German public opinion supports the thesis that humanitarian immigration is undesirable and not a mechanism to replenish the nation. Before the immigration debate began, public support for humanitarian immigration was small. Poll data show that in 1996, 21 per cent of the population rejected all immigration for asylum seekers; 66 per cent would restrict asylum-based immigration; and only 12 per cent supported unconstrained humanitarian immigration (Münz and Ulrich, 1998). In addition, the majority of Germans across all age groups rejected equal rights for asylum seekers, though not for Italians and Turkish people (Wasmer and Koch, 2003). Six years later, in 2002, when the immigration debate was in full swing and the notion of Germany as an immigration country still featured strongly in the debate, Germans continued to be more sceptical of humanitarian immigration than people in other European countries (Fertig, 2004: 1). Matthias Hell observes that the protection from asylum seekers (*Abschottung*) was an important theme of the immigration law debate (2005: 115–41). In fact, the arrival of desired immigrants and the intake of undesired asylum seekers were treated as dialectically opposed issues. In a poll conducted in the year 2000, 54 per cent of the sampled population supported the statement 'When we make an immigration law, asylum law must also be rearranged. Otherwise immigrants and refugees arrive simultaneously, which is too much.' Only 27 per cent of Germans agreed with the counter-statement that 'Germany must remain open to refugees. This must not change, it may not be restricted by an immigration law' (Köcher, 2000: 5). Apparently, in the public field, to permit desired immigration also often means to curb the intake of undesired refugees and asylum seekers.

In the media field, the discussions of the humanitarian aspect of immigration addressed mostly whether and why refugees and asylum seekers who were already in Germany should be permitted to stay, and under what circumstances they should be deported. The media discussions typically assumed that humanitarianism applies to 'internal "others"' (Ward, 2002: 233), not to people still abroad who wish to come to Germany for protection. In this respect, the German debate does not necessarily differ from the Canadian debate. However, compared to Germany, Canada's policies assume a much more proactive approach towards refugee admission: refugees are selected not only on the basis of their need for protection, but are also screened for their propensity to integrate into, and bring benefits to, Canada.[8] The German state, by contrast, plays a passive role in refugee admission.

This passivity is reflected in the German media's debate of immigration. Humanitarianism is represented as something in which the state participates passively, merely granting or denying permission to stay to foreigners who have managed to come to Germany on their own. The state is not supposed to actively select and bring humanitarian immigrants into the country. This perspective does not represent humanitarian immigration as an opportunity to select deserving immigrants, but rather as an obligation to conform to international law and moral values.

My analysis of the immigration debate revealed that the discussion of the humanitarian aspect followed these two themes. The first suggests that humanitarian assistance is Germany's *legal obligation* towards international law and legal practice. The second theme proposes that Germany has a *moral obligation* towards people in need. In the following sections, I discuss how the dialectical formation of national identity relates to these two themes.

Legal Obligation

The media presented a wide range of voices that supported the view that humanitarian immigration is Germany's legal obligation. Among these voices were Germany's Catholic and Lutheran churches.[9] For example, in the beginning of the immigration debate, in 2001, the *Frankfurter Allgemeine Zeitung* reported on how the two churches regarded the proposed immigration law as insufficient in meeting legal standards: 'The churches already demanded in 1996 in a joint statement about the challenges of refuge and migration that any regulation of immigration must conform to the claim of protecting human rights as well as the rule of legal clarity (*Rechtsklarheit*) and legal certainty (*Rechtssicherheit*). In regard to these claims, the proposed law is insufficient' (Deckers, 2001: 4).

More than two-and-a-half years later, in an interview with the *Süddeutsche Zeitung*, the bishop of Berlin and council president of the Lutheran Church in Germany, Wolfgang Huber, referred to the universality of human rights and Germany's legal obligation towards non-citizens: 'We are a country that is committed to human rights and not only to the civil rights of its citizens. The immigration law is the test of this [commitment]' (Drobinski, 2004a: 12).

The churches were not the only institutions that were defending humanitarian immigration on legal grounds. Next to churches, the media reported that international organizations were calling attention to Germany's legal commitments towards humanitarianism. For example, in an interview with the *Tageszeitung,* Stefan Berglund of the Office of the United Nations High Commissioner for Refugees reiterated that, with respect to the immigration law, 'Germany must fulfill its responsibilities towards public international law (*völkerrechtliche Verantwortungen*)' (Rath, 2003: 7).

In addition, press reporting presented politicians across the political spectrum as agreeing in principle on the legal obligation of Germany to humanitarianism. For example, an article in the *Süddeutsche Zeitung* presented the views of immigration experts Volker Beck of the Green Party and Wolfgang Bosbach of the Christian Democratic Union regarding humanitarian immigration. Although the two politicians disagreed on the contents and reference points (i.e., the European standard versus the Geneva Convention) of Germany's legal obligation, they both endorsed international law as the fundamental principle for humanitarian immigration to Germany.

> Beck: ... It has long been the European standard that non-state persecution is accepted [as a reason for immigration] – for example, when someone is pursued by paramilitary militias, but a state no longer exists that could protect from such acts.
>
> ...
>
> Bosbach: We are for the complete application of the Geneva Convention for Refugees. But what [the] Red-Green [coalition] wants clearly exceeds [the Convention] and can therefore not be done with us. (Grassmann, 2003a: 10)

The negation articulated through this theme of legal obligation constructs a particular *legal* identity for Germany. If the place where refugees and asylum seekers come from is portrayed as disrespectful of international law and universal human rights, then Germany appears as a country in which law and order creates a safe environment for its residents. Many articles used comparative images, discussing Germany's legal obligation in relation to the legal circumstances of the refugee-sending countries. This negation of the nation through the Other is expressed by a wide range of voices, including churches, non-governmental organizations, and politicians. For example, an interviewer from the *Süddeutsche Zeitung* asked Stephan Reimers of the German Lutheran Church if humanitarian immigration should be restricted because large numbers of people live in countries that practise torture and 'almost everyone from an Islamic country or a country of the Third World' could potentially claim refuge in Germany. Reimers answered: 'This argument worries me most. If we accept it, we undermine the absolute prohibition of torture in our constitutional state (*Rechtsstaat*). Should we say: Here in Germany torture is really bad, and abroad we don't care about it' (Drobinski, 2004b: 8). By supporting humanitarian immigration, Reimers affirms in this quote the identity of the German state as a champion of universal human rights, while 'abroad' these rights are disregarded.

Non-governmental organizations are also represented as endorsing this view. An article in the *Stuttgarter Zeitung* refers to Amnesty International to suggest that Germany's identity as a state that abides by international law would suffer if refugees were deported to places where they are threatened. In this case, the 'deportation' of refugees challenges the legal integrity of Germany: 'Amnesty sees the protection of refugees endangered [through German anti-terrorism policies] ... It would contradict the obligation of the Geneva Convention for Refugees, if conjectural supporters of 'terrorist' organizations can be deported [from Germany] without legal conviction, even if they are threatened at home [in other countries]' (*Stuttgarter Zeitung,* 2001: 1). Politicians were also presented as endorsing this position. When the prominent Green Party politician Claudia Roth discussed the humanitarian components of the proposed immigration law in an interview with the *Süddeutsche Zeitung,* she supported humanitarian immigration by suggesting: 'We would lose all credibility if we said that women who are prosecuted by the Taliban do not have the right to apply for asylum here' (Husemann, 2001: 11).

Interestingly, contrary to my expectations, the media did not emphasize images of desperate women, crying children, and graphic descriptions of victims of abuse who were deserving of compassion and protection. Instead, the press focused on representations of the deficient state which the immigrant was fleeing. For example, to explain the situation of refugees who would be affected by the ruling of Germany's constitutional court in 2002 to annul the immigration law, the *Stuttgarter Zeitung* published an article with the stories of several refugees, including descriptions of the circumstances they confronted in their countries of origin:

> The Turkish-Kurdish family Gökalp of the [German] region of Rastatt has been tolerated (*geduldet*) by German authorities for 13 years. Their asylum

> application failed because non-state persecution was and is not accepted as a reason for asylum. The background is that the Turkish military supposedly installed 'village protectors' (*Dorfschützer*) in the 80s in the Kurdish regions, who terrorized the population – also the Gökalp family because the father was considered a supporter of the PKK [*Partiya Karkerên Kurdistan*, or Kurdistan Workers Party, which is considered a terrorist organization by the Turkish state]. In the spring of 1989 they wounded his then four-year-old son Ali. (Ziedler, 2002: 2)

The image of paramilitary rule and insecurity at the place of origin and the presence of a repressive state that tramples the liberties of its citizens and terrorizes its population legitimates granting refugees the permission to stay in Germany.

The same article presents another case of a refugee family from the Balkans, which was affected by the court ruling. Under the 2002 version of the immigration law, the family would have been eligible to stay in Germany; after the court ruling it was threatened with deportation: 'The Sushicas from Kosovo must now worry about [deportation]. The father, Samir, is Roma, the mother, Duljeta, Albanian ... Radical Albanian militias – a non-state group – consider them ... collaborators of the Milosevic regime. Nevertheless, the family is not regarded as persecuted' (Ziedler, 2002: 2). The impression the reader gleans of the places of origin of these families is one of lawlessness, repression, and fear. The argument that the families should be accepted as refugees presumes, however, that Germany is a haven where law, freedom, and security exist.

I have presented above the main tendency of the legal-obligation theme to negate the nation through the image of the deficient state from which a refugee flees. This main tendency is complicated by a narrative suggesting that refugees should be assisted to return to their countries of origin. While this narrative does not challenge the image of the other country as the negation of the nation, it proposes that the return of refugees can assist in alleviating the deficiencies of the state abroad. In other words, if Germany provides refugees with the temporary opportunity to recover from an immediate threat, they can thereafter return to their countries of origin and help turn these states into ones of law, freedom, and security similar to Germany.

This repatriation (*Rückführung*) narrative appears in the newspapers through the voices of intergovernmental organizations and conservative politicians. In one interview, the *Tageszeitung* asked Bernd Hemingway of the International Organization for Migration (IOM) whether creating incentives for 'voluntary' return migration was not simply a strategy to avoid forced deportation. Hemingway responded: 'I regard [repatriation] as a very good alternative. And our long-standing experience shows that many people managed to re-establish themselves in their countries of origin through voluntary return migration, and even helped with the reconstruction of their country. To use this potential is, incidentally, also a matter of development-policy'[10] (*Tageszeitung*, 2004a: 7).

The following excerpt associates repatriation with the voice of a prominent conservative politician. The *Stuttgarter Zeitung* paraphrases Günther Beckstein:

> The [Christian Democratic and Christian Social] Union wants the 'strict deportation' of all foreigners who possess no residency entitlement (*Aufenthaltsrecht*). 30,000 such Afghan refugees without permanent right of residence (*Bleiberecht*) live in Germany who would be needed for the reconstruction of their country. (*Stuttgarter Zeitung*, 2002: 2)

That the media also challenges this repatriation narrative is exemplified by the following quote, which suggests that repatriation may be a valid idea, but in practice does not apply to any refugees in Germany:

> And what about voluntary return migration? 'We support refugees, if they voluntarily want to return to their home country (*Heimatland*),' said Danijela-Jelena Medved of the International Organization for Migration (IOM) – 'Voluntary return migration under pressure of otherwise threatened deportation is not voluntary, but forced,' replied Leyla Arslan of the Cologne counselling centre Agisra. She does not know a refugee who sees an alternative in voluntary departure. Rather, denied asylum applicants count on the possibility of continued migration (*Weiterwanderung*), toleration (*Duldung*), or movement into illegality. (Voigt, 2004: 4)

This challenge to the repatriation narrative illustrates the dialectical nature of media practice in relation to the humanitarian aspect of the immigration debate. In this respect, the press presents an argument and counter-argument in a way that can also be observed with respect to other aspects of the immigration debate in both Germany and Canada.

The counter-position, that repatriation is not applicable to refugees in Germany, can also be interpreted in light of Hegelian dialectics. In this context, the challenge of the repatriation narrative may be consistent with the earlier narrative, which negated the nation by Othering the places from which refugees are fleeing. The repatriation of refugees with the aim of creating a safe, liberal, and democratic state abroad would deny this negation of the nation. If the foreign state became as safe, lawful, and democratic as Germany, then the German nation would lose its dialectical counter-image of the foreign state that is unsafe, unlawful, and undemocratic. This condition would lead to the termination of the dialectical process. Sending refugees back to their countries of origin to successfully 'reconstruct' their country would be similar to the master killing the servant, which would reduce the master to a 'merely existing (*bloß seiende*) object' (Hegel, 2005 [1807]: 158). Challenging the repatriation narrative can thus be interpreted as an effort to sustain the image of the deficient state abroad and thereby maintain the principle of negation as an important step in the dialectical process of national subject formation.

Moral Obligation

The second theme of discussions of the humanitarian aspect of immigration suggests that humanitarian immigration is a moral obligation that the German nation owes. Similarly to the legal right to asylum, which is enshrined in the German constitution (article 16), the moral-obligation narrative is referenced in the German constitution. In particular, article 1 of the German constitutional law grants the 'indefeasibility of human dignity' to each human being and thereby sets a moral standard for the treatment of all people. In addition, the moral-obligation narrative relates to 'Christian values' that demand compassion towards people in need. In their role as Germany's moral authority, the Catholic and Lutheran churches are represented as the main proponents of the moral-obligation narrative. In fact, the two main Christian churches strongly support the moral claims of the constitution. For example, the *Frankfurter Allgemeine Zeitung* quoted the Catholic bishop Josef Voß, who, incidentally, was a member of the Süssmuth commission, in the following way: '"The church expects that the requirements for the fundamental protection of the dignity of human beings will not become a victim of negotiation," said the Bishop ... Even people who legally do not exist[11] are bearers of indefeasible human rights' (Deckers, 2003: 4).

In an interview with the *Süddeutsche Zeitung*, the Lutheran prelate Stefan Reimers also defended human rights. In answer to the question of whether he supported the detention of migrants involved in terrorist activities, he responded: 'Only as a final instrument, and I am only for it with discomfort. But I see the dilemma: on the one hand, the state has a legitimate security interest. On the other hand, we must never send a human being into torture and death, no matter how badly we think of his or her intentions or actions' (Drobinski, 2004b: 8).

Another article published in the *Süddeutsche Zeitung* indicates that the two churches agree that the plight of refugees should not fall victim to partisan politics. 'The two large [Catholic and Lutheran] churches ... warn of making refugees the "plaything (*Spielball*) of political interest." The parties should "leave aside nitpicking confrontations." "This is about people, not party-political confrontations," said the Munich cardinal Friedrich Wetter' (Rubner, 2002: 2). As 'people,' refugees possess basic moral and legal rights.

The importance of the 'Christian' values of compassion and kindness towards people suffering hardship[12] was also important in the moral-obligation theme. This importance became apparent, in particular, when the Christian Democratic Union and the Christian Social Union were accused of neglecting Christian values, and were reminded of the 'C' in their abbreviated names, CDU and CSU. Mainly politicians used this rhetorical tactic to point out the contradiction between the two conservative parties' political practice and their religious commitments, as signified by the 'Christian' in their names. For example, the *Frankfurter Allgemeine Zeitung* reported on how the chair of the government's commission on immigration, Rita Süssmuth of the Christian Democratic Union, criticised her own party: 'The former President of the Lower House of Parliament (*Bundestagspräsidentin*), Süssmuth, who chaired the government commission on immigration, pointed out to her own party that it must not oppose refugees, not least because of the Christian "C" in its name' (Leithäuser, 2001b: 3).

An article in the *Tageszeitung* shows that a cabinet member of the Social Democratic Party used the same rhetorical tactic against the two opposition parties: 'Even [federal minister of the interior] Schily's assertive reference to the Christian "C" in the initials of the Union parties and his appeal to the churches to persuade the Union to support the immigration law are unlikely to help: The CDU-leadership will not support the law, said the general-secretary Laurenz Meyer yesterday' (Oestreich, 2001: 3). Similarly, the Green Party's immigration expert, Volker Beck, in a debate with Günter Burkhardt, director of the refugee advocacy group Pro Asyl,[13] suggested that the 'Christian' parties should be held to their moral standards. In the *Tageszeitung*, Beck said: 'The actual problem is that there is no other party that clearly supports questions of human rights. Our assertiveness would be increased if some Christian Democrats would find their C and some Liberals would be involved with constitutional state liberalism (*Rechtsstaatsliberalismus*)' (Lang and Wallraff, 2003: 3).

According to a Hegelian interpretation of identity formation, the narrative of moral obligation – as it unfolded in the media – does not contribute much to the dialectical production of a German national identity. The image of a compassionate Christian nation does not seem to even enter the stage of the first negation. Unlike the legal-obligation narrative, the moral-obligation narrative generally fails to juxtapose the nation with the immorality of a dialectical opposite.

An expected counter-narrative against the acceptance of immigrants on moral grounds is that Germany does not possess the resources to accommodate everyone outside of Germany who is persecuted, maltreated, or otherwise morally deserving of protection. For example, in an interview with the *Tageszeitung*, a senator of Bremen, Kuno Böse of the Christian Democratic Union, was asked whether he supports ending the deportation of refugees who are victims of non-state and gender-specific persecution. He responded: 'This is very problematic. Excuse the example: genital mutilation. With recognition of this terrible problem, millions of women are affected. What happens if they want to come to Germany? How do we regulate this?' (Kahlcke, 2001: 22) This argument contradicts the general context of the debate of humanitarian immigration in the newsprint media. As I pointed out above, this debate focuses on the relatively small numbers of potential asylum seekers who are already in Germany or manage to get to Germany on their own. State institutions, such as the commissioner for foreigners of Berlin, have indeed advocated for the protection of African women from deportation if they are threatened with genital mutilation. The number of potentially affected immigrants, however, is small (Pohl, no year).

More important, in my eyes, is the effect that this counter-narrative has on the dialectical processes of national subject formation. A rejection of humanitarianism based on the principle of numbers does not even engage with the argument that Germany has a moral (or a legal) obligation. The discussion ends before the nation is negated through its counter-image. This non-engagement can be compared with the death of the servant in Hegel's work. If the abstract self is not negated by a material Other, then the dialectic of subject formation terminates prematurely.

The following excerpt from the *Stuttgarter Zeitung* can be interpreted in a similar manner. In this case, large numbers of refugees are presented as a challenge to 'internal peace' – a justification for their exclusion without resorting to any legal or moral arguments.

> In [1992], the Federal Republic [of Germany] admitted roughly 450,000 refugees and experienced a wave of hatred towards foreigners. In 2002, there were only 71,000 people who were accepted in Germany as political refugees. 'The solution of the problem by the large parties [Christian Democratic Union / Christian Social Union and Social Democratic Party] serves, in the end, also the internal peace,' remarks Bavaria's minister of the interior, Günther Beckstein, happily. (Ziedler, 2003: 5)

If the issue of humanitarian immigration is defined as a strictly internal matter that does not involve the representation of people and places outside the national context, then the humanitarian aspect of immigration fails to even make a contribution to the dialectical formation of national identity through the principle of negation. The counter-narrative of refugee numbers and limited resources appears to be of this nature: it does not matter what situations the refugees endure or what the circumstances abroad are; the issue is merely a matter of the state being unable to absorb the numbers.

Conclusion

By applying Hegel's ideas of dialectics to the humanitarian aspect of the immigration debate, I was able to gain a nuanced perspective on the role of humanitarianism in the formation of German national identity. My interpretation suggests that the humanitarian aspect has contributed to the formation of Germany's national identity through the first negation, which constructed a counter-image, or photographic negative, of an abstract national identity. The national image created in this way projects a legal identity. It presents Germany as a state that observes international law and protects human rights. This legal identity is consistent with the moral commitments that were enshrined in the post-war constitutional law of the Federal Republic of Germany in response to the humanitarian crimes committed by the Nazi German state.

In the debate on humanitarian immigration, 'cultural' factors, such as language and religion, play no significant role. Apparently, the humanitarian aspect does not involve the negation of a 'cultural' national self, and the German people do not acquire an identity opposite to the 'cultural' image of the refugee. The link between the humanitarian and danger aspects of immigration was not as strongly developed as the link between the 'culture' and danger aspects, which I discussed in the previous chapter. In fact, I suggest that the humanitarian aspect of the German immigration debate must be treated separately from other aspects. In this respect, the public and the media fields seem to hold corresponding views on immigration. According to polls, for example, the German public supports the reduction of refugees and asylum seekers with the implementation of a law that regulates immigration. In a way, the public proposed that either humanitarian or other types of immigration are possible, but not both (Köcher, 2000: 5). Similarly, the media does not seem to integrate humanitarian immigration into other aspects of the immigration debate.[14]

The humanitarian aspect of the immigration debate is interesting in other respects too. In particular, media debate in Germany stops short of considering the integration of humanitarian immigrants into the national community. As a result, the debate of the humanitarian aspect does not seek to resolve the boundary between the nation and the refugee Other. Although in the Canadian debate this discursive practice was rarely explicit, it was an implicit assumption that refugees become Canadians. In the German debate, however, refugees and asylum seekers remain trapped in the role of the Other. A second negation, or sublation, never occurs. With a separation maintained between the national subject and the material substance of the deficient countries from which the refugees and asylum seekers flee, the Hegelian dialectic of national subject formation is prevented from progressing towards sublation and remains underdeveloped. The dialectic does not reach the discursive stage that would be expected from a settler society, where refugees from abroad are absorbed into the national community.

The repatriation narrative, for example, illustrates that humanitarian immigration never moved beyond the initial negation and instead maintains the boundary between the self and the Other. Even the voices that challenged this repatriation sub-narrative can be interpreted as an effort to maintain this boundary. Both perspectives of the repatriation narrative suggest that the dialectic of national identity formation never entered the stage of sublation that would resolve the boundary between self and Other.[15] Similarly, the rejection of humanitarian immigration based on the large numbers of immigrants affected by human hardship sidelines Germany's moral and legal obligation towards refugees and asylum seekers as an issue. In this case, the dialectical process of national identity formation does not even enter the stage of the first negation, and thus humanitarian immigration is denied any role in the dialectical formation of German national identity.

This truncated dialectic suggests that, in Germany, refugees and asylum seekers do not fulfil the function of newcomers in an immigration country. Immigration is, by definition, important to the national subject formation of settler societies (Honig, 2001; Dauvergne, 2005). In Canada's case, this function is also extended to refugees – albeit to fewer numbers than, say, economic-class immigrants. In an ethnic nation, by contrast, collective identity hinges on the 'indigenous' population. In both ethnic nations and settler societies, the negation of the nation through the foreigner and the deficient state abroad may help to delineate the boundary of the national. I observed this situation in both the Canadian and German debates. In Canada, however, the first negation sets the stage for the second negation and the inclusion of refugees. This second negation indicates that Canada can be considered a settler society. In Germany, however, the dialectic ends with the first negation. My interpretation of the humanitarian aspect of the German immigration debate is that the German national community has not yet achieved the identity of an immigration country.

An additional important difference exists between Canadian and German humanitarian immigration policies and debates. In Canada, the state, represented by the staff of Citizenship and Immigration Canada, makes the decision about which refugees are selected to come to Canada under the Convention Refugee Abroad, the Country of Asylum, and the Source Country classes. The proactive selection practice represents an important form of agency on the part of the Canadian state. Seen through a Hegelian lens, this proactive selection practice can be interpreted as 'doing' (*Tun*) and a conscious engagement by the national subject with the material context beyond the boundaries of the nation. Such agency drives the dialectical processes of subject formation (Hegel, 2005 [1807]: 162–3). In the case of Canadian refugee policies, the self-reflecting nation engages with the outward-oriented selection of refugees as future members of the nation, and thereby 'discovers' its national identity. Conversely, in the German debate, this proactive, outward orientation of humanitarian immigration does not occur. Humanitarian immigration is not perceived as a process in which the state seeks out immigrants by selecting them while they are still abroad. Rather, the state is a passive entity, granting or denying the privilege to remain in Germany to refugees who are already in the country. In this passive role, the dialectical process of subject formation is inhibited from the very start because passivity, rather than 'doing,' characterizes the debate. Without such mediating proactive refugee and asylum policies, humanitarian immigration fails to elevate national identity to a higher level of meaning associated with an immigration country.

Despite the limited role of the humanitarian immigration aspect in the formation of German national identity, and its failure to contribute to the nation's identity as an immigration country, I am not suggesting that in settler societies the dialectic of national identity formation is complete or without contradiction. Quite the opposite is the case. In Australia, for example, Ghassan Hage observes, the inclusion of non-European refugees and immigrants in the national community never occurred. Rather, multiculturalism policy maintains a form of 'internal orientalism' (Hage, 1998: 17). In a Canadian context, writers such as Neil Bissoondath (1994), Richard Day (2000), and Cecil Foster (2007) have unveiled multiculturalism as a way of separating out and maintaining racialized groups as the Other. The immigration dialectic remains unfinished, but it continues in ways that differ between ethnic nations and settler societies.

Conclusion

In his work on French television, Pierre Bourdieu paints a rather pessimistic picture of the media. He laments the increasing obsession of market-driven journalism with audience ratings and argues that contemporary journalism favours 'pure entertainment' and 'mindless chatter' over serious debate (Bourdieu 1998a: 3). While I am sympathetic to a degree to such worrying tendencies in journalistic and media practice as outlined by Bourdieu and others, my interpretation of the media based on the analysis of the immigration debate is more optimistic. Journalistic practice and media debate have not become completely 'one-dimensional.' Rather, journalistic practice not only upholds the dialectical principle, but also engages actively in this dialectic. As the immigration debate progresses, the media will continue to shape and reflect this progression.

In this concluding chapter, I first re-examine the dialectical approach that I assumed to integrate various literatures, perspectives, and fields. Second, I discuss the main empirical findings of the previous chapters in light of their contribution to our understanding of the national imagination. Third, I explore the role of agency in media practice and the immigration–nation dialectic.

Reflections on Dialectics

To recap, immigration debates in Canada and Germany both follow a dialectical movement involving several dimensions. First, the media presents information related to immigration by juxtaposing oppositional positions. This practice represents a journalistic way of making sense of this information. In other words, it is the journalistic way of constructing, or 'discovering,' meanings of immigration and the identities of immigrants and nation. Second, the use of language and debate are connected to material practice and circumstances. In particular, the various positions on immigration, which the media articulates, are derived from concrete and material events that are reported as news. In the context of this study, these events related to legal immigration reforms. Although national histories and the material context of the political and legal fields differ between Canada and Germany, immigration debate is materially embedded in both countries. Third, the debate of immigration is linked to national identity. On the one hand, the media presents immigration in a manner that is a reflection of national identity. On the other hand, the roles and representations attributed to immigration shape national identity. In other words, the material practices and circumstances of immigration and abstract national identity engage in a dialectical relationship. Again, immigration debate in Canada and Germany shares the principle of this relationship, although its content is very different.

One of my main motivations for writing this book was to bring together the fields of immigration policy and practice, national identity formation, and critical discourse analysis, and apply the literatures related to these fields in the context of an empirical analysis. Following in the footsteps of well-known scholars such as Norman Fairclough, Ruth Wodak, and Teun van Dijk, I used critical discourse analysis as a method to explore the relationship between immigration, nation building, and the national imagination. However, I also moved a step beyond this existing literature. I consider the main conceptual contribution of this book to be the development and application of Georg W. F. Hegel's notion of dialectics. The dialectical framework proved enormously fruitful in respect to media analysis and an understanding of the formation of national identity. In fact, dialectics weaved throughout the ontological, epistemological, and methodological layers of the analysis and binds the pages of this book into a coherent piece of scholarship.

The comparison between Canada and Germany, too, is a reflection of the dialectical approach taken in this book. In particular, I chose to juxtapose two countries that are situated in different historical, geographical, and geo-political contexts. Analysing the cases of Canada and Germany provided important insights into how the nation–immigration dialectic contributes to the formation of national identity in these two countries. In particular, the analysis demonstrated that the formation of an abstract national identity based on the material fact of immigration relates to the particular material circumstances in which immigration occurs in Canada and Germany, and to the context-specific nature of dialectical contradiction as a linguistic practice of discovery. The three dialectical dimensions that characterize immigration debate interlock in a geographically contingent way.

The cross-country comparison showed that the dialectical movement of national identity is not only geographically contingent, but also remains open and ongoing. It would therefore be difficult to generalize from the immigration dialectic as it unfolds in the Canadian and German media. In fact, the dialectical framework rejects the very assumption that the categories of settler society and ethnic nation can be applied to Canada and Germany in unproblematic ways. Yet, these categories can be useful to a certain degree. Countries such as Australia and the United States of America share with Canada some elements of their settlement and colonial histories. I would therefore expect certain aspects of the immigration dialectic in these nations to unfold in a similar manner as in Canada. Conversely, many countries that have historically pursued the ethnic principle of national belonging are today confronting the material fact of international migration and permanent immigrant settlement within their borders. In these countries, I would expect similarities to Germany in respect to some aspect of the immigration dialectic. Unfortunately, it was beyond the empirical scope of this book to explore these similarities.

Immigration and the National Imagination

As a methodological point of entry, I started out with the basic observation that the national identities of Canada and Germany relate to different material circumstances and historical legacies. Viewed in this way, Canada represents a traditional settler society that has depended on immigration for its demographic and economic development and for *becoming* a nation in the first place. Germany has a different national legacy, one that has emphasized ethnic and 'cultural' characteristics. Surely, the two models of settler society and ethnic nation are also contested. Canada has a history of ethnic exclusion and continues this practice even in the context of contemporary multiculturalism policy (see, e.g., Day, 2000; Foster, 2007). By the same token, Germany has only reluctantly held on to the ethnic principle of belonging after the devastating endorsement of ethnic nationhood by the Nazi regime; it further challenged this principle of belonging with the acknowledgment that millions of contributing members of society have remained 'foreigners.'

Although the dialectical principle applies in both countries, the content of these dialectics differ substantially between Canada and Germany.[1] The analysis of media debates on immigration in the two countries revealed the details of the immigration dialectic and national imagination. In the analysis of the Canadian sample, I was initially surprised that the aspect of 'danger' not only dominated the Canadian debate but also did so long before the September 2001 airplane attacks in New York and Washington. The dialectical framework helped me to explain this phenomenon. Immigration and immigrants serve as the negation of the nation. By portraying immigration as a danger related to violence, organized crime, and terrorism, the press ascribes the opposite attributes to Canada. This representation of the unwanted immigrant is a structural element of Canadian national identity formation. At the same time, Canada acquires a positive identity of compassion by welcoming deserving refugees in humanitarian need. Implicit in Canadian immigration debate is the notion that deserving immigrants are being absorbed into the nation; they discard their identity as the immigrant Other and become integral members of the Canadian nation. This sublation of opposing immigrant and national identities presents a nuanced perspective of the process of identity formation. Although the Canadian debate is unique in that it discussed, for example, the cases of Jaballah, Ahani, and Suresh, or the particular situation of nine trafficked Chinese children, the dialectical processes of negation and sublation can be expected to occur also in other countries with similar settlement histories, such as Australia or the United States.

In the Canadian immigration debate, the expectation that immigrants integrate into society and the economy seems to be self-evident, uncontested, and unfit for media debate aimed at contested issues. For example, although Canada selects most of its immigrants based on economic criteria, the economic aspect is not on top of the agenda in the media debate on immigration. The press takes the immigration and integration of skilled and affluent foreigners into Canada for granted. The only contested issue worthy of significant media attention related to economic matters is whether economic immigration should follow laissez-faire or regulatory paradigms.

These observations can be linked to the existing literature of national identity formation in settler societies. While my interpretation of the media debate on immigration reform in Canada suggested a process of negation and sublation, this position is not free of contradiction or challenges. Cecil Foster (2007), for example, has acknowledged the dialectical process in the formation of the Canadian nation, but argues that even under multiculturalism policies, the Canadian national subject remains ethnically and racially divided and, in Hegelian terms, 'unhappy.' Richard Day (2000) even challenges a dialectical progression in the formation of multicultural national identity in Canada. A conclusion – which is supported by the dialectical approach of this book and its empirical analysis – is that the dialectic of national identity formation is neither complete nor stable. Rather, inherent contradictions and disagreements continue to characterize immigration debate, including the question whether Canada truly integrates, that is, sublates, newcomers into the nation. An important theoretical insight that follows from my empirical investigation is that not only is the nation a fluid discursive 'frame' (Brubaker, 2004a), but contradiction is an inherent element in the way in which a nation is dialectically imaged.

The case of Germany highlights the different character of the immigration dialectic in a nation that has historically embraced an ethnic identity. Despite this historical association between ethnic and national communities, the ethnic nation, or *Volk,* cannot be taken as an independent or pre-existing category (see, e.g., Behnke, 1997; Joppke, 1998). Still, the historically ethnic understanding of nationhood has presented immigration in a particular light. Compared to the debate on immigration reform in Canada, immigration in Germany is neither taken for granted nor is an unquestioned element of national identity. Rather, the German media engages in a debate of the fundamental benefits and consequences of immigration. The fact that the German media emphasizes the economic aspect of immigration speaks to the fundamental issues that are at stake in this debate. Blocking immigration altogether, if it harms the national economy, is a viable option – an option that was effectively implemented with the new German immigration law. The economic aspect of immigration debate was situated in a material context of domestic labour-market reforms – the so-called Hartz reforms – which pushed domestic workers into the economic role of flexible labour. In settler societies, immigrants often assume this function. Rather than replenishing the labour market through immigrants, the German state re-regulated its domestic labour to serve in this role. The humanitarian aspects of the German immigration debate also implied a national identity that differed from that of a settler society. In particular, asylum seekers and refugees are not represented as becoming Germans. Rather, they are treated as permanent Others who are to be repatriated.

Immigration debate, however, also challenges Germany's identity as an ethnic nation. While new immigration is rejected by many media commentators, the fact that millions of de facto immigrants are present in Germany is also acknowledged. An identity of Germany as an integration country achieves the dialectical sublation of the opposing positions of immigration and non-immigration country. The ethnic conception of nationhood thus did not persevere in the same manner in which it existed before; rather, it transformed into something new. Hegelian dialectics are able to explain this transformation towards a new national identity.

Hegelian dialectics also suggests that national identity remains unstable. When Thilo Sarrazin published a controversial book in 2010 in which he accused Muslims of not integrating into German society, a fierce debate ensued over the identity of Germany as an integration country.[2] Over the course of this debate, the German President, Christian Wulff, on the one hand declared that 'Islam also belongs to Germany' (Baur, 2010: 11), while, on the other hand, Chancellor Angela Merkel pronounced multiculturalism in Germany an 'utter failure' (Eddy, 2010: n.p.) Although this debate was too recent to be included in the above analysis, it suggests that the immigration dialectic has continued to evolve.

The debate on immigration reform in Canada and Germany is characterized by important omissions. These omissions further illustrate differences between the Canadian and German national imaginations. In Germany, the debate on immigration is exclusively about immigration from outside the European Union. Although international migration at the European scale is common and is promoted by German and European Union policies and institutions, it is not a topic of immigration reform in the media debate. On the one hand, this omission reflects material circumstances. The mobility of labour within European Union territory is regulated at the scale of the European Union and its institutions. National immigration law does not apply to European Union citizens, only to so-called third country nationals. Therefore EU citizens are not an object of debate. On the other hand, an upscaling of political structures may correspond to a transformation of the imagination of belonging, whereby the external Other is not conceived as a French or Italian European citizen, but rather as a non-European person.[3] While German nationhood in the nineteenth century was dialectically imagined in opposition to the French nation, today it may be constructed in juxtaposition to the non-European-origin Muslim, who is represented as lacking European civility and enlightenment. Although contemporary immigration debate in Germany appears to take place at the national scale, below the surface it seems also to be a debate about European belonging and non-European exclusion.[4] The media debate on immigration reform, however, did not extend into this European dimension, at least not explicitly. Rather, the nation served as the 'discursive frame' (Brubaker, 2004a: 11) in which immigration was discussed;[5] or, in Bourdieu's words, the media saw immigration through 'special glasses' that sharpened the national dimension and clouded the European dimension.

In the Canadian debate, a striking omission are Aboriginal Peoples and the First Nations. This is a noteworthy – albeit not unexpected – difference between the Canadian and German debates. In a country that embraces an ethnic national identity, the legitimacy to belong is conferred onto an ethnically defined 'indigenous' population. In the Canadian debate, however, this principle of belonging is disregarded. The First Nations fall out of the frames on the basis of which immigration reform is perceived. In fact, the ethnic principle of belonging would undermine the very foundation of liberal immigration policy and even challenge the legitimacy of Canada as a nation. The notion of a settler society seems to be negated by the presence of indigenous populations – and a reconciliation, or sublation, of the two opposing positions is empirically not discernible in the debate on immigration in the Canadian media. Although issues of immigration and indigenous peoples are historically related, they are discursively separated in Canadian immigration debate.

Aspects, Dialectics, and Agency

The dialectical movement of identity formation is necessarily fragmented, unstable, and unfinished. Immigration debates in Canada and Germany reflect these characteristics of the dialectical movement. The previous chapters illustrated, in particular, the various aspects of immigration and highlighted the polysemic nature of the debate. This treatment of immigration debate as fragmented into aspects resonates with a literature on positionality and situatedness, which has long demonstrated that knowledge is always partial and situated in a particular set of contexts and experiences (see, e.g., Haraway, 1991; Rose, 1997).

A hypothetical Archimedean vantage point is impossible to assume. Correspondingly, immigration means different things in different contexts. The media projects different images in relation to different frames of reference. By extension, national identity, as it dialectically relates to immigration, is fragmented and multifaceted.

A discussion of the term 'aspect' provides further insights into the nature of immigration debate and the formation of national identity. I deliberately chose this term to describe various perspectives on immigration because of the term's philosophical connotations. Ludwig Wittgenstein used 'aspect' to investigate how an object appears to the observer. When observers 'notice' an aspect, they perceive this object in a particular way (Wittgenstein 2001 [1945/6]: §1024 [part II, xi, a3]). With the 'dawning' of a new aspect, the observer recognizes a previously unrecognized meaning of the same object.[6] Using the term 'aspect' in a discussion of the immigration debate captures the polysemic nature of this debate. Furthermore, the media's ability to shift between economic, danger, humanitarian, and other aspects of immigration reflects a process that Wittgenstein (ibid.: §1028 [part II, xi, a18]) calls 'aspect-change' (*Aspektwechsel*).[7] Wittgenstein uses 'aspect' to convey the notion that meanings are not simply a matter of passive perception; rather, the construction of meanings is guided by context, experience, and anticipation.

The dialectical movement of the immigration debate, which I described in previous chapters, embraces this kind of aspect-seeing and the idea that meanings and concepts are never universal, complete, or fixed, but are always fragmented, partial, and open. Furthermore, critical theorists have warned that abandoning or denying the dialectical processes will stifle meaningful reflection, smother progressive thought, and bring social advancement to a catastrophic halt. They have therefore strived towards upholding oppositional, or negative, thinking, thereby affirming the continuation of the dialectical movement (Horkheimer and Adorno, 2004 [1947]; Marcuse, 1964). Accordingly, the concepts of immigration and nation must be recognized as inherently unstable. They are not universal or complete or fixed, nor would such a state be desirable. Rather, the impossibility of unifying the various aspects of immigration and national identity marks a defining moment in the ongoing dialectical movement. This dialectic involves not only passive observation but also anticipation. In other words, the debate on immigration and the ensuing national imagination not only *reflect* material practices, but also involve active *engagement* with these practices.

This discussion raises the question of agency in the media debates on immigration and the imagination of nationhood. In his work on journalism, Pierre Bourdieu proposes that the 'routines and habits' that govern 'the journalistic field represent the world in terms of a philosophy that sees history as an absurd series of disasters which can be neither understood nor influenced' (1998a: 8). This journalistic view of the world resonates with Hegel's passive idealism, which denies that philosophy can influence material practice. Hegel (1970 [1820], 59–60) famously wrote that philosophy's 'owl of Minerva takes flight only as dusk begins to fall,' suggesting that philosophy can only passively observe and interpret the world, but has no influence on material events.[8] Philosophy, according to Hegel, only exposes what has already happened. It is beyond the realm of philosophy to contemplate what will or should happen. Hegel's view of philosophy and Bourdieu's depiction of the journalistic field share common ground. According to this viewpoint, philosophy and journalism only passively observe the world. The media does not make the news, but reports it once it has happened.

As Bourdieu well realized, however, neither the media nor philosophy are purely passive observers. They are also active agents in the way they select news and interpret information. For example, journalists actively seek out contradiction, develop oppositional viewpoints, and anticipate audience responses when they craft their stories. This engagement may be habitual, but it is also active practice and a form of agency. In this way, Bourdieu's view of the media may resonate with a Hegelian understanding of identity formation, whereby self-awareness is achieved through 'doing' (*Tun*). Media work and journalism can be interpreted as acts of doing; they mediate between the acting subject and the material world. The authoring of news stories, commentaries, and articles on immigration, which the print media publishes, are acts of mediation between material events and the formation of meaning and identity. News related to immigration is the material reference point on which journalists act to construct meanings of the nation.

Again, parallels can be drawn between philosophy and journalism. While Marx, Engels, and critical theorists affirmed Hegel's dialectical principle (albeit in its materialist version), they also acknowledged the active role of the philosopher as educator. In 'Theses on Feuerbach,' Marx argued that philosophy is a 'revolutionary practice' that transforms material relations by producing the knowledge on the basis of which agents act (Marx, 1964 [1845]).[9] In this way, philosophy does shape material circumstances. In a similar way, the media not only reflects the material world, but also shapes this world by actively selecting and interpreting information, which subsequently informs politicians and cultural elites, and shapes everyday practices. Journalistic reporting becomes part of the knowledge base on which a wide range of agents act.[10]

The coexistence of multiple aspects and series of interlocking dialectical dimensions provides ample opportunities to exercise this agency. However, the capacity to engage in the construction of meanings and formation of identities is distributed highly unevenly among people. In media debates, privileged voices represent powerful national, political, and economic interests (van Dijk, 1987, 1991). While media reporting may, for example, express compassion towards human suffering and draw attention to injustice and hardship, marginalized people themselves tend to have little influence on this coverage. In particular, immigrants may be the object of news reporting, but few immigrants have opportunities to engage with and intervene in mainstream media debates. Nevertheless, the field of the media is connected to other fields, including academia and the everyday; the media is not an entirely closed system. The concepts and identities that circulate through the media are shaped and reformulated in other fields. Although this book has examined the nation–immigration dialectic as it occurs in the media, it is an invitation to people outside (as well as inside) the media to engage actively in this dialectic and thereby shape, reshape, and transcend the nation.

Epilogue: Towards a Critical Immigration Dialectic

Human agency is an integral part of the dialectical process. A related matter is the content of critical engagement in the immigration–nation dialectic. Marx's break with Hegel's (and Feuerbach's) passive scholarship created the opportunity for critical engagement in the dialectical movement. For Marx, an aim of critical engagement was to raise the self-awareness of a de facto existing working class and thereby instil agency in this class. Scholarship could, in a similar way, help raise the self-awareness of immigrants as acting subjects. However, this is not the argument that I pursue here.[1] Another way to take advantage of this opportunity of critical engagement is to insert 'the possible' into the dialectic, and juxtapose the possible with existing material practice. Henry Lefebvre noted that 'the "real" should not be permitted to obscure that of the possible. Rather, it is the possible that should serve as the theoretical instrument for exploring the real' (2001: 769). Similarly, more than thirty-five years ago, David Harvey called upon geographers to 'formulate concepts and categories, theories and arguments, which we can apply in the process of bringing about a humanizing change' (1972: 11). Recently, Harvey reiterated that utopian ideas 'could be the corevolutionary points around which social action could converge and rotate' (2011: 20). Along similar lines, Pierre Bourdieu, in a conversation with Günter Grass, remarked that 'intellectuals have an important responsibility . . . to restore a sense of utopian possibility' that challenges existing material practices of the dominant order (Grass and Bourdieu, 2002: 66).

The association between the constructions of the nation and the state strikes me as a taken-for-granted configuration in the immigration–nation dialectic that contradicts the possible. That the state is a problematic entity in relation to migration and immigration is not a new notion. Through immigration and refugee policy, the state makes decisions about people who do 'not democratically approve' of these decisions (Dauvergne, 2005: 53). Jacque Rancière suggests that democracy is defined precisely by the inclusion of subjects who do not correspond with the state or national society (2002: 109). In a context not related to immigration, Henry Lefebvre (2001) argued that the contemporary state is an undemocratic institution that acts in the interests of a few. And in the language of Hegelian dialectics, Lutz Hoffmann argues that if the state wanted to treat people equally, 'it would sublate (*aufheben*) itself' (Hoffmann, 2002: 221). Dissociating mobility, national imagination, and the state may open possibilities for progressive change that current immigration debate in neither Canada nor Germany has been receptive to.

I recently had the opportunity for an exchange with political scientist and psychoanalyst Stanley Renshon on the emotional attachments of immigrants to the nation state (Renshon, 2008; Bauder, 2008a). Although we disagreed on the necessity of the association between immigration and the state (in addition to many other issues), we found common ground in an appreciation of migration and mobility as an experience many people share. In settler societies, such as Canada, this experience is deeply engrained in the national imagination. In Germany, this experience was long denied, but has now been recognized in the identity of Germany as an integration country. The very experience of mobility and migration is a material commonality that, in my eyes, has not yet translated into a shared identity beyond the state.[2] I believe that there is enormous potential and opportunity in the immigration–nation dialectic to overcome the conventional political positions of today.

This book, however, is limited in its ability to propel this critical immigration dialectic forward. My empirical study has examined the link between the immigration debate and policy, which both occur at the scale of the nation state. Furthermore, since immigration policy is the domain of the state, my analysis and interpretations have been unable to unveil aspects of the immigration–nation dialectic that transcend the state. This starting position, which links immigration, nation, and state, is itself only a situated, partial, and incomplete aspect of the wider issue of mobility. While the link between immigration, nation, and state may represent today's material configurations, it should not obscure our view of the possible.

Appendix: Research Design

This appendix describes the approach that I took in conducting the research for this book; it explains in detail how I obtained, sampled, and analysed the data.

Approach

The research focuses on the media debate on the development and implementation of immigration policies in Canada and Germany. This focus situates the study at the intersection between media discourse and concrete legal practices towards immigration. This approach builds on existing studies, which either directly examine immigration law and legislative practices (e.g., van Leeuwen and Wodak, 1999; Dauvergne, 2005; Takle, 2007a) or investigate media representations of immigrants and immigration without directly linking these representations to concrete legal practice (e.g., Hier and Greenberg, 2002; Wengeler, 2003).

The focus on the media debate on immigration law enables me to link discursive and material processes; that is, I am able to examine the linguistic practices of media reporting in relation to the material, or substantive, practices of the nation state towards immigration. Thus, I am able, on the one hand, to explore the various dialectics related to immigration and the imagination of the nation that circulate through media discourse on immigration. An examination of the legislative process alone, in my eyes, would have been limited by the pragmatic and political nature of the parliamentary process. For example, Jan Semmelroggen and I conducted a study of immigration discourse in the German parliament (Bauder and Semmelroggen, 2009). We found that parliamentary statements on immigration are strategic stage performances that often distort and exaggerate the positions on the basis of which immigration policy is actually made.

On the other hand, the focus on the media debate on immigration law anchors discursive processes in concrete legal frameworks, and thus material practice. In another previous study on media representations of migrant workers in Ontario, I found it difficult to link the discursive practices by the media to the concrete material circumstances experienced by the migrants (Bauder, 2005, 2008b). By investigating the media debate on immigration law – rather than immigration in general – I address this difficulty. In particular, during periods of legal reform and the reorientation of national policies towards immigration, the media participates in the immigration debate and engages in the dialectic between immigration and national identity formation.

In preparing the empirical investigation, I assumed that media debates on immigration shape and are shaped by legal practices and immigration law. My approach thus acknowledges the dialectical relationship between discursive and material practice. This dialectic, which is an important theme of this book, has long been recognized by critical discourse analysts, such as Norman Fairclough (1992a), Ruth Wodak (e.g., Wodak et al., 1999, 2001; Wodak and Menz, 1990), and Teun van Dijk (1987, 1997b). This dialectic, however, is complex. Media opinions on immigration do not translate directly into immigration policy, nor does immigration policy always respond directly to public and media debate. In addition, the relationship between media debate on immigration and immigration law and policy is sensitive to social, political, national, and historical contexts. Thus, it is important that the media debates are interpreted in their material and discursive contexts.

A similarly complex and dialectical relationship exists between media debate and public opinion. Existing work by critical discourse scholars shows that the media tends to represent the interests of political, economic, and cultural elites, including members of government and civic administration, corporate directors and managers, as well as labour leaders, educators, and media workers. Therefore, with the research approach I have taken, I cannot claim to measure public opinion. Rather, my approach recognizes that the discussions of immigration and the formation of national identity in the media do not necessarily represent the everyday opinions and practices of the Canadian and German population. Moreover, the media does not blindly replicate the elite's interests, but rather, as I have noted in shapter 2, uses and modifies elite 'preformulations' to express its own opinions and perspectives. For example, the media often complements and contests elite interests by presenting viewpoints that reflect the interests of marginalized groups and individuals, non-governmental organizations, and other non-elite agents. The responsiveness of media coverage to the interests of diverse agents affirms the dialectical principle in the construction of meaning.

Data

For the empirical analysis, I used data from a systematic sample of articles published in German and English-language Canadian daily newspapers. The data consists of reports, features, columns, editorials, and letters to the editor. Teun Van Dijk (1991: 7) remarks that these types of newsprint articles are important elements in the propagation of public debate; they are therefore particularly interesting in the context of this study. With the help of student research assistants based at universities in Germany and Canada, I developed a Canadian and a German data sample. The two samples are independent of each other in that they contain data in different languages and are referenced in different national contexts. Nevertheless, the two samples were also coordinated with each other to enable a comparison of the debates on immigration legislation between the two national contexts.

Canadian Sample

The newspapers in the Canadian sample are the *Vancouver Sun, Calgary Herald, Toronto Star, National Post,* and *Ottawa Citizen*. The *Financial Post* was renamed the *National Post* in 1998. For the sake of clarity, I use the current name, *National Post,* throughout the book, although the analysis included articles published by the *Financial Post* (until 1998) and the *National Post* (from 1998). The five papers were chosen because they are among Canada's largest and most influential daily newspapers. In addition, they present a range of political and regional perspectives. The *Toronto Star* is Canada's largest daily newspaper and often portrays a left-leaning perspective. It serves mainly greater Toronto, which is Canada's largest immigrant gateway city. The coverage of the *National Post* is more conservative and targets a national audience, although the paper's headquarters are also located in Toronto. The *Vancouver Sun* serves another large immigrant gateway city of Canada, while the *Ottawa Citizen* targets the national capital region. Finally, the *Calgary Herald* servers an emerging major immigrant destination.

The five newspapers represent a wide range of opinions and perspectives on immigration. For example, the *National Post* often reflects corporate viewpoints; the *Toronto Star* tends to express a pro-immigrant and multicultural perspective; and the *Calgary Herald* sometimes privileges conservative views. Despite the variability captured by the sample, however, one cannot expect all opinions to be represented in the sample. For example, daily newspapers that serve smaller places, niche markets, and the ethnic community were not included in the sample. Thus, it can be anticipated that marginalized voices are underrepresented.

In addition, the five papers are based in the Canadian provinces of Ontario, British Columbia, and Alberta, in which the bulk of immigrants to Canada choose to settle. The province of Quebec, which also receives a significant portion of immigrants to Canada, was deliberately excluded from the analysis. According to Alan Simmons (1999b: 49), Quebec embraces a considerably different 'imagined future' with respect to immigration. I therefore anticipated that the media debate on immigration legislation there would be distinct from the rest of Canada. For reasons of methodological and analytical clarity, I chose to omit this province from the sample. The study instead concentrates on English-language media debate in Central and Western Canada.

Another reason for selecting the five newspapers was that they could be searched electronically for the period from 1996 to 2004 by using the search engine Canadian Newsstand. The identified material could then be downloaded and converted into a format suitable for analysis. The *Globe and Mail*, which I originally wanted to include in the sample, could not be searched and processed by the same method because its coverage in the search engine was incomplete at the time the sample was prepared. Unfortunately, the *Globe and Mail*'s own searchable database did not permit using the same search method and the output of the existing search method could not be processed in a manner consistent with that of the other newspapers. The additional resources for data acquisition and processing that would have been necessary to include the *Globe and Mail* in the analysis were beyond the project's budget. Data from the *Halifax Herald* could not be included in the sample for similar reasons.

In the Canadian context, the issue of newspaper ownership must be acknowledged. The *Toronto Star* is owned by TorStar Corporation. The *National Post* was owned, from 2000, by CanWest Global Communications Corporation; the *Vancouver Sun*, *Ottawa Citizen*, and

Calgary Herald were also acquired by CanWest during the study period (Canadian Newspaper Association, 2008). Now these four newspapers are owned by Postmedia Network Inc. The concentration of ownership of the newspapers in the sample may limit the range of perspectives represented in the sample. For example, the *Calgary Herald, Vancouver Sun,* and *National Post* published identical articles on several occasions. I did not double count reprinted articles in my analysis of the sample.

For the Canadian analysis, the sampling period ranged from 1 January 1996 to 31 December 2004. This period includes important dates of immigration reform in Canada and heightened media interest in immigration legislation. The first year included in the sampling period, 1996, was the year of the publication of the report *Not Just Numbers,* which led the Canadian government to review existing immigration and refugee policy and initiated a public debate on Canadian immigration legislation. The study period also included the passing of the Immigration and Refugee Protection Act in 2001. By the end of 2004, the new immigration legislation had been in effect for three years and the newsprint media's reporting on the act had tapered off.

After I experimented with methods to identify articles relevant for the analysis, I selected the combination of keywords 'immigration act' and 'Canada.' The five selected newspapers were subsequently searched using the keyword combination and the specified sampling period. A preliminary reading of the identified material examined whether an article indeed covered the topics of immigration and/or immigration legislation. Articles that contained the keywords but otherwise did not deal with the topics of immigration and/or immigration legislation were excluded from the final sample. Using a different search method, Minelle Mahtani and Alison Mountz found only 'little coverage of the introduction of Bill C-31, and later Bill C-11, to Parliament' (2002: 29) in newspapers published in the province of British Columbia. By using a different search method and by applying this method to a national sample, I was able to obtain a rich sample of sufficient size for meaningful analysis.

Table A.1 describes the final sample in terms of the newspapers in which articles were published and article lengths. Altogether, the Canadian sample included 490 articles. The *National Post* provided the most and on average longest articles on the topic; the *Calgary Herald* offered the fewest and on average shortest articles. Despite these differences, the average length of the articles (540–763 words) suggests that the search method identified articles in all five newspapers that cover

Table A.1 Description of the Canadian sample

Newspaper	Articles identified by search	Mean article length (in words)
Vancouver Sun	99	752
Calgary Herald	78	540
Toronto Star	111	763
Ottawa Citizen	89	762
National Post	113	774
Total	490	

immigration and immigrant legislation with considerable depth and detail.

German Sample

Initially, I intended to survey national and local German daily newspapers to obtain a matching sample that was sensitive to the potential regional differences that the Canadian sample might capture. A pilot survey revealed, however, that the inclusion of local papers was redundant because many articles on the immigration law were written by national or regional news agencies. The final selection of newspapers included in the sample consists of the *Frankfurter Allgemeine Zeitung, Stuttgarter Zeitung, Süddeutsche Zeitung, Tageszeitung,* and *Bild Zeitung.* The *Frankfurter Allgemeine Zeitung* and *Süddeutsche Zeitung* are typically described as reputable papers, with the *Frankfurter Allgemeine Zeitung* representing a right-centrist and the *Süddeutsche Zeitung* a left-centrist political perspective. These two papers are commonly used in content and discourse analyses (Niehr and Böke, 2000; Jung et al., 1997). The *Tageszeitung* and *Bild Zeitung* capture perspectives situated further to the left and the right of the political spectrum. These two newspapers were included in the sample to obtain a range of opinion reflective of the German political landscape. The *Stuttgarter Zeitung* is a centrist newspaper that offers a regional perspective. To keep the data sources consistent, I did not include weekly papers and magazines.

The *Frankfurter Allgemeine Zeitung, Süddeutsche Zeitung,* and *Tageszeitung* could be searched electronically and relevant articles could be downloaded through the search engines Legios and LexisNexis. In the case of the *Stuttgarter Zeitung,* only articles published in 2003 or later were available through these search engines. To obtain the data for 2002

Table A.2 Description of the German sample

Newspaper	Articles identified by search	Mean article length (in words)
Frankfurter Allgemeine Zeitung	137	524
Stuttgarter Zeitung	110	390
Süddeutsche Zeitung	132	583
Tageszeitung	173	441
Bild Zeitung	57	n/a*
Total	609	

* No electronic word count available

and earlier, I purchased the articles in electronic format directly from the publisher. Unfortunately, articles published in the *Bild Zeitung* were not available in electronic format and efforts to obtain electronic copies from the publisher failed. Therefore, hard copies of *Bild Zeitung* were searched manually. To limit the parameters of this search, twenty-three significant events were identified in the debate or the implementation of the immigration law. Then the five daily issues that followed these events were searched manually. The relevant articles and images were photographed, catalogued, and organized using a similar method applied to the articles from other newspapers.

The time frame covered by the analysis ranges from 4 July 2001, the day the Süssmuth commission presented its final report, to 10 August 2005, when the immigration law had been in effect for more than eight months and media interest in the topic had dwindled.

A pilot search revealed that the single search term 'Zuwanderungsgesetz' (immigration law) identified relevant articles. The initial search, however, produced almost 5000 hits in the five German newspapers combined. To reduce the final sample to a size both manageable and comparable to the Canadian sample, the search was restricted to articles containing the term 'Zuwanderungsgesetz' more than once: three or more times in the cases of the *Stuttgarter Zeitung, Süddeutsche Zeitung,* and *Tageszeitung*; and two or more times in the case of the *Frankfurter Allgemeine Zeitung*. This restriction eliminated articles which mention 'Zuwanderungsgesetz' only in a peripheral context and selected mostly longer articles that offer more in-depth discussions.

The description of the final sample is shown in table A.2. The German sample contains 608 articles, a larger number than the Canadian sample. However, on average, the German articles were shorter than their

Canadian counterparts. Thus, the two samples are comparable in terms of quantity of included material. All papers included in the German sample are written in the German language. I analysed and contextualized the data in the original German language (Fairclough, 1992b: 196) and only translated the quotes for the purpose of presenting them to an English-speaking audience.

Analysis

The data from both samples were analysed using a similar method, consisting of coordinated content and discourse analyses. Initially, separate analyses were conducted for the Canadian and German samples. At later stages, the preliminary interpretations of the data in both samples were cross-referenced to conduct comparisons between national contexts.

The first step of the analysis was inspired by linguists who developed the analysis of 'topoi' (Böke et al., 2000; Wengeler, 1995, 2003). The term is the plural of the Greek word *topos* and represents 'patterns of argumentation' (*Argumentationsmuster*) (Böke et al., 2000: 24) and 'modes of thinking' (*Denkweisen*) that express a distinct rhetorical perspective (ibid.: 25). In the text, I refer to these topoi as 'aspects.' I assumed that this terminology is more reader-friendly and that readers are more likely to be familiar with the term aspect. In addition, I chose aspect, rather than 'theme,' to indicate that I am investigating different perspectives and viewpoints on immigration which themselves stand in a dialectical relationship with each other (I elaborated on this use of the term aspect in the Conclusion). Wengeler's analyses of topoi seek to identify distinct patterns of argumentation embedded in a given text or text passage, organize these topoi, and analyse their occurrence in a systematic manner. By recognizing and exploring multiple perspectives simultaneously, I was able to cope with the multidimensional nature of the media debate and juxtapose various thematic positions that underpin immigration discourse.

In a series of empirical studies, Martin Wengeler (1995, 2000, 2003) examined topoi in the context of immigration discourses in German-speaking countries. In one particular study of immigration-related media coverage in Austria, Germany, and Switzerland in the 1970s, Wengeler (2000) identified sixteen topoi that occurred in a sample of newspaper articles, including economic-utility, danger, humanitarian, political-utility, and 'culture' topoi. In my analysis of the German sample, I used the topoi description from this study as an initial guide to develop 'recording instructions' for an a priori coding of text sequences (Stemler, 2001). I modified Wengeler's 16-topoi scheme to fit the data represented in the German sample.

The coding of the Canadian sample by aspect (i.e., topoi) followed a related process. In their study of immigration to British Columbia, Mahtani and Mountz (2002) had grouped media coverage into five categories: economic implications of immigration, human interest stories, social and health dimensions of immigration, criminal association with immigration, and factual articles. In my analysis, however, I use different categories. Rather than classifying the debate on immigration according to media-specific themes, I focused on particular perspectives on immigration that situate migration in the context of distinct models of argumentation. In the Canadian case, I was able to use the aspects that I developed for the German sample as a guide. I modified and coordinated these aspects to suit the data and context of both the Canadian and German samples.

Assigning aspects to text passages is not always a straightforward task. The wider context and the rest of the article in which a particular text passage appears must be carefully considered. Many articles and text passages were assigned multiple aspects, since different patterns of argumentation and modes of thinking often interlocked or were presented within a single article or paragraph.

Multiple researchers were involved in coding the data. To address the issue of reliability and to ensure consistent application of the recording instructions, I collaborated closely with a team of research assistants, with whom I had regular discussions during the coding process. As we came across text sequences for which coding was potentially ambiguous, we discussed the issue of consistency in the interpretation of the recording instructions (Weber, 1990). To further ensure the reliability of the coding procedure, we regularly checked our coding against articles that were coded at earlier points of the analysis. My participation in the coding of both the Canadian and German samples ensured reliability and consistency between the two national samples.

Content Analysis

The content analysis provided a quantitative overview of the debate on immigration in the two data samples. The results of this analysis form the basis of chapter 3. For this analysis, I identified a small number of 'dominant' aspects in terms of their frequency of occurrence. To be sensitive to the particularities of national contexts, I conducted separate analyses for the Canadian and German samples. The combinations of dominant aspects thus differ for the Canadian and the German samples.

Four aspects dominated each sample in a quantitative and qualitative sense (see chapter 3). First, they occurred more frequently than other aspects. Second, I examined the nature of the arguments to ensure that the four aspects would not present weak arguments and to avoid excluding aspects that were less frequent but represented strong arguments. This examination revealed that the more frequent aspects were generally associated with strong arguments. For example, the text sequences coded 'economic' or 'danger' often presented arguments that lawmakers also addressed in the proposed and/or final legislation, such as the need to coordinate immigration policy with the demand for skilled and unskilled workers by the national economy, or the potential danger of terrorism emanating from immigration.

I aggregated the remaining aspects under the category 'other.' Due to an overlap among aspects and the multiple coding of individual text passages, many of the text sequences that were categorized as 'other' also appeared under one of the four dominant aspects. For example, consider the following excerpt of text: 'on the one side, we admit immigrants to complete simple work and, on the other side, we pay social assistance to Germans who do not want to work. In addition, one cannot expect relief of the social insurance system from foreigners' (*Frankfurter Allgemeine Zeitung*, 2002a: 37). In this case, the 'stress' aspect (aggregated under 'other') occurs in the context of an economic argument and was also coded 'economic.' Such overlap between aspects occurred frequently in the sample. Thus, much of the information represented under the label 'other' was also included in the four dominant aspects.

The quantitative content analysis examined the frequency with which particular aspects were deployed in the sampled newspaper articles. This examination enabled me to assess which aspects were used more often than others. In addition, the frequency of aspects could be examined in their temporal context and related to various stages or periods of the immigration debate and to external events, such as the 2001 attacks in New York and Washington in the United States and the 2004 bombings in Madrid, Spain. In addition, the content analysis permitted a comparison between Canadian and German media reporting on immigration reform in terms of the dominance of aspects and their frequency distribution over time.

In a separate publication based on data from the Canadian sample, I examined whether the contents of aspects construct positive, negative, or neutral arguments related to immigration and immigration policy (Bauder, 2008c). This analysis provided interesting insights into the nature of the immigration debate. However, in the context of this book, a separate analysis based on the positive, negative, or neutral characters of aspects is redundant, since I offer detailed qualitative assessments of individual aspects in parts 2 and 3 of the book. Furthermore, it is beyond the scope of quantitative content analysis to explore in detail the linguistic practices that are enacted in newsprint media coverage. Therefore, I conducted a discourse analysis (see below) that presents a qualitative assessment of aspects and the contexts in which they occur.

Within the samples, differences exist between newspapers. For example, in the German sample, articles in the *Frankurter Allgemeine Zeitung* were less likely to be coded with aspects that represented particular models of argumentation due to the factual manner in which this newspaper reported on the immigration law. Conversely, the *Tageszeitung* presented information in a much more opinionated manner and often offered interpretations that applied particular models of argumentation. Although the *Bild Zeitung* is famous for its controversial and blunt opinions, many articles identified in the search were too short to articulate a structured argument that could be associated with an aspect. In addition, the relative distribution of aspects varied between newspapers. For example, the economic aspect occurred in 58 per cent of all relevant articles in the *Süddeutsche Zeitung*, but in only 38 per cent of the articles in the *Tageszeitung*. Conversely, the humanitarian aspect appears in 31 per cent of the articles in the *Tageszeitung*, but in only 13 per cent of the articles in the *Frankurter Allgemeine Zeitung*. Based on the literature, I expected this variability (Crespi, 1997; Taylor, 2001). In addition, the newspapers were selected in the first place to cover a range of opinions and journalistic approaches.

'Discourse' Analysis

Media debates are complex and the analysis of such discourses is not a straightforward undertaking. Rather, media debates can be analysed at different levels of examination, with varying methods, and deploy diverse theoretical approaches (e.g., van Dijk, 1991; Wetherell et al., 2001; Fairclough, 1992a). In the context of Germany, Karin Böke and her colleagues suggest three ways to investigate immigration 'discourse':

word analysis, metaphor analysis, and argument analysis (Böke et al., 2000: 18–28). Word and metaphor analyses attempt to unveil the political and cultural meanings embedded in particular words and terms. Argument analysis, by contrast, emphasizes the explicit justification of a particular position or perspective. This form of analysis has been linked to Jürgen Habermas's ideas of rational communication between actors and applied, for example, in a recent study of parliamentary immigration debate in Germany (Takle, 2007a).

While my analysis of immigration debate in the media is sensitive to the uses of symbolic words, phrases, and metaphors, it consists mainly of argument analysis. This method of analysis examines particular patterns of argumentation and modes of thinking for their qualitative contents in relation to their material, historical, and substantive contexts. The argument analysis was closely coordinated with the earlier content analysis, which categorized the data according to aspects. Böke et al. (2000: 25) suggest that arguments relate to a body of 'collective knowledge' (*kollektives Wissen*) shared among groups and communities. Given my research topic of national identity formation, I am particularly interested in the question of how arguments related to immigration reveal and construct collective national identities.

The qualitative analysis involved a reiterative process of developing sub-codes, recording nodes and linkages, and contextualizing the coded text sequences. As the analysis progressed, the coding tree, linkages between codes, and the contextualization of the data grew increasingly complex, enabling me to explore the nature of given aspects, capture subtle meanings and symbolisms, investigate the connections between aspects, and situate the aspects in their wider political, national, and temporal contexts. At the same time, the relatively mechanical method of coding was important for identifying multiple viewpoints and narratives that typically characterize complex debates (Wodak et al., 1999; van Dijk, 1991; Wetherell et al., 2001; Taylor, 2001). I aimed at an intermediary-level interpretation that was neither entirely abstract nor too context-particular for the data to be grouped (Böke et al., 2000).

Through this analysis, I was eventually able to organize the data into distinct narratives and positions, revealing representations of immigrants and immigration law, and processes of national identity formation (Jäger, 2004; Klammer, 2005). The quotes I present in the empirical chapters of this book are examples that illustrate these narratives and positions. Since newspaper articles are carefully scripted texts that present selected evidence designed to convey particular viewpoints, I interpreted these texts and their meanings as strategic presentations (Fairclough, 1992a; 2000).

The analysis illustrated the dialectical nature of media discourse. As expected, based on the existing literature and my previous research, I encountered the challenge of navigating through a debate that presents multiple aspects and narratives, and various positions and perspectives. Many articles included in the sample contained inconsistencies and contradictions, and they juxtaposed various opinions and positions – which, as I have shown in chapter 2, are common strategies of journalistic practice. By focusing on the representation of oppositional perspectives, I was able to interpret the media debate of immigration as a dialectical process.

Some commentaries, however, also presented singular viewpoints. In the Canadian sample, for example, the *National Post* occasionally featured rather blatant commentaries by immigration critics Martin Collacott and Diane Francis (a similar observation was made by Francis Henry and Carol Tator [2002]). When placed into their wider discursive context, however, these commentaries typically represent one side of a wider argument, with the other side being presented in other articles.

At a different level of analysis, the media debate on immigration reform in Canada and Germany shows how the linguistic articulation of particular arguments links with the formation of collective national identity. This link resonates with the Hegelian viewpoint that language is a mechanism that mediates the dialectic of identity formation (Hegel, 2005 [1807]: 87). The research design for this book has built on an established literature on national identity formation that places language, narration, and linguistic representation at the centre of the imagination of national communities (e.g., Wodak et al., 1999: 7–48).

Notes

Preface

1 Prominent examples of this tradition include Hegel (2002 [1832–45]), Marx and Engels (1953), Horkheimer and Adorono (2004 [1947]), and Marcuse (1964).
2 Slavoj Žižek (2006: 13) concludes that 'Hegelian dialectics can be used to analyse anything.'
3 Even the notion of dialectics seems to have come into the Anglo-American social sciences via French philosophers such as Henry Lefebre (e.g., Soja, 1996). Still, to be fair, I must acknowledge that Marxian and Hegelian dialectics have not been entirely neglected (e.g., Harvey, 1973) and the Frankfurt School's critical theory has been on the radar screen (e.g., Brenner, 2009).
4 For example, it encompasses the physical and the human worlds, the fundamental and applied sciences, theory and techniques, positive and normative approaches, and so on.
5 I have elaborated on this perspective of critical geography in the introduction to the open-access textbook *Critical Geographies: A Collection of Readings,* which I co-edited with my colleague and friend Salvatore Engel-Di Mauro (Bauder and Engel-Di Mauro, 2008).
6 The literature is so large that I even find it difficult to keep track of the work that reviews it. As initial points of entry, I suggest Lees (2004) and Müller (2008).
7 The media, in particular, has been a popular field for studies of migration and immigration in the tradition of critical discourse analysis (e.g., Bauder, 2005, 2008b; Finney and Robinson, 2008; Hier and Greenberg, 2002; Mahtani and Mountz, 2002; Tsoukala, 2008a, 2008b; van Dijk, 1991; Wengeler, 2003).

Introduction

1 Aboriginal peoples should not be neglected in this context. It is important not only to acknowledge the presence of aboriginal peoples but also to recognize their historical and contemporary contributions to Canadian society. Despite these contributions, however, Canada is often conceived as a settler society because the majority of the contemporary population has settler roots. Aboriginal peoples constitute a minority. In the 2006 Canadian census, 4.0% of the population declared a full or partial ethnicity (i.e., single and multiple responses) of North American Indian; 1.3% declared being Metis and 0.2% Inuit (calculation based on Statistics Canada, 2009).

2 Marianne Takle (2007b) uses these terms as ideal types of national communities to examine the recent transformations of immigration policy in Germany. 'Demos' relates to the *jus soli* principle of citizenship and a political understanding of nationhood. 'Ethnos' links to *jus sanguinis* and understandings of nationhood based on heritage, language, and ancestry. Rogers Brubaker (1992) applies a similar distinction to a comparative study of citizenship and nationhood in France and Germany.

3 For exceptions that do offer such comparisons, see Schultze (1994), Reitz et al. (1999), Winter (2001), Geißler (2003), Triadafilopoulos (2004, 2006), Bauder (2006b), Bendel and Kreienbrink (2008), and Schidtke (2010).

4 According to the 2006 Canadian census, 24.8 million or 79.3%, of Canada's total population of 31.2 million are non-immigrants who obtained Canadian citizenship at birth (Statistics Canada, 2009).

5 According to the German Federal Office of Statistics (*Statistisches Bundesamt*) 15.3 million, or 19% of all residents of Germany, have a background in migration. Of these, 8 million possess German citizenship and 7.3 million are foreigners. Approximately three million are naturalized Germans (*Migration und Bevölkerung*, 2006).

6 In the past, setter societies, such as Canada, tended to select immigrants based on their race and ethnicity. This racial and ethnically biased immigrant selection was supposed to facilitate the integration of immigrants as full members of an equally racially and ethnically biased society. In recent decades, however, the expectation that immigrants become full members of society has been detached from race and ethnic origin. Canada, like other settler societies, has officially renounced policies that would select immigrants based on race or ethnicity or origin (Liston and Carens, 2008).

7 Joppke (2005: 240–50) even observes a corresponding international trend towards the 're-ethnicization' of migration politics.

8 Homi Bhabha (1990: 2) further problemtizes the nation as a hybrid and 'ambivalent figure.' He draws on Hanna Arendt (1998 [1958]: 256), who sees the emergence of the modern nation as substitution for the home and the family, and a fusion of the public and private realms.

9 Lora Wildenthal (1997) suggested that Brubaker's book neglected the role of race and gender in shaping German citizenship, and Kathleen Canning (2004) critiqued it for not paying sufficient attention to gender and class.

10 Others, such as Eli Nathans (2004: 6), share this critique of Brubaker's book.

11 In his work on history, Hegel (2002 [1832–45]) states explicitly that 'law and legislation' (*Gesetz und Recht*) are 'substantive matter' (*substantielle Gegenstände*) in which the human spirit appears. According to Hegel's idealist perspective, they are the result of human agency and freedom. While I put greater emphasis on the material basis of the dialectical process, I adopt Hegel's view that law and legislation are substantive and material entities that are dialectically related to national identity.

12 I say 'assumed' because I do not wish to suggest that an independent, or natural, 'subject' of the nation exists. Furthermore, representing a national subject by the voices expressed in the media is, of course, a reduction and simplification of anything that could be considered a national collective. Nevertheless, the media is an important institution that reflects and engages in processes of national identity formation. It reports on controversial practices, extraordinary events and the hot topics of the day, and thereby is located near the centre of where the formation of identity occurs (Habermas, 1981).

13 Wittgenstein used the term 'aspect' to explain how an object can appear to an observer in multiple and seemingly unrelated forms. He illustrates, for example, that a single object can contain multiple aspects by presenting the so-called rabbit-duck-head, a picture that can be seen as the head of a rabbit or the head of a duck (Wittgenstein, 2001 [1945/6], §1024 [part 2, xi, a3]). In another example, he uses the image of a triangle to show that it can be perceived as apex, mountain, wedge, or 'virtually unlimited' other aspects (Aidun, 1982: 111). Undeniably, substantial differences exist between Hegel's and Wittgenstein's work, in particular the irreconcilability of Hegel's idealism and Wittgenstein's emphasis on practice and context (Cook, 1984). Yet, Hegel arguably uses a similar idea as Wittgenstein – without using the term 'aspect' – when he notes the different perspectives of a concept, such as salt, which can be defined by simultaneously being 'white *and* sharp *and* cubic *and* of a particular mass, etc.' (Hegel, 2005 [1807]: 98, original emphasis). More importantly, however, both philosophers treat contradiction

as a productive moment (Frenzel, 1999/2000; Earle, 2002). This feature is also central to the argument I develop in this and the following chapters. Resonating with my materialist interpretation of dialectics, Wittgenstein suggests that aspect-seeing relates to context and material use. I elaborate on this link between aspect-seeing and dialectics in greater detail elsewhere (Bauder, forthcoming).

14 Of course, language is important to all kinds of material practices, not only those related to neoliberalism. Language, for example, can be a propaganda tool for military intervention and imperialism (Chomsky, 2007).

15 I have heard an alternative interpretation that the reason for this lack of understanding was that Hegel's students (and perhaps Hegel himself) were regularly intoxicated. I personally like to believe that Adorno's interpretation is correct.

16 Although I too was born and raised a Swabian, I do not feel that I benefited in the same way as Horkheimer did from this linguistic connection. To me Hegel's texts have remained ambiguous and sometimes intangible.

1. The Nation–Immigration Dialectic

1 To use a famous example, the psychoanalyst Jacques Lacan (1982 [1949]: 2) suggests that the formation of the 'I' as the 'dialectic of identification with the other' begins in the infant child, which recognizes its external image in the mirror.

2 The position of Karl Marx on the topic of dialectics is often associated with his Theses on Feuerbach, in which Marx acknowledges the material basis of the dialectical process. However, he also criticizes Feuerbach's view for its passive materialism, according to which the scholar is a mere bystander of the dialectical process. Marx instead suggests that scholarship not only has the possibility but also the responsibility to actively engage in the dialectical process. The possibility of intervention continues to be an important aim of critical theory.

3 Drawing on Jean Hyppolite's interpretation of Hegel, Michel Foucault explicitly rejected Hegel's 'phenomenological approach' (Foucault, 1970: xiv) and total system (Foucault, 1972: 235–6). In fact, he argued that his understanding of 'discourse is very unfaithful to the Hegelian *logos*' (Foucault, 1984: 134, emphasis in original).

4 The so-called new cultural geography of the late 1980s and 1990s and an enormous body of literature that followed the associated 'cultural turn' have offered important understandings of how meanings of territory and place are constructed through practices of Othering.

5 Or the 'East' as negation of the 'West.'

6 The juxtapositioning of Canadian and American identities is common (e.g., Adams, 2004; Smith, 1994; Sumara et al., 2001), although measurable differences also exist (e.g., Hardwick et al., 2010). Elke Winter (2009) unveiled a more nuanced dialectical formation of English-speaking Canadian identity in relation to Quebec, on the one hand, and the United States, on the other. My analysis in the empirical chapters does not include the case of Quebec. Such an inclusion may have revealed interesting dialectical positions. However, in an effort to keep the entire project manageable, I narrowed the scope of my investigation to the dialectic between the English-speaking Canadian nation and immigration. Similarly, the German analysis focuses on a 'West' German experience and does not engage extensively with the West–East dialectic (e.g., Schlottmann, 2005).

7 To the contemporary reader with little prior exposure to Enlightenment philosophy, the language used by Hegel may be difficult to grasp. The German terms that are central to Hegel's argument are rarely used in everyday conversation. For example, a concept (*Begriff*) may exist abstractly (*Ansichsein*), but it is defined through its negation (*Anderssein*), which constructs the boundary of identity. The second negation, or sublation (*Aufhebung*), integrates both perspectives into a higher meaning (*Fürsichsein*). While I retain some of this terminology, such as negation and sublation, I spare the reader the entire arsenal of Hegel's terminology.

8 Without negation, the concept of tree would be meaningless; without recognizing that a rock does not have leaves or a bush does not have a trunk, it would not make sense to identify a tree as having leaves and a trunk.

9 I loosely translated Hegel's original terms. Other English translations sometimes refer to 'master' and 'slave.' Hegel's (2005 [1807]: 153) original title of this discussion, 'Herrschaft und Knechtschaft,' would be more accurately translated as 'reign and servitude.'

10 In recent decades, negation has been a focal point of critical scholarship, including in the areas of feminism, Marxism, and cultural studies. This scholarship has examined constructions of identities of ethnicity, gender, race, sexuality, and other categories through dualisms, juxtapositions, and representations of the Other (e.g., Butler, 1990; Kobayashi and Peake, 1994; Castree, 1996; Chouinard, 2006).

11 I use the passive voice deliberately to indicate that there is no pre-existing national subject, i.e., that there is no a priori national community that could actively imagine or discover 'itself.'

12 Pierre Bourdieu (1991: 122) calls this a 'magical boundary' and astutely observes that this boundary not only serves to define who is on the outside but also disciplines the people on the inside to embrace their attributed identities.

13 These practices of racialization and humiliation of immigrants are blatantly apparent, for example, in letters to the editor published in daily newspapers (Shattell and Villalba, 2008).
14 This United States–based research echoes David Sibley's study on Gypsies in the countryside of the United Kingdom as a 'polluting presence' (1995: 104).
15 The recent literature has illustrated the role of race in dialectially defining the Canadian nation (e.g., Thobani, 2007; Austin, 2010).
16 The use of the term 'illegal' is also problematic for a different reason. It is derogatory and technically incorrect. Legality (and illegality) cannot be attributed to a person but merely, from the state's perspective, to the manner in which a person crosses the border and sets up residence. The massive protests by immigrants in the United States in 2006 had the partial aim of claiming legal and symbolic membership in the national community, although these claims and the strategies to achieve them are, in my eyes, not unproblematic (Bauder, 2006a, 2008a).
17 Similarly, the depiction of immigrants as racialized Others in European and North American countries has material-historical roots in colonialism (e.g., Pratt, 2004; Thomas, 2007).
18 In her book *Home Economics,* Nandita Sharma (2006) illustrates that this labour force and the associated exploitation is not restricted to the agricultural sector, but represents a growing phenomenon in the Canadian labour market as a whole. Recent statistics published by Citizenship and Immigration Canada (2009b) confirm the growing numbers of termporary foreign workers, especially relative to permanent immigration to Canada.
19 This tension has long been acknowldeged by immigration scholars such as Stephen Castles (2000).
20 The previous citizenship study guide, which was in effect until early 2010, listed 'democratic values' of 'equality,' 'respect for cultural differences,' 'freedom,' 'peace,' and 'law and order,' and defined 'multiculturalism,' 'volunteerism,' and 'protecting the environment' as distinctly Canadian values (Citizenship and Immigration Canada, 2007a).
21 The Federal Republic of Germany signed agreements with Italy (1955), Spain and Greece (1960), Turkey (1961), Morocco (1963), Portugal (1964), Tunesia (1965), and the former Yugoslavia (1968).
22 In a study that inspired the empirical method used for this book, Martin Wengeler (2000, 2006) identifies the topos 'economic utility' as an important feature of the media discourse of immigration in post-war Germany. I adopt the label of this topos in chapters 3 and 7 (see also the appendix for details).

23 Drawing on Ulrich Herbert (e.g., 2001), they even suggest that this continuity includes the Nazi's use of foreign labour: 'The founders of the Federal Republic [of Germany] never confronted this part [i.e., foreign labour recruitment] of the Nazi legacy. As Herbert has observed, the scale of other Nazi crimes, such as the Holocaust, obscured the brutal record of their treatment of foreign labor. In the interval between the defeat of the Nazis in 1945 and the FRG's [Federal Republic of Germany] resumption of foreign labor recruitment in 1955, memories of the former receded' (Klusmeyer and Papademetriou, 2009: 90).

24 Next to article 16, which constitutes the cornerstone of Germany's asylum law, the Constitutional Law also guarantees the 'indefeasibility human dignity' (article 1) and assures the right to legal recourse in upholding these constitutional rights (article 19). The combination of these articles gave West Germany the reputation of possessing 'one of the most "liberal" asylum laws anywhere' (Klusmeyer and Papademetriou, 2009: 134), until article 16 was changed in 1993.

25 Article 116 of the Constitutional Law extended German citizenship to refugees and expelled persons with German ethnicity (*Volkszugehörigkeit*).

26 These new configurations will contain their own contradictions, as Foster acknowledges: 'There will always be contradictions, even when we end up dialectically at higher and deeper levels of understanding. The difference will be that they would be *new* contradictions and that most of the old ones will have been clarified in the process, whether through negation or refutation, and that they may very well be included in some of the newer contradictions, and challenges, and in the new meanings' (2007: xxvii, original emphasis).

27 Catherine Dauvergne remarks that the humanitarian aspect of immigration 'is vague enough that all nations can aspire to it while taking very different actions' (2005: 219). This statement seems to apply to the concept of immigration in general.

28 The literature elaborates on these debates (e.g., Hinrichs, 2003; Färber et al., 2008; Beck-Gernsheim, 2007), and I will return to them in later chapters.

29 Through 'doing,' the knowing subject engages with the material world. For example, gardening can be interpreted as an activity through which individuals 'discover' themselves by moving soil, seeding plants, and pulling weeds, and thus mediating between their existence as pure subjects and the material world of plants and soil. In the subject–substance dialectic, 'doing' can refer to a range of activities, including the physical labour process, as understood by Karl Marx, who lamented the alienation of the factory worker from meaningful talks. It can also refer to mental forms of

labour, through which a subject engages with material substance (Adorno, 1963: 35).

2. The Field of the Media

1 A growing literature has documented the complex nature of dialectics in the media and journalism. For example, a recent study of media reporting on the Human Geonome Project and race-based medication uncovered a series of nested dialectics that juxtapose 'race' as functions of genetics or social context and of geography or ancestral origin (Lynch, 2008: 273). Other recent research has investigated the dialectical nature of language use and journalistic argumentation (Walton, 2007). The linguists and the media scholars who have applied the framework of critical discourse analysis have also contributed to the understanding of dialectics in the media (e.g., Wodak, 2001, 2006).

2 I am not claiming that these three dimensions are an exhaustive list of possible dialectics related to media practice. They merely represent the dimensions that are relevant to the empirical investigation that I discuss in parts 2 and 3. The three dimensions reflect my interpretation of the empirical data. A study that focuses on different empirical contexts, that asks different research questions, and/or that applies different methods may uncover different dialectical dimensions.

3 Although Bourdieu (1998a) speaks of the 'journalistic' field, rather than the media field, I use the two terms interchangeably.

4 This understanding of media as a separate field has recently attracted considerable scholarly attention in media studies as well as in other disciplines (e.g., Hesmondhalgh, 2006; Benson and Neveu, 2005; Marlière, 1998, Couldry, 2003a, 2003b; Benson, 2006).

5 For example, depending on national contexts, the media entertains more or less close relations to government and the state. Governments typically regulate the media. In many countries the media is state-funded and the state sometimes actively intervenes in programming and hiring (Marlière, 1998). Governments also feed selected information to the media via designated spokespersons, public relations professionals, and 'spin doctors' who manipulate the media to achieve political aims. The state scripts some of its activities that the media reports as political events and news in ways that they capture media attention and to produce tailored audience effects. Conversely, the 'journalistic field produces and imposes on the public a very particular vision of the political field,' which politicians rely on for legitimacy and 'symbolic support' (Bourdieu, 1998a: 2, 4).

To use another example, the media field entertains complex and powerful linkages to the field of business. In fact, many media firms *are* businesses that are privately owned and that operate within the business field and according to business principles. The dependence of the media on private advertisers further solidifies the journalism–business relation. In addition, the fields of journalism, politics, and business are linked through the principle of competition and market exchange. In their famous 'propaganda model,' Edward Herman and Noam Chomsky (2000) present the media more as an extension of private corporations and state interests than as an independent field.

6 In an era when reporters have to work with declining resources, smaller budgets, and fewer staff, news reporting increasingly reproduces the narratives provided by spin doctors and public-relations professionals who are representing powerful interests, while investigative and critical journalism are in decline (e.g., Schimmeck, 2009).

7 These critical interpretations are, in turn, fed back to the media. The relation between the media and other fields is recursive and multi-directional.

8 This apparent 'distance' should not obscure the constraints imposed by business, politics, and hegemonic bourgeois ideologies (Gitlin, 1980; Herman and Chomsky, 2000).

9 Bourdieu developed this notion in, among other places, a series of books (Bourdieu, 1977, 1984, 1998b).

10 Bourdieu however, did apply the notion of habitus to the field of academia (1988: 37), which, arguably, shares with journalism some of the rules of ethics and norms of professionalism.

11 Which events and information editors and journalist deem newsworthy, of course, is also a matter of hegemonic structures imposing 'incentives, pressures, and constraints' (Herman and Chomsky, 2000: xi).

12 Bourdieu discusses the link between language and habitus in *Language and symbolic power* (1991).

13 For key authors who developed this concept, see Gitlin (1980), Goffman (1974), and Tuchman (1978).

14 The concept of 'discourse' also reflects this classical Greek interpretation of dialectics as a method of argument (e.g., Burke, 1969 [1945]). In fact, the very word 'discourse' has its origin in the Latin verb *discurrere,* meaning 'running back and forth' (Wodak, 2006: 596).

15 Walton (2007: 153) suggests that journalism that does not explicitly juxtapose opposing viewpoints can also be 'dialectical in nature.' For example, when media reporting seeks to evoke fear or pity, it often fails to present oppositional perspectives. Even in the absence of contradictory viewpoints, journalistic reporting anticipates the audience's reaction of fear and compassion, and therefore simulates the audience's involvement in a dialogue. This dialogue imitates the dialectical engagement between journalist and audience, as if both parties participated in a conversation.

16 In a revealing way, the slogan 'fair and balanced' was also adopted by the US-based Fox News television channel to gain legitimacy (Fox News Channel, 2009). Many readers who do not embrace right-wing views will likely find that Fox News presents their viewpoints only in a very biased and unfair way. Nevertheless, the fact that other views *are* represented, albeit in biased and unfair ways, speaks to the importance of the dialectical practice in the media of representing equally biased right-wing positions as legitimate.

17 In a similar way, journalists practise a variation of this first dialectical dimension by continual 'code-switching' (Schudson, 2002: 263) between presenting themselves as objective observers of events and moral interpreters of these events, and by applying 'profession narratives,' following their journalistic values, and 'cultural narratives,' following a practice of myth building when they report news (Nossek and Berkowitz, 2006).

18 Bourdieu (1998a: 35) relates this journalistic practice of presenting contradictory viewpoints to the language games explored by Ludwig Wittgenstein (2001 [1945/6]), suggesting that journalism uses language in a manner that is always context-particular, and that meanings are never fixed but are revealed in the use of language.

19 Beyond the particular context of Germany, media scholars have noted the impact of the 2001 airplane attacks in New York and Washington on the manner in which immigrants are framed as security threats (e.g., Tsoukala, 2008a, 2008b; Vukov, 2003). In chapter 4, I challenge some of the conventional perspectives of these events.

20 Bourdieu (1988a) already noted this tendency in *On television and journalism*. Since then this trend continued, if not accelerated.

21 I'm not clear whether, in the eyes of the translator, the American field of the media represents a general model of the field that applies in all English-speaking countries, whether non-American English-speaking audiences would be more familiar with the American than the French characteristics of the media field, or whether non-American English-speaking audiences were simply not important enough of an audience to be considered in the translator's remarks.

22 To present another example of the national differences within the media field, in the Netherlands, foreign affairs journalists work independently and experience relative autonomy, while in the United States they experience greater pressure and competition (Cohen, 1995).

23 Other geographical scales, including urban and regional scales, also matter in the way in which immigrants and immigration are represented in the press. For example, when the local media in Cardiff reported on the

national settlement dispersal program of asylum seekers, it framed immigrants in the context of cosmopolitan local identity and constructed asylum seekers as one of 'us.' The local media in Leeds, by contrast, presented asylum seekers as labour competition and portrayed immigrants as deviant 'others' (Finney and Robinson, 2008). Apparently, political, economic, and social circumstances at the local scale provide different material points of reference for the formation of asylum seekers' identities.

24 In other national contexts these nation–immigration dialectics unfold in the media in yet other ways. In Israel, for example, the media produces an ethnic national identity in opposition to an Arab ethnic population (Frosh and Wolfsfeld, 2006).

25 I will elaborate on these events and their significance in the next chapter.

26 Harper (2006) spoke of the Québécois as an independent 'sociological, cultural group,' apparently linking language not only to nationhood but, arguably, also to a separate linguistic habitus.

27 In the French context, Bourdieu supports Anderson's idea when he argues that the standardization of language practices and nation building went hand-in-hand (1991: 48).

3. The Immigration Debate in Canada and Germany

1 An interesting connection existed between Canadian and German colonial projects. Germany wanted to retain German-origin farmers to pursue its territorial expansion eastward. Canada was interested in attracting the same population as immigrants for its own territorial claims on the Prairies. According to Jonathan Wagner (2006: 151), 'For both Canada and Germany, the migration issue had become intertwined with not only the state's expanding role but also with the maturation of each country's nationalism. Both state pretensions and national ambitions contributed directly to the impasse that developed between Germany and Canada in the 1890s over migration. The impasse obstructed or prevented Reich farmers from participating as they might have in the settlement of Canada's west.'

2 *Jus soli* refers to the practice of granting citizenship on the basis of birthplace, i.e., birth on a territory's 'soil.' The *jus soli* principle is often juxtaposed with the *jus sanguinis* principle of citizenship based on ancestry, i.e., 'blood.' Conversely, the *jus domicilii* refers to the principle of citizenship based on place of residence.

3 Furthermore, the federal government has agreements, so-called Provincial Nominee Programs, which allow the provinces and territories to nominate immigrants.

4 For example, in 1983, 54.9% of all immigrants belonged to the family class, 27.1% to the economic class, and 15.7% were refugees (2.3% were 'other' immigrants). By 1996, the share of the family class had declined to 30.2%, the economic class increased to 55.5%, and 12.6% were refugees (1.7% were 'other' immigrants) (Citizenship and Immigration Canada, 2008).

5 Canada's identity as a highly developed industrial nation does not contradict the counter-image of a resource-based Canadian economy. In fact, Harold Innis and William Archibald Mackintosh's staples theory has resolved this contradiction by arguing that Canada's resource base was instrumental in the country's industrial development.

6 Although the Liberal Party of Canada had a mandate to govern a maximum term of five years, it called an early election only three years after the previous election. The Liberals, under the leadership of Prime Minister Jean Chrétien, emerged victorious with a majority of seats and thus won a third consecutive term.

7 According to the terminology used by the Canadian government, refugees are not a 'class' (as I explain in chapter 5). However, in an attempt to keep the text reader-friendly, I speak of 'three immigration classes,' which includes refugees.

8 Between 1996 and 2004 – the period of this book's empirical study – the economic class captured between 54.7% (2003) and 62.1% (2001) of the annual immigration to Canada, the family class between 24.2% (2004) and 30.2% (1996), and refugees between 11.0% (2002) and 13.9% (2004). Between 0.1% (2001) and 4.2% (2003) were 'other immigrants' who did not belong to any of the three classes (Citizenship and Immigration Canada, 2008).

9 In Li's words, the debate incorporated the 'subjective perceptions and normative values Canadians hold about Canada's past and its future' (2003: 163).

10 I put 'culture' and 'cultural' in quotes to recognize the essentialized nature in which the term is applied in this context (for a discussion of the term, see Mitchell, 1995; and Williams, 1983: 87–93).

11 Herder (1966 [1772]: 104–12) called the development of various national languages a 'natural law.' In the particular context of German national identity, Arndt wrote in 1812: 'Was ist des deutschen Vaterland, ist's Preußenland, ist's Schwabenland, ist's wo die deutsche Rebe blüht, ist's wo am Rhein die Möve zieht? Oh nein, sein Vaterland muß größer sein . . . so weit die deutsche Zunge klingt . . . das ganze Deutschland sell es sein' (quoted in Oberndörfer, 1992: 36). Following the principle of negation, Arndt speaks of the 'hatred' against the French as a unifying feature of German identity: 'Dieser Haß glühe als die Religion des deutschen Volkes,

als ein heiliger Wahn in allen Herzen und erhalte uns in Treue, Redlichkeit und Tapferkeit' (quoted in Busse, 1997: 32).

12 Although the German word *Volk* can be translated as 'the people,' it encompasses meanings of ethnic nationalism based on common folklore, history, and ancestry.

13 The influential study by Rogers Brubaker (1992) exemplifies the oppositional character of citizenship and nationhood in Germany and France.

14 Interestingly, Eli Nathans (2004: 28–9) emphasizes a different role Hegel played in the formation of nation and nationhood in Germany. According to Nathans, Hegel's (1970 [1820]) philosophy of right helped facilitate the rise of liberal and universal citizenship in Prussia and other German states. Nathans suggests that 'Hegel's philosophy . . . implied that states had a powerful capacity to integrate foreigners, both those currently in the country and those immigrating from the outside' (2004: 28).

15 The Weimar Republic existed between 1919 and 1933. After the First World War and the fall of the emperor, the German Reich received a democratic constitution in August 1919. The Weimar era ended with the takeover by Nazi dictator Adolf Hitler.

16 My discussion of the post-war period up to 1990 focuses on West Germany, i.e., the Federal Republic of Germany. Migration also existed in East Germany, i.e., the German Democratic Republic, although in a very different political context. Furthermore, perception of national identity, and the role of foreigners in this context, differed between East and West Germany (Fulbrook, 1996).

17 West German politicians evoked common culture, heritage, and fate to uphold the idea of unity between West and East Germany in the 1960s. Some politicians continued this practice after reunification (Knischweski, 1996).

18 Throughout German history, policies towards foreign residents attempted to balance the indispensable economic need for immigrant labour with the objective of excluding non-German migrants from the ethnically defined nation state (e.g., Bade, 2004; Oltmer, 2005).

19 Lafontaine later left the Social Democratic Party and became the chairperson of a newly formed party, *die Linke,* positioned at the left of the political spectrum.

20 These laws included the Integration Adjustment Act (*Eingliederungsanpassungsgesetz*) and the Resettler Reception Law (*Aussiedleraufnahmegesetz*) of 1990 and the Law on Settling the Consequences of the War (*Kriegsfolgenbereinigungsgesetz*) of 1993. Christian Joppke (2005: 204–15) provides an

excellent review of the 'demise' of Germany's ethnic nationhood model that was expressed in the policies towards the repatriation of ethnic Germans.

21 The Green Party, however, did not mention immigration explicitly in its election program (Hell, 2005: 93–4).

22 In academic debate, the question of whether Germany is an immigration country was raised much earlier, for example, by Friedrich Heckmann (1981), who published a book in the early 1980s that contained this question in the title. A decade later, Rogers Brubaker observed that 'the undeniable fact of immigrant settlement does not make Germany – according to its own self-understanding – a country of immigrants' (1992: 174). Another decade later, Edda Currle and Tanja Wunderlich (2001) still phrased the issue of whether Germany is an immigration country as a question in the title of their edited volume.

23 The contentious issue of whether Germany is an 'immigration country' has not been put to rest. As I am making revisions to the manuscript, the secretary general, Alexander Dobrindt, of the Christian Social Union (CSU) publicly criticized the federal minister of education and research, Annette Schavan, of the sister-party, the Christian Democratic Union, for declaring that 'Germany is an immigration country' and argued that 'openness (*Weltoffenheit*) and tolerance shouldn't be equated with unregulated immigration' (Deutscher Depeschendienst, 2010).

24 The law, which took effect on 1 January 2000, provided, for example, the children of immigrants who settled permanently in Germany with German citizenship. If these children possess the additional citizenship of the parents, they need to choose between one of those citizenships before the age of 23. In December 2007, parliament initiated a review of this legislation. Most invited experts recommended axing the 'model of choice' (*Optionsmodel*) of citizenship in favour of multiple citizenship (Deutscher Bundestag, 2008).

25 The Green Card was not as popular as anticipated by the German government. Of the 20,000 Green Cards available, only 14,876 were issued between August 2000 and July 2003 (Kolb, 2005: 2).

26 The commission received its name from its chairperson, Peter Müller, president of the state of Saarland. Although the Müller commission supported immigration in general, it also differed from the Süssmuth commission's recommendations in that it emphasized the Christian roots of the German nation.

27 In a personal conversation, Ms Süssmuth told me that the commission did in fact reach out and promote the need for immigration but was unsuccessful in changing public opinion because resistance was too strong.

28 In the former East Germany it increased between 2000 and 2003.

29 Although the periods of legal reform in both countries may not be identical, a comparison is possible. Karin Böke and her colleagues (2000) develop a particular framework for the international comparison of immigration discourse. They suggest that international comparisons are feasible between similar discourses in different countries or varying discourses in different countries that occur at similar times. In my analysis, I examine similar discourses of 'immigration' in a similar time period.

30 By focusing on the debate of the law, I am able to examine discursive practices in relation to laws with concrete social, political, economic, and thus material consequences (see appendix for details on the research design).

31 The sample of newspaper articles contained all aspects, or 'topoi' (see appendix), identified by Wengeler (2000) in previous research. For analytical clarity, I summarized less frequent aspects (stress, human utility, political utility, exploitation, justice, political aim, displacement, foreign aid, contradiction, responsibility, and realist) under the label 'other.'

32 A 'legal' aspect was also represented in the samples. However, I excluded this aspect from the analysis because the sampling procedure selected newspaper articles that discussed immigration law and therefore sampled this aspect. Given that all articles discuss the immigration law, the interpretation of this aspect relative to other aspects would be difficult and redundant.

33 Although the political aspect obviously plays an important role in Canada's immigration debate, it is likely that the high frequency of this aspect is partially attributable to the sample selection procedure, which focused on the process of creating a new law and therefore may have over-sampled political considerations of immigration. Although I retain this aspect in the analysis for this chapter, I do not pursue it in the analysis in part 2. A closer look at the data showed that this aspect addresses the processes and practices of strategic politics and bargaining, which are less interesting in the context of national identity formation than the other aspects. This observation is supported by the finding that the majority of occurrences of the political aspect were neutral towards immigration, which suggests that the discussion of this aspect takes a strong side neither for nor against immigration, but generally discusses the strategic points of immigration policymaking.

34 They represent 24% (danger) and 23% (humanitarianism) of occurrences of the coded articles in the sample.

35 Nevertheless, I would have expected the overall frequency of the danger aspect to be lower because the study period included considerable more time (60 months) before 11 September 2001 than after (39 months).
36 In fact, only 21 articles in the entire Canadian sample of newspaper articles contained at least one passage associated with a 'cultural' argument.
37 This observation must be qualified. The years in the beginning and towards the end of the study period also represent phases in the debate at which the overall number of articles was low (see figure 3.2). Due to the small number of observations for these years, greater fluctuations than in other years can be expected.
38 The data are organized into six-month intervals. With these intervals the horizontal axis of the graphs for the German data (figures 3.4 and 3.5) and the Canadian data (figures 3.2 and 3.3) have roughly the same number of intervals. Optically, the data of the two countries are thus comparable. However, an interpretation and comparison of the data must recognize that the scales of the horizontal axes differ on the Canadian and German graphs.
39 When I shifted the scale of analysis to three-month intervals, I found that media attention actually peaked in the second quarter (between 1 April and 30 June), and thus immediately after the Madrid attacks.
40 The study period ended before the end of 2005. The count for the second half of 2005 is therefore lower than if the study had continued until the end of the year.
41 A recent opinion survey supports my interpretation that economic utility of immigration is a commonly accepted and relatively uncontested idea: 75% of polled Canadians believe that 'immigrants create jobs in Canada' and 70% opposed the suggestion to reduce the intake of highly skilled immigrants (Gustin and Ziebarth, 2010: 981).

4. Immigration as Danger

1 Scholarship confirms that the terrorist attacks in New York and Washington and the intensification of the war on terror are often associated with key changes in migration law and discourses (e.g., Tsoukala 2008a, 2008b; Nicol, 2005; Olmedo and Soden, 2005). Similarly, Catherine Dauvergne argues that the attacks on the World Trade Center and the Pentagon in the United States 'are a key marker' for the global security agenda that shaped immigration law in Canada and other 'Western' countries (2007b: 533; also Dauvergne, 2008).

2 Mark Krikorian of the United States–based right-wing think tank Center for Immigration Studies illustrates this association between danger and immigration: 'Our enemies have repeatedly . . . insert[ed] terrorists by exploiting weaknesses in our immigration system. A Center for Immigration Studies analysis of the immigration histories of the 48 foreign-born Al-Qaeda operatives who committed crimes in the United States from 1993 to 2001 (including the 9/11 hijackers) found that nearly every element of the immigration system has been penetrated by the enemy' (2004: no page). A similar argument can be made for the Canadian case.

3 This politically charged and methodologically opaque report proposes 'limitations on immigration, including a more selective approach to certain Middle Eastern nationals' in the name of American citizens' right to protection (McGowan, 2003: 9).

4 These parentheses are part of the original quote.

5 The think tank clearly affirms the dialectic among discursive media practice, law, and material outcomes.

6 A study by Anastassia Tsoukala (2008a, 2008b) on British press reporting does not examine records prior to 11 September 2001. Apparently, Tsoukala assumes that the security threat emerged as a result of the attacks.

7 The Royal Canadian Mounted Police (RCMP) is Canada's federal law enforcement agency. The Canadian Security and Intelligence Service (CSIS) is the federal agency responsible for collecting security intelligence. Citizenship and Immigration Canada (CIC) is the federal department responsible for immigration and citizenship issues. Although these agencies serve different roles, they belong to what Didier Bigo (2002, 2008) calls a 'field' of (in)security professionals that shares a certain *habitus* in dealing with issues of 'terrorism, organized crime, and the so-called migratory invasion or reverse colonialization' (Bigo, 2008: 11; see also Bigo and Tsoukala, 2008).

8 Another indication that the Canadian government responded to the perception of danger prior to September 2001 is the declining proportion of refugees – an immigrant group that is often associated with security risks – of all landing immigrants to Canada. Statistics indicate that this proportion declined before 11 September 2001, from 13.1% in 1998 to 11% in 2001; after 2001, this proportion actually increased to reach 13.9% in 2003 (Citizenship and Immigration Canada, 2006).

9 Bill C-42 was a response to the attacks of 11 September 2001 in the United States and one of three pieces of 'anti-terrorism' legislation (Government of Canada, 2003).

10 The same survey also showed that most Canadians disagree that immigrants to Canada should have their religious beliefs and values screened before they are allowed to enter Canada, and three out of four agree that Muslim immigrants make a positive contribution to Canada. Apparently, the fear of terrorism is not associated with a categorical rejection of Muslim immigration. Rather, the fear of terrorism is a particular theme in a complex debate.

11 The press reported on numerous other cases (e.g., O'Connor, 2002). The three cases I am showcasing here were the most frequently covered ones in my data sample.

12 Although it did exist, as exemplified by an article in the *Ottawa Citizen,* which quoted a Canadian government's lawyer: 'Every Canadian citizen, every visitor, every permanent resident . . . deserves protection from people like Mr. Jaballah,' lawyer Donald McIntosh said. 'They deserve protection from people who, if left to their own devices, would assist and facilitate the kinds of diabolical acts like those of Sept. 11' (Duffy, 2004).

13 The press coverage of Ahani and Suresh's cases also presented the other side of the argument. For example, an article by the same author published in both the *Ottawa Citizen* and the *Calgary Herald* acknowledged that 'several of the nine justices . . . appeared skeptical of the federal Immigration Act provisions allowing the government to weed out suspected terrorists deemed to be a threat to Canada's security' (Tibbetts, 2001d).

14 An article published on the same day in the *National Post* reiterated these statements using similar language (Tibbetts, 2001b).

15 In comparison to the residents of other countries, however, relatively few Canadians associate immigration with crime. Only 17% agreed or strongly agreed in 1995 with the statement that immigrants increase crime. Although this number increased to 27% in 2003, it was far below the 56% (1995) and 62% (2003) in the former West Germany or the 68% (1995) and 67% (2003) in the former East Germany who agreed with this statement (Simon and Sikich, 2007: 960).

16 The original article repeats the legal text of the Immigration Act's definitions of 'inadmissible classes.' I summarize portions of this text to convey the point that the press presents various themes of danger. The full text is more comprehensive than these excerpts.

17 Health risks associated with immigration were only a minor theme in the sampled newspaper articles. In addition, the low frequency of reporting

did not permit a reliable interpretation of media representations of this theme.

18 Although the arrival of the four boats was covered in the media debate of immigration reform, a direct link between these immigrants and concrete dangers to Canadian society was made relatively infrequently in the sampled newspaper articles. In most cases, these immigrants were represented as 'queue jumpers' who entered Canada 'illegally' and constitute an economic liability, rather than presenting a concrete danger to Canada and Canadian's safety and security.

19 I could trace the term 'securitization' back to Ole Waever (1995); it was developed by others in relation to immigration (e.g., Burke, 2002; Bigo, 2008; Bigo and Tsoukala, 2008).

20 This dialectic of security varies between contexts. For example, in different countries and regions, the media constructs dangers of crime and threats of terrorism in different ways (Hewitt, 1992; Jiwani, 2005). Furthermore, the link between media reporting on international crime and terrorism, and policy responses, varies between national contexts. A study of television news coverage during election campaigns found that in Russia and the United States 'international security and terrorism were not discussed on the same rational level' (Oates, 2006: 434) as other election issues; the media exaggerated terrorism threats. Conversely, in Britain, the issue of terrorism was debated in a less distorted manner. I therefore expect that the danger narrative differs in content and structure between media reporting in Canada and in Germany.

21 In Faist's (2000) words, international migration serves as a 'meta-issue,' mediating between the politics of fear and the restructuring of national and global order.

5. Humanitarian Immigration

1 'Convention refugees' are defined by the United Nations as having a well-founded fear of persecution based on their race, religion, nationality, or membership in a group. A second group, which Canada recognizes as refugees, are 'people who are in refugee-like situations for whom no other durable solution can be found' (Minister of Public Works and Government Services Canada, quoted in Abu Laban et al., 1999, no page). The Canadian government further distinguishes between government-sponsored and privately sponsored refugees.

2 Beyond these formal similarities, however, refugees may experience settlement in Canada very differently from other groups due to their histories and circumstances of migration.

3 Citizenship and Immigration's website explicitly warns applicants and sponsors that 'applications for permanent residence made on humanitarian and compassionate grounds are only approved in exceptional circumstances and it could take up to several years to process an application' (Citizenship and Immigration Canada, 2009a).
4 This history also included less honourable episodes, including Canada's refusal (along with other countries, including the USA) in 1939 to permit entry to the more than 900 Jewish refugees on board the ship St Louis, who had escaped from Nazi Europe. After being forced to return to Europe, many of the passengers died in concentration camps. The recently unveiled memorial 'Wheel of Conscience,' designed by Daniel Libeskind and located at Pier 21 in Halifax, commemorates this tragic event (*Toronto Star,* 2011).
5 The case of Ms. Baker and her children is not unique, and the press reported on numerous similar cases. For example, the *Toronto Star* (1998: 1) supported a court decision in favour of a single mother and refugee claimant whose two Canadian-born children were scheduled for deportation. An article in the *Calgary Herald* (Marshall, 1999a: B8) criticized the lack of compassion in a decision by Citizenship and Immigration Canada to deport a Sri Lankan refugee, although her husband and two children possessed Canadian citizenship. An article in the *National Post* (Martinez, 1999: A14) laments that 'family unity is often disregarded, particularly in deportation cases.'
6 Although – in dialectical fashion – the article presents the counter-argument that war crimes were often committed by coerced peasants, the authors express their opinion by ending with a quote from a spokesperson of the Centre for Latin American Vancouverites Ethnic Society: 'No-one has the right to torture another human being, even if you're involved in a civil war. Everyone has a choice.'
7 The German press spelled the name 'Zündel,' although it did not relate this case to the debate on the immigration law.

6. Economic Utility

1 Karl Marx (2001 [1867]) observed long ago that migrants are in a more vulnerable labour-market position than non-migrants and therefore suffer disproportionately from exploitation. Migrant workers have been in this vulnerable position relative to non-migrant workers throughout the history of industrial capitalism, and they continue to be (Castells, 1975; Piore, 1979; Sassen, 1988; Balibar, 2002).

2 In Canada, a range of cultural and institutional mechanisms exist that devalue immigrant labour. In the German labour market, migrants and foreigners also sell their labour power under value. In the German context, the lack of formal inclusion and citizenship are an important mechanism of labour devaluation.

3 For example, on both sides of the Atlantic, the label 'illegal migrants' is increasingly applied in political and public debate. This label denies the migrants the most basic rights and allocates their entire existence to the realm of illegitimacy.

4 Although the gendered language was removed in later policy documents and public debates, implicit gendered assumptions of male immigrants as economic actors and female immigrants as reproductive domestic or care-taking labour remain deeply embedded in contemporary law, policy, and public debate (e.g., Spijkerboer and van Walsum, 2007). It is important to acknowledge these gender assumptions.

5 Correspondingly, the majority of immigrants to Canada were selected for economic considerations. The economic class constituted 55.5% of all immigration to Canada in 1996 and 56.7% in 2004. During the study period, it peaked in 2001 at 62.1% (Citizenship and Immigration Canada, 2008).

6 I am not suggesting that there will not be a period or place where such ideas will be questioned. Rather, my observation applies to the particular context of the economic aspect of the media debate of immigration between 1996 and 2004.

7 Simmons and Keohane (1992) suggest that Canadian policymakers have relatively successfully attempted to limit the coverage of their labour-supply-driven immigration policy as a major issue of media debate.

8 Other viewpoints on how immigration can produce economic benefits for Canada were also present. For example, non-racial immigration policy can create international business networks that result in foreign investment from Asia and broaden exports (Martin, 1999: A13; Samuel, 1998: 1). Or, immigration is a 'key component [of] the purchasing power of our consumer base' (*Toronto Star,* 1999: 1) and stimulates growth in particular industries, such as language education (*Vancouver Sun,* 2004: A14). These viewpoints, however, occurred with much lower frequency (typically only once in the analysed articles) than the two main viewpoints discussed in this section.

9 The points system rewards applicants between the ages of 21 and 49 with the maximum of 10 points for their age. The points system thereby favours 'prime working age' immigrants who have completed their costly education in childhood and adolescence, but who will likely remain productively in the labour

force for at least fifteen years before they retire and the average costs for their health care and social services increase again. The argument presented in the press differs from this 'prime working age' argument and focuses instead on the demographic development of Canada vis-à-vis its competitor nations.

10 To a certain degree, different newspapers present different viewpoints. In the context of the theme of victims and perpetrators, the *Vancouver Sun* tended to focus on immigrant deskilling, while the *National Post* was more concerned with the negative impact of immigration on the welfare state. This bias in reporting corresponds with the *National Post*'s reputation as a pro-business newspaper. In the reporting of other themes, however, this association between individual newspapers and the representation of a certain viewpoints was not clearly discernible.

11 Between 2004, the end of the study period, and 2008, these numbers increased from 112,553 to 192,519 (Citizenship and Immigration Canada, 2009b).

7. Nation of *Wirtschaftswunder*?

1 I am referring to the new citizenship law that took effect on 1 January 2000, and which incorporates elements of the territorial principle (*jus soli*). I elaborated on this law in chapter 3. Despite this new law, for the vast majority of cases, citizenship continues to be bestowed following the principle of *jus sanguinis.*

2 Between 1960 and 1965, 36% of newsprint articles sampled by Wengeler used this argument; between 1970 and 1975, 29.5% of articles did so. In the 1980s the rank of the economic utility argument dropped from first to sixth place relative to other arguments, appearing in only 12.4% of sampled articles (Wengeler, 2003).

3 German policies were by no means unique in this respect but followed the policies of other European and North American countries that also used immigration to regulate national labour markets (Luccasen, 1998; Pellerin, 1999).

4 Despite the recruitment stop, migration to Germany continued because fewer workers than expected decided to return to their countries of origin. These workers had accumulated post-national rights and privileges that enabled them to stay and work in Germany (Soysal, 1994). Many decided to bring their families, with the result that immigration continued, despite the official policy of a 'recruitment stop.' For all practical purposes, these migrants are not 'guest workers' but immigrants. Or, as Max Frisch allegedly said: 'We called for workers, but people came.'

5 According to Martin Wengeler, throughout the 1960s, the 1970s, and the early 1980s, the view prevailed in German migration debate that migrants should produce a benefit to the national economy and labour market (Wengeler, 2003: 385–91). After 1982, this economic viewpoint declined in significance (Wengeler, 2006: 16–17).
6 The euro (€) replaced the German mark.
7 Nor were they allowed to assume German citizenship without revoking their citizenship of birth, or other acquired citizenships.
8 For example, the so-called Agenda 2010 aimed at reforming Germany's economy, labour market, and social security system along neoliberal lines. Although Agenda 2010 was announced in 2003 – three years after the Green Card – it symbolizes the political and economic trends of the time.
9 A comparison with a similar opinion poll taken before the German immigration debate began in 2000 confirms the earlier trend from the positive towards the negative representation of the economic aspect of immigration. In 1995, 38% of West Germans and 32% of East Germans believed that immigrants were good for the economy, while only 27% of West Germans and 43% of East Germans were of the opinion that immigrants take away jobs from Germans (Simon and Sikich, 2007: 958–9).
10 For example, the argument that immigrants fill important labour market gaps appeared in 61 articles, while the suggestion that they increase unemployment was present in only 28 articles.
11 The negative perspective of the economic aspect occurred in several clusters: towards the end of 2001 and the beginning of 2002, in spring of 2003, and in summer of 2004. These clusters were not in any discernible way related to the political process of the making of the immigration law or other prominent news incidents.
12 While most electronic records of the sampled newspapers did not contain the photographs (see appendix for sampling and analysis details), the records did indicate whether a photograph or figure accompanied an article. This figure or photograph could then be examined by locating the article on micro-film or micro-fiche.
13 Interestingly, the positive association of immigration with business's need for labour seems to be a position that newspapers across the political spectrum assumed. In the sample, it was represented in both centrist and left-wing newspapers. Unfortunately, the coverage in the *Bild Zeitung* was not detailed enough to assess whether this positions also represents right-wing media views.

14 Newspapers did not spell Green Card consistently; variations include 'Green Card,' 'Greencard,' and 'Green-Card.' For the sake of consistency I translated all variations as 'Green Card.'
15 The 'recruitment stop,' ending Germany's guest worker program of 1955–73, was still official policy in 2002.
16 The European Central Bank fixed the exchange rate of DM 1.95583 to €1.00.
17 The idea that immigration should contribute to the flexibilization of the lower segments of the labour market was notably absent in the reporting of the left-wing newspaper *Tageszeitung*.
18 Mostly articles in the centrist newspapers argued in this way.
19 I generalize based on the reporting in centrist and left-wing newspapers. In most cases, the right-wing *Bild Zeitung* did not contain sufficient detail for a meaningful, in-depth analysis.
20 Although the media repeatedly expressed this position, there was no consensus. For example, some articles emphasized the need to replenish the labour market with immigration to sectors that are not typically associated with the knowledge economy, including nursing and the restaurant industry. This disagreement indicates that the immigration dialectic has not reached a point of stability.
21 The German government continued to block the immigration of skilled labour *and* continued to use neoliberal rhetoric. For example, the law to regulate labour migration (*Arbeitsmigrationssteuerungsgesetz*) of 2009, which fine-tuned areas of the immigration law, is still insufficient to significantly improve Germany's position in the global competition for skill and talent. Nevertheless, the explanation of the law begins with defining the 'problem' in this way: 'Germany's position in the international competition for highly qualified workers must be strengthened' (Deutscher Bundestag, 2008: 1).
22 For eight of the ten new member countries the so-called 2+3+2 model specified that the labour mobility restrictions applied for an initial two years, but could be renewed for three years and after that for an additional two years. Cyprus and Malta were exempt from this regulation.

8. From Immigration to Integration

1 Jürgen Habermas (1979), in particular, suggests that constitutional patriotism (*Verfassungspatriotismus*) and the identification with the constitution have replaced ethnic nationalism in post-war Germany (see also Sternberger, 1990). Dieter Oberndörfer (1992) applied a similar civic understanding of nationhood to an immigration context, advocating for a

republic that is 'open' to individuals who embrace Germany's constitutional order, independent of their ethnic origin.

2 Poll data show that 70% of Germans associate Islam with a tendency towards violence, revenge, and retaliation. Conversely, Christianity is linked by 80% of the German population to kindness, and by 71% to human rights and charity.

3 The media also often fails to make distinctions between Arab immigrant populations, who are the object of the fear of terrorism, and Germany's existing Turkish immigrant communities (Ewing, 2008).

4 Prantl echoed the Green Party, which withdrew from the negotiations of the immigration law shortly before politicians and the media linked the case of Metin Kaplan with the immigration law. The Greens explained their withdrawal with the words 'We will not follow the path to Guantanamo' (Jox and Weikert, 2004: 24).

5 The fact that Kaplan was a 'Turkish Islamist' who did not represent the Arab-based groups linked to al-Qaeda and the New York and Washington attacks speaks further to the practice of homogenizing all Muslims (see Ewing, 2008: 206–11).

6 Schavan is well known for her later role in federal politics as the minister of education and research in the cabinet of Angela Merkel.

7 Net migration has already been negative since 2003. According to data collected by the Federal Office of Statistics (Statistische Bundesamt), 95,262 fewer foreigners lived in Germany in 2008 than in 2003. Only in the period between 2004 and 2005 was the trend reversed, as Germany gained 1196 foreigners (Bundesamt für Migration und Flüchtlinge 2009: 4–5).

8 The discussion of the parallel society bears similarities to the underclass debate in the United States, with which North American readers may be more familiar. The concept of the underclass suggests that the exclusion of African American and Latino populations in US inner cities is a matter not only of material deprivation but also of cultural pathology on the side of the minority group. The main proponent of the underclass concept, William J. Wilson (1987), drew on Oscar Lewis's (1966) work on the 'culture of poverty.' While Lewis suggested that cultural pathology is learned early on in a person's life and inherited within a community, Wilson traces the origin of pathology to economic deprivation. Both scholars, however, embrace the problematic idea that 'culture' can be dysfunctional. According to some proponents of the underclass concept, cultural dysfunction spreads through minority neighbourhoods and communities like a disease. Prolonged exposure to the minority group breeds cultural dysfunction. The proposed solution to cure this disease is mixing immigrant and minority populations

with so-called mainstream society – which, presumably, is not culturally dysfunctional. Although developed by academics, the underclass concept has been applied by planners, policymakers, and politicians, and has served as a powerful ideological tool of Othering and legitimating the assimilation of marginalized social groups (Gans, 1990; Bauder, 2002a, 2002b). The term parallel society evokes similar connotations of a pathological community that suffers from cultural dysfunction because it is socially isolated and spatially secluded. Breaking up isolated immigrant communities, demolishing secluded ethnic neighbourhoods, and dispersing immigrant populations would be considered important steps towards the cultural integration of immigrants.

9 In some instances, politicians and the media also addressed the integration and improvement of the legal status of refugees and asylum seekers already in Germany, many of whom are not Turkish.

10 Petra Rostock and Sabine Berghahn (2008) have identified gender, in particular the construction of Muslim women as headscarf-wearing Others, as a pivotal moment in the redefinition of German identity. Anna Korteweg and Gökçe Yurdakul (2008) draw attention to gendered practices of boundary-drawing through discourses on honour killings.

11 This invitation is similar to the opportunity extended to African American and Latino members of the US 'underclass' to become members of mainstream America.

12 In her book *Stolen Honor,* Katherine Pratt Ewing (2008) unpacks the complex relations between Germany's problematic history, the valorization of the constitution, and the representations of Muslim immigration and Islam.

13 Between German and US citizens, however, there is little difference. Although figures for Canada are not available in this study, this situation raises the issue of whether public opinion in Germany reflects that of a settler nation in this particular context.

14 For example, the *Kaiserreich* discriminated against non-German-speaking Poles and other Eastern European groups who resided in German territory in 'an effort to "strengthen Germandom"' (Brubaker, 1992: 15).

15 Fairclough made these remarks in the context of developing an application of the concept of 'intertextuality' to discourse analysis.

16 The recent coalition contract between the conservative Christian Democratic and Christian Social Unions and the liberal Free Democrats exemplifies the lasting material effect of the position that Germany is an integration country. The contract contains a section, 'Integration and Immigration,' that clearly emphasizes 'integration' over 'new immigration' and focuses on integration measures, such as language training for

migrants and their children. This contract also mentions the intention to establish 'integration contracts' with new immigrants and migrants who already live in Germany to achieve their 'successful inclusion into German society and the German labour market' (CDU, CSU, and FDP, 2009: 75).

17 I am not suggesting that this two-way street is uncontested or unproblematic, as I illustrated in a review of this book (Bauder, 2009). Yet, this two-way street does represent a viewpoint that is common among key groups that shape the immigration debate in Canada, including policymakers, government administrators, and some academics.

9. Refugees and Asylum Seekers

1 The new immigration law regulates both asylum seekers and refugees according to the Geneva Convention under the rubric 'humanitarian immigration' (Bosswick, 2008: 128–9).

2 For example, Susan Musarrat Akram (2000) illustrates the role of neo-Orientalism in the framing of refugee and asylum claims.

3 The working paper *Die Organisation der Asyl- und Zuwanderungspolitik in Deutschland* by Jan Schneider (2009) provides a detailed overview of the administrative organization of asylum and immigration policies and practices in Germany.

4 In the year 2000, the largest group of asylum applicants came from Iraq (14.8%), followed by the former Yugoslavia (14.2%) and Turkey (11.4%). But 2005, these patterns changed; the largest group came from Serbia and Montenegro (19.1%), followed by Turkey (10.2%) and Iraq (6.9%) (Bundesamt für Migration und Flüchtlinge, 2008: 19–20).

5 For comparative purposes, Canada, which has a considerably smaller population, accepted 27,919 refugees in 2001 and 32,687 in 2004 (Citizenship and Immigration Canada, 2007b).

6 Although the final law did not allow for significant numbers of selected immigrants, the debate began with this position. The Süßmuth commission, for example, suggested a points system to select immigrants based on human-capital criteria.

7 Before and during the Second World War, Berlin was the undisputed centre of the German state that unified the German nation. After the Second World War and during the Cold War, the government of West Germany was seated in Bonn, that of East Germany in East Berlin. After the East German state was dissolved in 1990, the government of the unified Germany remained initially in Bonn. With unification, however, a debate emerged – the so-called *Hauptstadtdebatte* (capital debate) – about the proper seat of government. In 1991, parliament decided to relocate from

Bonn to Berlin. Since 1999, the lower house of parliament, the Bundestag, has held sessions in the renovated building of the former Reichstag in Berlin. The relocation from Bonn to Berlin (and especially into the former Reichstag building) symbolized a newly found national identity.

8 For example, under the Convention Refugee Abroad Class, Canada admits people whom the United Nations High Commission for Refugees (UNHRC) classifies as Convention Refugees. However, not all such cases are admitted nor are they selected on a random basis. Rather, Citizenship and Immigration Canada and, ultimately, an immigration officer decide 'whether the person identified meets the requirement of Canada's Refugee and Humanitarian Resettlement Program, and if the person will be admitted to Canada' (Citizenship and Immigration, 2009c: n.p.). Canada also entertains a Country of Asylum Class and a Source Country Class, under which the admission of refugees and asylum seekers is also subject to the discretion of Citizenship and Immigration Canada and its staff. In an effort to block entry by refugees who were not actively selected by the Canadian state, Canada signed a Safe Third Country Agreement with the United States in 2004.

9 On its website, the Evangelische Kirche translates its own name as 'Evangelical Church' (http://www.ekd.de/english/index.html). I chose the translation 'Lutheran Church' to avoid confusion with other Evangelical churches. The Roman Catholic and Lutheran churches are the main Christian denominations in Germany. The churches operate the charities Caritas and Diakonie.

10 Interestingly, in a different study, I came across a similar argument of 'development policy' in a Canadian context. In an analysis of newspaper coverage of Canada's Commonwealth Caribbean and Mexican Seasonal Agricultural Workers Program, I found that the press depicted the temporary nature of the seasonal foreign labour program as necessary, allowing the workers to deliver their earnings back to the poor families and communities in the Caribbean and Mexico. The temporary foreign labour program is thus considered a form of development assistance to foreign countries (Bauder, 2005). This argument is used against extending permanent residency to the workers.

11 Voß is referring to the situation of the 'hundred of thousands of illegals [i.e., irregular migrants] in Germany' whose lives are not addressed in the German immigration law.

12 In the context of his narrative, the reference to 'Christian' values emphasizes morality and compassion over self-interest. Generally, the newspaper articles did not juxtapose the values of Christianity against those of other religions. A rare exception is the editorial of *Süddeutsche Zeitung* editor

Heribert Prantl, who contrasted the 'C' in the two conservative parties' names (i.e., CDU, for Christian Democratic Union, and CSU, for Christian Social Union) with the maltreatment of women in countries with 'fundamentalist regimes.' Prantl wrote: 'A party which carries the "C" in the name should welcome the protection of women maltreated by fundamentalist regimes. However, an election campaign approaches, and then such a thing does not count' (Prantl, 2001a: 4). This article, however, was the only reference I found in the context of the moral-obligation narrative in which the values of different religions were juxtaposed, and then only implicitly.

13 Pro Asyl is a well-respected non-governmental organization that engages in a variety of activities, ranging from individual legal assistance to refugee applicants to political lobbying and furnishing legal opinions.

14 Arguably, the political field also differed from the public and media fields. In this context of humanitarian immigration, media debate in the new Berlin Republic did not follow the initial political program of the Social Democratic/Green government coalition. This program sought to reconfigure Germany as an 'Open Republic' (Oberdörfer, 1992) that not only welcomes and integrates immigrants but also admits refugees based on generous humanitarian principles. In this way, the political debate of the immigration law connected humanitarian and other aspects of immigration. It did not treat them as dialectically opposing aspects.

15 Interestingly, the repatriation narrative mirrors the policy that Germany practised towards its own 'diaspora' until the 1990s. In this case, *Aussiedler* were considered Germans who were to be repatriated (Joppke, 2005: 158–218). This practice defined German nationhood in ethnic terms. Although the empirical data that I collected in this respect is too thin to present an empirically informed interpretation, an interesting thesis would be that the repatriation narrative applies an ethnic understanding of nationhood to both Germany and the country of refugee origin. Put bluntly: 'Migrants should return to the places where they naturally belong.'

Conclusion

1 The interpretation here of the immigration–nation dialectic in both countries was certainly influenced by the empirical research design and the selection of the sample. Had the investigation focused not only on the material context of Canadian immigration reform but also on Canadian multiculturalism policy, I may have been able to observe a dialectic around the concept of integration that bears similarities to the German debate.

2 There was widespread public outrage over Sarrazin's assertions across Germany. A group of researchers tested his theses and concluded that he used data selectively and that his research did not meet standards of academic rigour (Foroutan et al., 2010). Calls for condemnation, however, were countered by claims that Sarrazin was expressing what many Germans think, but are reluctant to articulate in public (e.g., *DISS-Journal*, 2010).

3 In the wake of the Nazi catastrophe and the Third Reich, German ethnic nationalism lost its moral authority and Germans were searching for substitute identities. European integration offered an alternative to ethnic national identity. German foreign policy became a driving force in the material creation of European supranational bodies, including the European Coal and Steel Community in 1952 and the European Economic Community in 1957. The upscaling of economic structures, political processes, and legal institutions from the national to the regional level also gave rise to new European identity politics. The German population began increasingly to identify as Europeans (Knischweski, 1996: 134). Poll data from the 1990s confirm that Germans tend to be more accepting of Italian than of non-European Turkish neighbours (Böltken, 2003), and that a majority of Germans favour equal rights for Italian but not for Turkish immigrants (Wasmer and Koch, 2003). Other commentators who assume a perspective of European integration not centred on Germany but related to migration agree. According to Ian Ward, the European Union legally defines itself relative to an 'external "other"' (2002: 229), referring to refugees who are outside of the European Union's borders, and 'internal "other"' (233), referring to third-country nationals who are already inside the European Union. Étienne Balibar confirms that 'notions of interiority and exteriority . . . are undergoing a veritable earth quake' (2001: n.p.) in light of the geographical upscaling of belonging that occurs in Europe.

4 Nevertheless, it would be difficult to argue, I think, that a European identity will replace national identities. What Joppke pointed out more than a decade ago still applies: 'European citizenship is not decoupled from but premised on a person's nationality' (1998: 30). In a similar way, what continues to make Germans Europeans is their 'Germanness.'

5 To a degree, the significance of the national scale may have been reinforced by the topic and method of analysis I chose. In particular, I chose to examine *national* media discourse, opted to conduct *national* comparisons, and selected the topic of *national* immigration reform. If anything, this methodological choice illustrates how entrenched the category of the nation is in relation to the debate of people's mobility and belonging.

6 Wittgenstein applied 'aspect' mostly to visual and sensual perception (Park 1998). Others, however, have expanded on his original use of the term. For example, Debra Aidun (1982) suggests that Wittgenstein conceived of the entire field of philosophy as aspect-seeing. I too expand on Wittgenstein's original use of 'aspect' and the idea of 'aspect-seeing' beyond visual and sensual perception and apply it to the media debate on immigration law, which constructs different meanings of immigration and nation.

7 In other words, when it comes to the debate on immigration in Canada or Germany, the media is not 'aspect-blind,' which is how Wittgenstein (2001 [1945/6]: 1058 [part 2, xiv]) describes people who see only the rabbit or the duck, but not both meanings of the rabbit-duck head (see Introduction, n. 13).

8 The entire quote reads: 'When philosophy paints its grey in grey, then a configuration of life has grown old, and cannot be rejuvenated by this grey in grey, but only understood; the Owl of Minerva takes flight only as dusk begins to fall' (Hegel 1970 [1820]: 59–60).

9 Marx's famous eleventh thesis on Feuerbach forcefully establishes the counter-position to Hegel's passive idealism and expresses the responsibility of scholarship to engage in material processes: 'The philosophers have only interpreted the world in various ways; the point, however, is to change it' (1964 [1845]).

10 Correspondingly, Wodak identifies an additional 'dimension' of critical discourse analysis, aimed towards the 'improvement of communication' and social transformation (2001: 65; see also Wodak, 1997). This dimension resonates with the reflective nature of Marxian-inspired critical theory.

Epilogue

1 And it would be condescending for academics to assume that immigrants and activists cannot effectively organize without their help, although academics can play a role (Bauder, 2006a).

2 However, commentators such as Ulrich Beck and Edgar Grande (2007) have called for a European identity that embraces precisely the notion of mobility.

Bibliography

Abu-Laban, Baha, Tracey Derwing, Harvey Krahn, Marlene Mulder, and Lori Wilkinson. 1999. The settlement experience of refugees in Alberta. Website of Prairie Centre of Excellence for Research on Immigration and Integration and Population Research Laboratory, http://pcerii.metropolis.net/Virtual%20Library/RefugeeStudy.

Abu-Laban, Yasmeen. 1998. welcome/STAY OUT: The contradictions of Canadian integration and immigration policies at the millennium. *Canadian Ethnic Studies* 30(3): 191–211.

Adams, Michael. 2004. *Fire and ice: The United States, Canada and the myth of converging values.* Toronto: Penguin Canada.

Adelman, Howard. 2002. Canadian borders and immigration post 9/11. *International Migration Review* 63(1): 15–28.

Adorno, Theodor W. 1963. *Drei Studien zu Hegel.* Frankfurt am Main: Surkamp Verlag.

Aidun, Debora. 1982. Wittgenstein, philosophical method and aspect-seeing. *Philosophical Investigations* 5(2): 87–164.

Akram, Susan Musarrat. 2000. Orientalism revisited in asylum and refugee claims. *International Journal of Refugee Law* 12(1): 7–40.

Am Orde, Sabine. 2002. Deutschkurse auf Chipkarte. *Die Tageszeitung,* 28 March: 21.

Anderson, Benedict. 1991. *Imagined communities: Reflections on the origin and spread of nationalism.* Revised edition. London: Verso.

Anderson, Kay. 1991. *Vancouver's Chinatown: Racial discourse in Canada 1875–1980.* Montreal and Kingston: McGill-Queen's University Press.

Arar, Maher. 2006. *Maher Arar: Chronology of Events.* http://www.maherarar.ca.

Arar Commission. 2006. *Maher Arar commission of inquiry.* http://www.ararcommission.ca.

Arat-Koç, Sedef. 1999. Neo-liberalism, state restructuring and immigration: Changes in Canadian policies in the 1990s. *Journal of Canadian Studies* 34(2): 31–56.
Arendt, Hanna. 1998 [1958]. *The human condition.* Chicago: University of Chicago Press.
Austin, David. 2010. Narratives of power: Historical mythologies in contemporary Québec and Canada. *Race and Class* 52(1): 19–32.
Avunca, Berna. 1999. Turkish-Canadians can't rescue destitute relative. *Ottawa Citizen,* 18 September: B5.
Bade, Klaus J. 1994. *Ausländer, Aussiedler, Asyl.* Munich: C.H. Beck.
– 2004. *Sozialhistorische Migrationsforschung.* Studien zur historischen Migrationsforschung, vol. 13, ed. Michael Bommes and Jochen Oltmer. Göttingen: V & R Unipress.
Bade, Klaus J., ed. 1997. *Fremde im Land.* Osnabrück: Universitätsverlag Rasch.
Balibar, Étienne. 2000. What we owe to the *san-papiers.* In *Social insecurity,* ed. Len Guenther and Cornelius Heesters, 42–4. Toronto: Anansi.
– 2001. At the border of Europe. http://makeworlds.org/node/80.
– 2002. *Politics of the other scene.* Translated by Christine Jones, James Swenson, and Chris Turner. London: Verso.
– 2004. *We, the people of Europe: Reflections on transnational citizenship.* Translated by James Swenson. Princeton: Princeton University Press.
Ballett, Gerry. 2004. Helping people to stay here. *Vancouver Sun,* 22 July: B2.
Basok, Tanya. 2002. *Tortillas and tomatoes: Transmigrant Mexican harvesters in Canada.* Montreal and Kingston: McGill-Queens's University Press.
Bathelt, Harald, and Meric S. Gertler. 2005. The German variety of capitalism: Forces and dynamics of evolutionary change. *Economic Geography* 81(1): 1–9.
Bauder, Harald. 2002a. Neighbourhood effects and cultural exclusion. *Urban Studies* 39(1): 85–93.
– 2002b. *Work on the west side: Urban neighborhoods and the cultural exclusion of youths.* Lanham, MD: Lexington Books.
– 2003. Equality, justice and the problem of the international border: A view from Canada. *ACME – An International Journal of Critical Geographies* 2(2): 167–82.
– 2005. Landscape and scale in media representations: The construction of offshore farm labour in Ontario, Canada. *Cultural Geographies* 12(1): 41–58.
– 2006a. And the flag waved on: Immigrants protest, geographers meet in Chicago. *Environment and Planning A* 38(6): 1001–4.
– 2006b. *Labor movement: How migration regulates labor markets.* New York: Oxford University Press.

– 2008a. Emotional attachment . . . to what? A reply to Stanley Renshon. *Migrations and Identities* 1(2): 187–93.

– 2008b. Foreign farm workers in Ontario (Canada): Exclusionary discourse in the newsprint media. *Journal of Peasant Studies* 35(1): 100–18.

– 2008c. Immigration debate in Canada: How newspapers reported, 1996–2004. *Journal of International Migration and Integration* 9(3): 289–310.

– 2009. Review of *Immigration and Integration in Canada in the Twenty-First Century,* ed. J. Biles, M. Burnstein, and J. Frideres, in *The Canadian Geographer* 53(3): 381–2.

– Forthcoming. Towards a critical geography of the border: Engaging with the dialectic of practice and meaning. *Annals of the Association of American Geographers.* In press.

Bauder, Harald, and Salvatore Engel-Di Mauro. 2008. Introduction: Critical scholarship, practice and education. In *Critical geographies: A collection of readings,* ed. Harald Bauder and Salvatore Engel-Di Mauro. Kelowna, BC: Praxis (e)Press. http://www.praxis-epress.org/CGR/1-intro.pdf.

Bauder, H., and Jan Semmelroggen. 2009. Immigration and imagination of nationhood in German parliament. *Nationalism & Ethnic Politics* 15(1): 1–26.

Baur, Uli. 2010. Wegbügeln funktioniert nicht mehr. *Focus,* 18 October: 11.

Baxter, James. 2002. Coderre unveils changes to immigration act. *Ottawa Citizen,* 12 June: A6.

Beaulne, Jacques. 2001. Easy target. *Ottawa Citizen,* 1 November: A17.

Beck, Ulrich, and Edgar Grande. 2007. *Das kosmopolitische Europa: Gesellschaft und Politik in der Zweiten Moderne.* Taschenbuchausgabe. Frankfurt am Main: Surkamp Verlag.

Beck-Gernsheim, Elisabeth. 2007. *Wir und die Anderen: Kopftuch, Zwangsheirat und andere Mißverständnisse.* Erweiterete Ausgabe. Frankfurt am Main: Surkamp Verlag.

Beckstein, Günther. 1999. Annäherung and die Leitkultur. *Zeitschrift für Kulturaustausch.* Rev. 21 July 2004. http://www.ifa.de/zfk/themen/99_3_hysterie/dbeckstein.htm.

Behnke, Andreas. 1997. Citizenship, nationhood and the production of political space. *Citizenship Studies* 1(2): 243–65.

Beise, Marc. 2004. Wirtschaft macht Druck bei der Zuwanderung. *Süddeutsche Zeitung,* Wirtschaft, 25 May: 19

Bell, Stewart. 2001a. Alleged Islamic terrorist goes on trial in U.S. *National Post,* 10 March: A8.

– 2001b. Court ruling could make Canada 'haven' for terrorists, assassins. *National Post,* 17 February: A1.

– 2001c. CSIS links Toronto teacher to Jihad. *National Post,* 28 August: A1.
– 2001d. No way to fight terrorism. *National Post,* 18 July: A15.
– 2003. Zundel ordered held as a national security risk. *National Post,* 1 March: A4.
Bencivenga, Ermanno. 2000. *Hegel's dialectical logic.* New York: Oxford University Press.
Bendel, Petra. 2004. Totgesagte leben länger: Das deutsche Zuwanderungsgesetz. *Gesellschaft – Wirtschaft – Politik* 53(2): 205–12.
Bendel, Petra, and Axel Kreienbrink, eds. 2008. *Kanada und Deutschland: Migration und Integration im Vergleich.* Nürnberg: Bundesamt für Migration und Flüchtlinge.
Benson, Rodney. 2005. Mapping field variations: Journalism in France and the United States. In *Bourdieu and the journalistic field,* ed. Rodney Benson and Erik Neveu, 85–112. Cambridge, UK: Polity.
– 2006. News medias a 'journalistic field': What Bourdieu adds to new institutionalism, and vice versa. *Political Communication* 23: 187–202.
Benson, Rodney, and Erik Neveu, eds. 2005. *Bourdieu and the journalistic field.* Cambridge, UK: Polity.
Bergen, Bob. 1998. Molester's release angers kid's mom. *Calgary Herald,* 18 June: B1.
Berger, John. 1972. *Ways of seeing.* London: Viking Press.
Bhabha, Homi K. 1990. Introduction: Narrating the nation. In *Nation and narration,* ed. Homi K. Bhabha, 1–7. London: Routledge.
Bigo, Didier. 2002. Security and immigration: Toward a critique of the governmentality of unease. *Alternatives* 27: 63–92.
– 2008. Globalized (in)security: The field and the ban-opticon. In *Terror, insecurity and liberty: Illiberal practices of liberal regimes after 9/11,* ed. Didier Bigo and Anastassia Tsoukala, 10–48. London: Routledge.
Bigo, Didier, and Anastassia Tsoukala. 2008. Understanding (in)security. In *Terror, insecurity and liberty: Illiberal practices of liberal regimes after 9/11,* ed. Didier Bigo and Anastassia Tsoukala, 1–9. London: Routledge.
Biles, John, Meyer Burstein, and James Frideres, eds. 2008. *Immigration and integration in Canada in the twenty-first century.* Montreal and Kingston: McGill-Queen's University Press.
Bissoondath, Neil. 1994. *Selling illusions: The cult of multiculturalism in Canada.* Toronto: Penguin Books.
Blommaert, Jan, and Jef Verschueren. 1998. *Debating diversity: Analyzing the discourse of tolerance.* London: Routledge.
Böke, Karin, Matthias Jung, Thomas Niehr, and Martin Wengeler. 2000. Vergleichende Diskurslinguistik: Überlegungen zur Analyse national

heterogener Textkorpora. In *Einwanderungsdiskurse: Vergleichende diskurslinguistische Studien,* ed. Thomas Niehr und Karin Böke, 11–36. Wiesbaden: Westdeutscher Verlag.

Böltken, Ferdinand. 2003. Social distance and physical proximity: Day-to-day attitudes and experiences of foreigners and Germans living in the same residential areas. In *Germans or foreigners? Attitudes towards ethnic minorities in post-reunification Germany,* ed. Richard Alba, Peter Schmidt, and Martina Wasmer, 233–54. New York: Palgrave Macmillan.

Borovoy, Alan. 1996. Deportation rules test Canada's sense of fairness. *Toronto Star,* 1 January: A11.

Bosswick, Wolfgang. 2008. Immigration policy in Germany. In *Migration and globalization: Comparing immigration policy in developed countries,* ed. Atsuschi Konda, 107–38. Tokyo: Akashi Shote.

Bourdieu, Pierre. 1977. *Outline of a theory of practice.* Translated by Richard Rice. Cambridge: Cambridge University Press.

– 1984. *Distinction: A social critique of the judgement of taste.* Translated by Richard Rice. Cambridge: Harvard University Press.

– 1988. *Homo academicus.* Stanford, CA: Stanford University Press.

– 1991. *Language and symbolic power.* Edited by John B. Thompson, translated by Gino Raymond and Matthew Adamson. Cambridge, MA: Harvard University Press.

– 1998a. *On television and journalism.* London: Pluto.

– 1998b. *Practical reason: On the theory of action.* Stanford, CA: Stanford University Press.

– 2002. Against the policy of depoliticization. *Studies in Political Economy* 69 (Autumn): 31–41.

Bradimore, Ashley, and Harald Bauder. 2011. Mystery ships and risky boat people: Tamil refugee migration in the newsprint media. *Metropolis BC Working Paper* no. 11–02. http://riim.metropolis.net/assets/uploads/files/wp/2011/WP11-02.pdf.

Braun, Stefan. 2003. Abschied auf leisen Sohlen. *Stuttgarter Zeitung,* 23 October: 2.

Braun, Stefan, and Heinrich Halbig. 2002. Regierung und Opposition nach dem Urteil zur Zuwanderung. *Stuttgarter Zeitung,* Dritte Seite, 19 December: 3.

Brenner, Neil. 2009. What is critical urban theory? *City* 13(2–3): 198–207.

Bröll, Claudia. 2001a. Euphorie und Ernüchterung nach einem Jahr Green Card. *Frankfurter Allgemeine Zeitung,* Wirtschaft, 31 July: 13.

– 2001b. Mittelständler wirbt für 'Green Card' auf indonesisch. *Frankfurter Allgemeine Zeitung,* Wirtschaft, 5 July: 19.

– 2003. Green Card noch ein Jahr länger. *Frankfurter Allgemeine Zeitung,* Wirtschaft, 8 July: 12.

Bronskill, Jim. 1997. Lawyer fears for woman's life. *Ottawa Citizen,* 19 March: A1.

– 1998. Iranian 'assassin' to be deported. *Ottawa Citizen,* 30 April: A5.

– 2001. Alleged terrorist eluded justice. *Ottawa Citizen,* 16 January: A1.

Bronskill, Jim, and Rick Mofina. 2002. Deportee faces drug charges. *Calgary Herald,* 10 January: A13.

Brosius, Hans-Bernd. 1993/4. Verändern Schlüsselereignisse journalistische Selektionskriterien? Framing am Beispiel der Berichterstattung über Anschläge gegen Ausländer und Asylanten. *Rundfunk und Fernsehen* 41: 512–30.

Brubaker, Rogers W. 1992. *Citizenship and nationhood in France and Germany.* Cambridge, MA: Harvard University Press.

– 2004a. *Ethnicity without groups.* Cambridge, MA: Harvard University Press.

– 2004b. In the name of the nation: Reflections on nationalism and patriotism. *Citizenship Studies* 8(2): 115–27.

Bundesamt für Migration und Flüchtlinge. 2005. Teilstatistik: Migration und Asyl. http://www.bamf.de.

– 2008. *Asyl in Zahlen 2008.* Nürnberg.

– 2009. *Ausländerzahlen 2008.* Nürnberg. http://www.bamf.de.

– 2010. *Ausländerzahlen 2009.* Nürnberg. http://www.bamf.de.

Bundesgesetzblatt. 2008. Gesetz zur arbeitsmarktadäquaten Steuerung der Zuwanderung Hochqualifizierter und zur Änderung weiterer aufenthaltsrechtlicher Regelungen (Arbeitsmigrationssteuerungsgesetz). 20 December. Vol. 1, no. 63. Bonn. http://217.160.60.235/BGBL/bgbl1f/bgbl108s2846.pdf.

Bundesministerium des Innern. 2001a. *Schily verbietet islamische Vereinigung 'Kalifatsstaat.'* Press release. http://www.bmi.bund.de/nn_165140/Internet/Content/Nachrichten/Archiv/Pressemitteilungen/2001/12/Schily_verbietet_islamistische_Id_65050_de.html.

– 2001b. *Zuwanderung gestalten – Integration fördern.* Bericht der unabhängigen Kommission 'Zuwanderung.' Berlin: Zeitbild Verlag.

– 2004. *Gesetz zur Steuerung und Begrenzung der Zuwanderung und zur Regelung des Aufenthalts und der Integration von Unionsbürgern und Ausländern (Zuwanderungsgesetz).* http://www.bmi.bund.de.

– 2005. Zuwanderung: Zeitstrahl. www.zuwanderung.de/1_zeitstrahl.html.

Bundesministerium der Justiz. 2004. *Gesetz zur Steuerung und Begrenzung der Zuwanderung und zur Regelung des Aufenthalts und der Integration von Unionsbürgern und Ausländern.* http://217.160.60.235/BGBL/bgbl1f/bgbl104s1950.pdf.

Burke, Anthony. 2002. Aporias of security. *Alternatives* 27: 1–27.

Burke, Kenneth. 1969 [1945]. *A grammar of motives.* Berkeley: University of California Press.

Busse, Dietrich. 1997. Das Eigene und das Fremde: Annotationen zu Funktion und Wirkung einer diskurssemantischen Grundfigur. In *Die Sprache des Migrationsdiskurses: Das Reden über 'Ausländer' in Medien, Politik und Alltag,* ed. Matthias Jung, Martin Wengeler, und Karin Böke, 17–35. Wiesbaden: Westdeutscher Verlag.

Butler, Judith. 1990. *Gender trouble: Feminism and the subversion of identity.* New York: Routledge.

Buzan, Barry, Ole Waever, and Jap de Wilde. 1998. *Security: A framework for analysis.* Boulder, CO: Lynne Rienner Publishers.

Calgary Herald. 2001. Senate ponders new immigration law. 19 September: A5.

Canadian Newspaper Association. 2008. Daily paid newspaper circulation data. http://www.cna-acj.ca/en/aboutnewspapers/circulation.

Canadian Press. 2004. More immigrants needed for workforce: Minister. *Toronto Star,* 29 October. http://www.thestar.ca.

Canning, Kathleen. 2004. Class vs. citizenship: Keywords in German gender history. *Central European History* 37(2): 225–44.

Carstens, Peter. 2004. Fragen an Bundesinnenminister Schily. *Frankfurter Allgemeine Zeitung,* Politik: 4.

Casey, John P. 2009. Open borders: Absurd chimera or inevitable future policy? *International Migration* 48(5): 14–64.

Castells, Manuel. 1975. Immigrant workers and class struggles in advanced capitalism: The western European experience. *Politics and Society* 5(1): 32–66.

Castles, Stephen. 2000. *Ethnicity and globalization: From migrant worker to transnational citizen.* London: Sage.

Castree, Noel. 1996. Birds, mice and geography: Marxism and dialectics. *Transactions of the Institute of British Geographers* ns 21(2): 342–62.

CDU Deutschland. 2001a. *Abschlussbericht der Kommission, Zuwanderung und Integration.* http://www.jum.baden-wuerttemberg.de/servlet/PB/show/1142470/m_ller_kommission_abschlu_bericht_28.4.01_.doc.pdf.

– 2001b. *Zuwanderung steuern und begrenzen: Integration fördern.* Resolution by the CDU of Germany of 7 June 2001, Berlin. http://www.cdu.de/doc/pdfc/070601_zuwanderung_steuern.pdf.

– 2007. *Freiheit und Sicherheit: Grundsätze für Deutschland. (Grundsatzprogramm),* passed at the 21st party convention in Hannover, 3–4 December. http://grundsatzprogramm.cdu.de.

CDU, CSU, and FDP. 2009. *Wachstum – Bildung – Zusammenhalt: Koalitionsvertrag zwischen CDU, CSU und FDP,* 17. Legislaturperiode. http://www.cdu.de/doc/pdfc/091026-koalitionsvertrag-cducsu-fdp.pdf.

Center for Immigration Studies. 2007. About the center for immigration studies. http://www.cis.org/aboutcis.html.

Ceyhan, Ayse, and Anastassia Tsoukala. 2002. The securitization of migration in Western societies: Ambivalent discourses and policies. *Alternatives* 27: 21–39.

Chavez, Leo R. 2008. *The Latino threat: Constructing immigrants, citizens, and the nation.* Stanford: Stanford University Press.

Chomsky, Noam. 2007. Twenty years of propaganda. Lecture delivered at Windsor, Ontario, 17 May.

Chouinard, V. 2006. On the dialectics of differencing: Disabled women, the state and housing issues. *Gender, Place and Culture* 13(4): 401–17.

Chwialkowska, Luiza. 2001a. Ottawa fears labour time bomb, *National Post,* 25 June: A1.

– 2001b. Refugees' case has developed into showdown of ideologies. *National Post,* 21 May: A8.

– 2001c. Terrorist deportation policy can withstand challenge, McLellan says. *National Post,* 3 October: A10.

Cisneros, David J. 2008. Contaminated communities: The metaphor or 'immigrant as pollutant' in media representations of immigration. *Rhetoric and Public Affairs* 11(4): 569–602.

Citizenship and Immigration Canada. 1999. *Building on a strong foundation for the 21st Century: New directions for immigration and refugee policy and legislation.* Ottawa: Ministry of Public Works and Government Services Canada.

– 2002. Fair and equitable response from minister. News release 2002-01. Ottawa. http://www.cic.gc.ca/english/press/02/0201-pre.html.

– 2006. *Facts and figures: Immigration overview 2005.* Ottawa.

– 2007a. *A look at Canada.* Ottawa. http://www.cic.gc.ca/english/look/look-00e.html.

– 2007b. *Facts and figures 2006,* Ottawa. http://www.cic.gc.ca/english/pdf/pub/facts2006.pdf.

– 2008. *Facts and figures: Immigration overview 2007.* Ottawa. http://www.cic.gc.ca/english/resources/statistics/menu-fact.asp.

– 2009a. Applying for permanent residence from within Canada: Humanitarian and compassionate considerations (IMM 5291). http://www.cic.gc.ca/english/information/applications/guides/5291E.asp.

– 2009b. *Facts and figures: Immigration overview 2008.* Ottawa. http://www.cic.gc.ca/english/resources/statistics/facts2008/index.asp.

– 2009c. Resettlement from outside Canada: Convention refugees abroad class. http://www.cic.gc.ca/english/refugees/outside/convention.asp.

– 2010. *Discover Canada: The rights and responsibilities of citizenship,* 2010 edition. http://www.cic.gc.ca/english/pdf/pub/discover.pdf.

Citrin, Jack, and John Sides. 2008. Immigration and the imagined community in Europe and the United States. *Political Studies* 56: 33–56.

Cobb, Chris. 2001a. Palestinian plays system for 15 years: Convicted terrorist remains in Canada legally while case grinds through appeal process. *Ottawa Citizen,* 3 October: A1 (also published in the *Vancouver Sun*).

– 2001b. Terrorist loses another appeal to stay. *Ottawa Citizen,* 3 November: A3.

Coell, Murray. 2004. The welcome mat is out for skilled immigrants. *Vancouver Province,* 10 June. http://www.canada.com/vancouver/theprovince.

Cohen, B.C. 1995. *Democracies and foreign polity: Public participation in the United States and the Netherlands.* Madison: University of Wisconsin Press.

Cohen, Robin. 1987. *The new helots: Migrants in the international division of labour.* Aldershot, UK: Avebury.

Collacott, Martin. 2001a. More workers, not more voters, *National Post,* 2 November: A12.

– 2001b. Political will needed to guard the border. *National Post,* 22 October: A10.

– 2001c. We're not ready for an open-door policy. *National Post,* 7 June: A16.

– 2002. Canada's immigration policy: The need for major reform. *Public Policy Sources* 64. Vancouver: The Fraser Institute.

– 2003. Immigration's flaws. *National Post,* FP (Financial Post), 15 December: 13.

Cook, Daniel. 1984. Hegel, Marx and Wittgenstein. *Philosophy and Social Criticism* 10 (Fall): 49–74.

Couldry, Nick. 2003a. Media meta-capital: Extending the range of Bourdieu's field theory. *Theory and Society* 32: 653–77.

– 2003b. *Media rituals: A critical approach.* London: Routledge.

Coyne, Andrew. 1998. Those hordes at the gates awaiting citizenship are a myth. *Vancouver Sun,* 8 January: A19.

Crespi, Irving. 1997. *The public opinion process: How the people speak.* London: Lawrence Erlbaum Associates Publishers.

Currle, Edda, and Tanja Wunderlich, eds. 2001. *Deutschland – Ein Einwanderungsland? Rückblick, Bilanzen und neue Fragen.* Stuttgart: Lucius & Lucius.

Curry, Bill, and Stewart Bell. 2003. Germany wants Zundel extradited. *National Post,* 21 February: A4.

Dahlstedt, Magnus, and Fredrik Hertzberg. 2007. Democracy the Swedish way? The exclusion of 'immigrants' in Swedish politics. *Scandinavian Political Studies* 30(20): 175–203.

Dauvergne, Catherine. 2005. *Humanitarianism, identity, and nation: Migration laws in Canada and Australia*. Vancouver: UBC Press.

– 2007a. Citizenship with a vengeance. *Theoretical Inquiries in Law* 8(2): 489–506.

– 2007b. Security and migration law in the less brave new world. *Social and Legal Studies* 16(4): 533–49.

– 2008. *Making people illegal: What globalization means for migration and law*. New York: Cambridge University Press.

Day, Richard J. F. 2000. *Multiculturalism and the history of Canadian diversity*. Toronto: University of Toronto Press.

Deckers, D. 2001. Kirchen kritisieren Entwurf des Zuwanderungsgesetzes. *Frankfurter Allgemeine Zeitung*, 9 September: 4.

– 2003. Einwanderungsgesetz ungenügend. Katholische Bischöfe dringen weiter auf umfassende Neuregelung. *Frankfurter Allgemeine Zeitung*, 30 August: 4.

De Haas, Hein. 2005. International migration, remittances and development: Myths and facts. *Third World Quarterly* 26(8): 1269–84.

Dench, Janet. 1997. Refugee policy contradicts itself. *Toronto Star*, 20 January: A13.

Deutsche Presse Agentur. 2004a. Baden-Württembergs Kultusministerin Annette Schavan (CDU) hat eine Pflicht für Imame gefordert in Moscheen in deutscher Sprache zu Predigen. Stuttgart, 14 November.

– 2004b. Kaplans Familie vor Ausweisung? *Frankfurter Allgemeine Zeitung*, 7 June: 4.

Deutscher Bundestag. 2007. Innenausschuss: Einbürgerung / Staatsangehörigkeit – Stellungnahmen der Sachverständigen, 10 December 2007. http://www.bundestag.de/ausschuesse/a04/anhoerungen/Anhoerung10/Stellungnahmen/index.html.

– 2008. Beschlussempfehlung und Bericht des Innenausschusses (4. Ausschuss), Drucksache 16/10914. 12 December. http://dip21.bundestag.de/dip21/btd/16/109/1610914.pdf.

Deutscher Depeschendienst. 2010. Zuwanderung: Schavan eckt in Union an. *Südwest Presse*, 28 July: 2.

DeVoretz, Don J., ed. 1995. *Diminishing returns: The economics of Canada's recent immigration policy*. Toronto and Vancouver: C.D. Howe and the Laurier Institution.

Dietrich, Stefan. 2004. Überbrückbare Gegensätze. *Frankfurter Allgemeine Zeitung*, 25 May: 1

Dillon, C.C. 1999. Compassion has limits when humanitarian laws are abused. *Vancouver Sun,* 3 August: A15.

Dimmock, Gary. 2001. The secret life of Mahmoud Jaballah. *Ottawa Citizen,* 27 September: A1.

DISS-Journal: Zeitung des Duisburger Instituts für Sprach- und Sozialforschung. 2010. Vol. 20. http://www.diss-duisburg.de/DISS-Journale.htm.

Downing, John, and Charles Husband. 2005. *Representing race: Racism, ethnicities and media.* London: Sage.

Drobinski, M. 2004a. Faire Chancen zur Integration: Bischof Huber fordert großzügige Zuwanderungsregelung. *Süddeutsche Zeitung,* 12 March: 12.

– 2004b. Keinen in den Tod schicken. Kirchen: Anti-Terror-Kampf nicht mit dem Zuwanderungsrecht. *Süddeutsche Zeitung,* 30 April: 8.

Duffy, Andrew. 1999. Immigration targets unrealistic, lawyers say. *National Post,* 28 September: A11.

– 2000a. New law subjects refugees to immediate criminal checks. *Ottawa Citizen,* 6 April: A 3 (also published in *Calgary Herald* and *National Post*).

– 2000b. UN envoy urges Canada to remain open to refugees. *Vancouver Sun,* 2 February: A6.

– 2004. The fight for the soul of Canada's justice system. *Ottawa Citizen,* 12 January: A1.

Durchdenwald, Thomas. 2001. Zuwanderungsdebatte stört das Klima in der Koalition. *Stuttgarter Zeitung,* 22 December: no page.

– 2002. Goll gibt Teufels Klage keine Chance. *Stuttgarter Zeitung,* 6 July: no page.

Earle, Bo. 2002. Hegel, Wittgenstein, and the dialectic of philosophy and anthropology. *Idealistic Studies* 32(2): 101–19.

Eddy, Melissa. 2010. Multiculturalism in Germany 'utterly failed,' Merkel says. *Globe and Mail,* 17 October: n.p. http://theglobeandmail.com.

El Refaie, Elisabeth. 2001. Metaphors we discriminate by: Naturalized themes in Austrian newspaper articles about asylum seekers. *Journal of Sociolinguistics* 5(3): 352–71.

Esses, Victoria M., John F. Dovidio, Lynne M. Jackson, and Tamara L. Armstrong. 2001. The immigration dilemma: The role of perceived group competition, ethnic prejudice, and national identity. *Journal of Social Issues* 57(3): 389–412.

Euler, Ralf, and Helmut Schwan. 2002. Zuwanderung besser steuern. Interview mit Minister Bouffier zur Ausländerpolitik. *Frankfurter Allgemeine Zeitung,* Rhein-Main Titelseite, 27 January: R1.

EUMC (European Montoring Centre on Racism and Xenophobia). 2005. *Majorities' attitudes towards minorities: Key findings from the Eurobarometer and the European social survey.* Vienna: Manz Crossmedia.

Ewing, Katherine Pratt. 2008. *Stolen honor: Stigmatizing Muslim men in Berlin.* Stanford, CA: Stanford University Press.

Fairclough, Norman. 1992a. *Discourse and social change.* Cambridge: Polity Press.

– 1992b. Discourse and text: Linguisitc and intertextual analysis within discourse analysis. *Discourse and Society* 3(2): 193–217.

– 2000. Language and neoliberalism. *Discourse and Society* 11(2): 147–8.

Fairclough, Norman, and Ruth Wodak. 1997. Critical discourse analysis. In *Discourse as social interaction – discourse studies: A multidisciplinary introduction,* ed. Tuen A. van Dijk, vol. 2: 258–84. London: Sage.

Faist, Thomas. 2002. 'Extension du domaine de la lutte': International migration and security before and after September 11, 2001. *International Migration Review* 36(1): 7–14.

Family Service Association of Toronto. 2003. Factsheet on Bill-18: The Citizenship of Canada Act. http://www.fsatoronto.com/programs/social/BillC18Feb03.pdf#search=%22Bill%20C-18%22.

Färber, Christine, Nurcan Arslan, Manfred Köhner, and Renée Parlar. 2008. *Migration, Geschlecht und Arbeit: Probleme und Potenziale von Migrantinnen auf dem Arbeitsmarkt.* Opladen: Budich UniPress.

Fertig, Michael. 2004. *Die gesellschaftliche Akzeptanz von Zuwanderern in Deutschland.* Nuremberg: Bundesamt für Migration und Flüchtlinge.

Feuerbach, Ludwig. 1986 [1841]. *Das Wesen des Christentums.* Ditzingen: Reclam.

Fife, Robert. 1999. Airlift of refugees causing a rift in NATO alliance. *National Post,* 7 April: A12.

– 2001. Liberals spar over changes to Immigration Act. *National Post,* 19 March: A7.

Finney, Nissa, and Vaughan Robinson. 2008. Local press, dispersal and community in the construction of asylum debates. *Social and Cultural Geography* 9(4): 397–413.

Fleury, Jean-Guy. 2004. Impacts of the events of September 11, 2001 on the IRB. Paper presented at the Council of Canadian Administrative Tribunals 3rd International Conference: Bringing Administrative Justice to the People of the World, 20–23 June, Toronto. http://www.irb–cisr.gc.ca/en/media/speeches/2004/ccat_e.htm.

Florida, Richard. 2002. *The rise of the creative class: And how it's transforming work, leisure, community and everyday life.* New York: Basic Books.

Focus Migration. 2008. Zuwanderung ausländischer Fachkräfte erleichtert. *Newsletter* 7/08. http://www.migration-info.de/migration_und_bevoelkerung/archiv/ausgaben/ausgabe0807.pdf.

Fong, Petti. 2002. Accused Chinese smuggler ordered out. *Vancouver Sun*, 22 June: A4.

Foroutan, Naika, Korinna Schäfer, Coskun Canan, and Benjamine Schwarze. 2010. Sarrazins Thesen auf dem Prüfstand: Ein empirischer Gegenentwurf zu Thilo Sarrazins Thesen zu Muslimen in Deutschland. Berlin. http://www.heymat.hu-berlin.de/sarrazin2010.

Foster, Cecil. 2007. *Blackness and modernity: The colour of humanity and the quest for freedom*. Montreal and Kingston: McGill-Queen's University Press.

Foucault, Michel. 1970. *The order of things: An archaeology of the human sciences*. New York, Pantheon.

– 1972. *Archaeology of knowledge*. Ed. A.M. Sheridan Smith. New York: Harper Colophon Books.

– 1977. *Discipline and punish*. New York: Pantheon.

– 1984. The order of discourse. In *Language and politics*, ed. Ian McLeod and Michael J. Shapiro, 108–37. Oxford: Basil Blackwell.

Fox News Channel. 2009. Fox News: Fair & Balanced. http://www.foxnews.com.

Francis, Diane. 1999. Refugee system needs total overhaul: Criminals allowed in at expense of real victims. *National Post*, 22 April: C3.

– 2002. A $150-million-a-year deadbeat dilemma. *National Post*, FP (Financial Post), 12 October: 3.

– 2003. Dangerous strangers in our midst. *National Post*, 6 December: C3.

Frankfurter Allgemeine Zeitung. 2002a. Die Länder sollen ihre Steuern selbst bestimmen. 17 February: 37.

– 2002b. Das wäre ein verheerender Fehler. *Politik*, 18 January: 2.

Freeman, Gary P. 1995. Modes of immigration politics in liberal demographic states. *International Migration Review* 29(4): 881–902.

Frenzel, Leif. 1999/2000. Weltbegriff und Widerspruch: Zu einer sprachanalytisch-logischen Strömung des 20. Jahrhunderts. Presentation to Research-Colloquium of Prof. Dr Wolfgang Welsch, Institut für Philosophie. Jena: Friedrich-Schiller-Universität. http://www.leiffrenzel.de/papers/inkons.html.

Frosh, Paul, and Gadi Wolfsfeld. 2006. ImagiNation: News discourse, nationhood and civil society. *Media, Culture & Society* 29(1): 105–29.

Fulbrook, Mary. 1996. Germany for the Germans? Citizenship and nationality in a divided nation. In *Citizenship, Nationality and Migration in Europe*, ed. David Cesarani and Mary Fulbook, 88–105. London: Routledge.

Gans, Herbert J. 1990. Deconstructing the underclass: The term's dangers as a planning concept. *Journal of the American Planning Association* 56(3): 271–7.

Gaus, Bettina, and Ulrike Herrmann. 2002. Stimmungssieg für Schröder. *Die Tageszeitung*, Inland, 28 February: 10.

Gauweiler, Peter. 2002. Wählen heißt auswählen. *Bild Zeitung,* 4 March: 2.

Gee, James Paul. 2003. *An introduction to discourse analysis: Theory and method.* 4th edition. London: Routledge.

Geißler, Rainer. 2003. *Multikulturalismus in Kanda – Model für Deutschland? Aus Politik und Zeitgeschichte* 26(23 June): 19–25.

Gellner, Ernest. 1983. *Nations and nationalism.* Ithaca, NY: Cornell University Press.

Gerdes, Jürgen, and Thomas Faist. 2006. Von ethnischer zu republikanischer Intergration: Der Diskurs um die Reform des deutschen Staatsangehörigkeitsrechts. *Berliner Journal für Soziologie* 16(3): 313–35.

Gillespie, Kerry. 2001. Security-risk testimony turns cryptic. *Toronto Star,* 19 December: 18.

Gillis, Charlie. 1999. Police jail 13 more migrants as possible organizers and security threats. *National Post,* 6 September: A5.

Gitlin, Todd. 1980. *The whole world is watching: Mass media in the making and unmaking of the new left.* Berkeley: University of California Press.

Go, Avvy. 2004. Refugee system lacks compassion. *Toronto Star,* 20 July: A18.

Goddar, Jeannette. 2001. Klassenziel: Einbürgerung. *Süddeutsche Zeitung,* 24 November: V1, V7.

– 2002. Beckstein bleibt sich treu. *Tageszeitung,* 17 September: 3.

Goffman, Erving. 1974. *Frame analysis: An essay on the organization of experience.* Cambridge, MA: Harvard University Press.

Göl, Ayla. 2005. Imagining the Turkish nation through 'othering' Armenians. *Nations and Nationalism* 11(1): 121–39.

Government of Canada. 2003. Bill C-42: The Public Safety Act. http://dsp-psd.communication.gc.ca/Pilot/LoPBdP/LS/371/371c42-e.htm.

Grass, Günter, and Pierre Bourdieu. 2002. Dialogue: The 'progressive' restoration. *New Left Review* 14: 76–7.

Grassmann, Philip. 2003a. Drei Türen in der Deutschen Festung. *Süddeutsche Zeitung,* 12 December: 10.

– 2003b. Union stimmt gegen Zuwanderungsgesetz. *Süddeutsche Zeitung,* 10 May: 5.

Grassmann, Philip, and Susanne Höll. 2002. Abstimmung im Bundesrat Votum Brandenburgs entscheidet über Zuwanderungsgesetz. *Süddeutsche Zeitung,* 22 March: 1.

Green, Alan G., and David A. Green. 1999. The economic goals of Canada's immigration policy: Past and present. *Canadian Public Policy* 25(4): 425–51.

Gustin, Delancey, and Astrid Ziebarth. 2010. Transatlantic opinion on immigration: Greater worries and outlier optimism. *International Migration Review* 44(4): 974–91.

Habermas, Jürgen. 1979. Einleitung. In *Stichworte zur geistigen Situation der Zeit,* ed. Jürgen Habermas, 7–35. Frankfurt: Suhrkamp.

– 1981. *Theorie des kommunikativen Handelns.* Volumes 1 and 2. Frankfurt am Main: Surkamp.

Hage, Ghassan. 1998. *White nation: Fantasies of white supremacy in a multicultural society.* Annandale, NSW: Pluto Press Australia.

Hall, Stuart. 1980. Encoding/decoding. In *Culture, media, language,* ed. Stuart Hall, Dorothy Hobson, Andrew Lowe, and Paul Willis, 128–38. London: Routledge.

– 1996 [1989]. New ethnicities. In *Stuart Hall: Critical dialogues in cultural studies,* ed. David Morley and Kuan-Hsing Chen, 441–9. London: Routledge.

Hallin, Daniel C. 1996. Commercialism and professionalism in the American news media. In *Mass Media and Society,* 2nd ed., ed. James Curran and Michael Gurevitch, 243–62. London: Arnold.

Haraway, Donna. 1991. *Simians, cyborgs and women: The reinvention of nature.* New York: Routledge.

Hardcastle, Leonie, Andrew Parkin, Alan Simmons, and Nobuaki Suyama. 1994. The making of immigration and refugee policy: Politicians, bureaucrats and citizens. In *Immigration and refugee policy: Australia and Canada compared,* ed. Howard Adelman, 95–124. Melbourne: Melbourne University Press.

Hardwick, Susan W., Rebecca Marcus, and Marissa Isaak. 2010. Education and national identity in a comparative context. *National Identities* 12(3): 253–68.

Harles, John. 1998. Multiculturalism, national identity, and national integration: The Canadian case. *International Journal of Canadian Studies* 17: 217–48.

Harper, Stephen. 2006. Stephen Harper recognizes Québécois nation. http://www.youtube.com/watch?v=hwf44j6sWws&feature=related.

Harvey, Bob. 1997. Church leaders demand better treatment for refugees. *Ottawa Citizen,* 4 April: A4.

Harvey, David. 1972. Revolutionary and counterrevolutionary theory in geography and the problem of ghetto formation. *Antipode* 4(2): 1–13.

– 1973. *Social justice and the city.* Baltimore, MD: Johns Hopkins University Press.

– 2011. Roepke Lecture in Economic Geography: Crises, geographic disruptions and the uneven development of political responses. *Economic Geography* 87(1): 1–22.

Hastings, Adrian. 1997. *The construction of nationhood.* Cambridge: Cambridge University Press.

Heckmann, Friedrich. 1981. *Die Bundesrepublik: Ein Einwanderungsland? Zur Soziologie der Gastarbeiterbevölkerung als Einwanderungsminorität.* Stuttgart: Klett-Cotta.

– 1992. *Ethnische Minderheiten, Volk und Nation: Soziologie inter-ethnischer Beziehungen.* Stuttgart: Ferdinand Enke Verlag.

Hegel, Georg W.F. 1961 [1837]. *Vorlesungen über die Philosophie der Geschichte.* Stuttgart: Reclam.

– 1970 [1820]. *Grundlinien der Philosophie des Rechts oder Naturrecht und Staatswissenschaft im Grundrisse.* Stuttgart: Reclam.

– 2002 [1832–45]. *Vorlesungen über die Philosophie der Geschichte.* Stuttgart: Reclam.

– 2005 [1807]. *Phänomenologie des Geistes.* Paderborn: Voltmedia.

Hell, Matthias. 2005. *Einwanderungsland Deutschland? Die Zuwanderungsdiskussion 1998–2002.* Wiesbaden: VS Verlag für Sozialwissenschaften.

Henkel, H.-O. 2003. Die Steuerung der Zuwanderung durch ein Zuwanderungsgesetz aus bevölkerungs- und wirtschaftspolitischer Sicht. *Zeitschrift für Ausländerrecht und Ausländerpolitik* 2003/4: 124–6.

Henry, Frances, and Carol Tator. 2002. *Discourses of domination: Racial bias in the Canadian English-language press.* Toronto: University of Toronto Press.

Heptner, Bernd. 2002. Koch sieht sich im lauten Protest bestätigt. *Frankfurter Allgemeine Zeitung,* Rhein-Main/Hessen, 19 December: 56.

Herbert, Ulrich. 2001. *Geschichte der Ausländerpolitik in Deutschland: Saisonarbeiter, Zwangsarbeiter, Gastarbeiter, Flüchtlinge.* Munich: C.H. Beck

Herder, Johann Gottfried. 1966 [1772]. *Abhandlung über den Ursprung der Sprache.* Stuttgart: Reclam.

Herman, Edward S., and Noam Chomsky. 2000. *Manufacturing consent: The political economy of the mass media.* Updated edition. New York: Pantheon Books.

Herod, Andrew. 2000. Workers and workplaces in a neoliberal global economy. *Environment and Planning A* 32: 1781–90.

Hesmondhalgh, David. 2006. Bourdieu, the media and cultural production. *Media, Culture & Society* 28(2): 211–31.

Hewitt, Christopher. 1992. Public's perspective. In *Terrorism and the Media,* ed. David L. Paletz and Alex P. Schmid, 170–207. London: Sage.

Hier, Sean P., and Joshua L. Greenberg. 2002. Constructing a discursive crisis: Risk problematization and illegal Chinese in Canada. *Ethnic and Racial Studies* 25(3): 490–513.

Hinrichs, Wilhelm. 2003. *Ausländische Bevölkerungsgruppen in Deutschland: Integrationschancen 1985 und 2000.* Berlin: Wissenschaftszentrum Berlin für Sozialforschung.

Hobsbawn, Eric J. 1989. *Nations and nationalism.* London: Cambridge University Press.

Hoffmann, Lutz. 2002. Zuwanderung und kollektive Identität. In *Was schulden wir Flüchtlingen und Migranten? Grundlagen einer gerechten Zuwanderungspolitik,* ed. Alfredo Märker and Stephan Schlothfeldt, 215–35. Wiesbaden: Westdeutscher Verlag.

Höfle, Nicole. 2004. Das sind keine eindeutigen Signale. *Stuttgarter Zeitung,* Lokales, 18 June: 23.

Honig, Bonnie. 2001. *Democracy and the foreigner.* Princeton, NJ: Princeton University Press.

Horkheimer, Max, and Theodor W. Adorno. 2004 [1947]. *Dialektik der Aufklärung: Philosophische Fragmente.* 15th edition. Frankfurt am Main: Fischer Verlag.

Hume, Stephen. 1997. A region forged by immigrants' diversity. *Vancouver Sun,* 1 November: A1.

Husemann, Ralf. 2001. Kampfansage: Die Grünen-Chefin Claudia Roth zum Zuwanderungsgesetz. *Süddeutsche Zeitung,* Themen aus Deutschland, 13 December: 11.

Hutchinson, Brian. 2002. Canadian deportees dumped in war zone. *National Post,* 9 March: A1.

Immigration Legislative Review Advisory Group. 1997. *Not just numbers: A Canadian framework for future immigration.* Ottawa: Ministry of Public Works and Government Services Canada.

Inacker, Michael. 2002. Union will zuspitzen. *Frankfurter Allgemeine Zeitung,* 15 September: 1.

International Migration Review. 2002. Reflections on international migration after 9/11: Perspectives from around the world. 36(1): 5–6.

Institut für Demoskopie Allensbach. 2002. Das Zuwanderungsgesetz: Der Bundespräsident hat ein Gesetz unterschrieben, an dessen Qualität die Mehrheit zweifelt. *Allensbacher Berichte,* no. 11. Allensbach am Bodensee.

Jacobi, Robert. 2003. Grün ist die Hoffnung. *Süddeutsche Zeitung.* Nachrichten, 7 July: 1.

Jäger, Siegfried. 2004. *Kritische Diskursanalyse.* Duisburg: Diss Verlag.

Jasper, Ulla. 2004. Humanität und Qualität. *Die Tageszeitung,* 30 December: 2.

Jimenéz, Marina. 1999a. Children's fate key in deportation cases. *National Post,* 10 July: A8.

– 1999b. Terrorist ordered deported after 12-year legal process. *National Post,* 27 April: A1.

– 2000a. Journey of desperation. *National Post,* 30 March: B1.

– 2000b. Ottawa plans much looser refugee policy. *National Post,* 11 March: A1.

– 2006. Women's rights trump cultural habits, poll finds. *Globe and Mail,* 14 November: A5.

Jiwani, Yasmin. 2005. 'War talk' engendering terror: Race, gender and representation in Canadian print media. *International Journal of Media and Cultural Politics* 1(1): 15–21.

Joppke, Christian. 1998. Immigration challenges the nation state. In *Challenge to the nation-state: Immigration in Western Europe and the United States*, ed. Christian Joppke, 5–46. New York: Oxford University Press.

– 2005. *Selecting by origin: Ethnic migration in the liberal state*. Cambridge, MA: Harvard University Press.

Jox, Markus, and Eva Weikert. 2004. Hutschnur auf dem Holzweg gerissen. *Die Tageszeitung*, Nord Aktuell, 4 May: 24.

Joyce, Greg. 2001. Couple permitted to live at home under strict security. *Vancouver Sun*, 3 February: B1.

Jung, Matthias, Martin Wengeler, and Karin Böke, eds. 1997. *Die Sprache des Migrationsdiskurses: Das Reden über 'Ausländer' in Medien, Politik und Alltag*. Wiesbaden: Westdeutscher Verlag.

Kahlcke, Jan. 2001. Rein oder nicht rein. *Die Tageszeitung*, Bremen Aktuell, 15 November: 22.

Karaokcu, Gurel. 1999. Turkish-Canadians should be able to rescue relatives. *Ottawa Citizen*, 25 September: B5.

Karatani, Rieko. 2005. How history separated refugee and migration regimes: In search of their institutional origins. *International Journal of Refugee Law* 17(3): 517–41.

Kari, Shannon. 2002. Alleged extremist in legal limbo. *Ottawa Citizen*, 23 August: A1.

Kastner, Susan. 1997. Strangers in a strange land. *Toronto Star*, 31 May: L1.

Kelley, Ninette, and Michael J. Trebilcock. 1998. *The making of the mosaic: A history of Canadian immigration policy*. Toronto: University of Toronto Press.

Kermani, Navid. 2008. Der fundamentale Irrtum. *Der Spiegel, Spiegel Special* 2: *Allah im Abendland*, 14–21.

Klammer, B. 2005. *Empirische Sozialforschung*. Konstanz: UVK Verlag.

Kloosterman, Robert, and Jan Rath, eds. 2003. *Immigrant entrepreneurs: Venturing abroad in the age of globalization*. Oxford: Berg.

Klusmeyer, Douglas B., and Demetrios G. Papademetriou. 2009. *Immigration policy in the Federal Republic of Germany: Negotiating membership and remaking the nation*. New York: Berghahn Books.

Knischewski, Gerd. 1996. Post-war national identity in Germany. In *Nation and identity in contemporary Europe*, ed. Brian Jenkigs and Spiros A. Sofos, 125–51. London: Routledge.

Knowles, Valerie. 1997. *Strangers at our gates: Canadian immigration and immigration policy, 1540–1997*. Toronto: Dundurn Press.

– 2000. Forging our legacy. Ottawa: Public Works and Government Services Canada. http://www.cic.gc.ca/english/department/legacy/.

Kobayashi, Audrey, and Linda Peake. 1994. Unnatural discourse: Race and gender in geography. *Gender, Place and Culture* 1(2): 225–43.

Köcher, Renate. 2000. Von Luftballons und Schicksalsfragen: Der Bevölkerung fehlt das Vertrauen in die politische Gestaltung der Zuwanderung. *Frankfurter Allgemeine Zeitung*, 19 April: 5.

Kolb, Holger. 2005. The German 'Green Card.' *Focus Migration*, Policy brief no. 3. http://www.focus-migration.de.

Koopmans, R. 1999. Germany and its immigrants: An ambivalent relationship. *Journal of Ethnic and Migration Studies* 25(4): 627–47.

Korteweg, Anna, and Gökçe Yurdakul. 2008. Islam, gender, and immigrant integration: Boundary drawing in discourses on honour killing in the Netherlands and Germany. *Ethnic and Racial Studies* 31(2): 218–38.

Krause, Christina C. 2004. *Neue Zuwanderungspolitik? Entwicklung in der 14. Legsilaturperiode in Deutschland.* PhD dissertation. Christian-Albrechts-Universität zu Kiel.

Krikorian, Mark. 2004. *Keeping terror out: Immigration policy and asymmetric warfare.* Washington, DC: Center for Immigration Studies. http://www.cis.org/articles/2004/mskoped050104.html.

Kritz, Mary M. 2002. Time for a national discussion on immigration. *International Migration Review* 36(1): 33–6.

Lacan, Jacques. 1982 [1949]. The mirror stage as formative of the function of the I as revealed in psychoanalytic experience. In *Écrits: A Selection*, ed. Jacques Lacan, 1–7. New York: W.W. Norton & Co.

Lachenmann, Akiko. 2003. Green Card in der Region beliebt. *Stuttgarter Zeitung*, Aus den Nachbarkreisen, 10 March: 25.

Laclau, Ernesto, and Chantal Mouffe. 1985. *Hegemony and socialist strategy: Towards a radical democratic politics*, ed. Winston Moore and Paul Cammack. London: Verso.

Landy, Keith M. 2001. Scale up the war against terrorism. *National Post*, 12 July: A19.

Lang, S., and L. Wallraff. 2003. Das ist einfach Quatsch: Pro-Asyl-Geschäftsführer Günter Burkhardt wirft den Grünen vor, zu viele Kompromisse zu machen. Volker Beck wehrt sich. *Die Tageszeitung*, 3 September: 3.

Lee, Jeff. 1999. Ship dumps migrants on remote B.C. island. *Vancouver Sun*, 12 August: A1.

Lee, Jeff, and Craig McInnes. 2000. B.C. ignores agreement to import overseas nurses. *Vancouver Sun*, 22 November: A1.

Lefebvre, Henry. 2001. Comment on a new state form. *Antipode* 35(5): 769–82.

Leithäuser, Johannes. 2001a. FDP lobt Schilys Gesetzentwurf. *Frankfurter Allgemeine Zeitung,* Politik, 8 August: 2.

– 2001b. Der zweifache Machtkampf um die Einwanderung. *Frankfurter Allgemeine Zeitung,* 28 November: 3.

Leitner, Helga. 2003. The political economy of international labor migration. In *A companion to economic geography,* ed. Eric Sheppard and Trevor J. Barnes, 450–67. Malden, MA: Blackwell.

Leon, Leonard. 1998. Pirate guides undercutting local tourism. *Ottawa Citizen,* 4 April: B5.

Lewis, Oscar. 1966. The culture of poverty. *Scientific American* 125(4): 19–25.

Ley, David. 2003. Seeking homo economicus: The Canadian state and the strange story of the business immigration program. *Annals of the Association of American Geographers* 93(2): 426–41.

Li, Peter S. 2001. The racial subtext in Canada's immigration discourse. *Journal of International Migration and Integration* 2(1): 77–97.

– 2003. *Destination Canada: Immigration debates and issues.* Don Mills, ON: Oxford University Press.

Libfeld, Sheldon. 2002. We need more Michaels from Malta. *Toronto Star,* 23 February: M19.

Liston, Mary, and Joseph Carens. 2008. Immigration and integration in Canada. In *Migration and globalization: Comparing immigration policy in developed countries,* ed. Atsuschi Konda, 207–27. Tokyo: Akashi Shote.

Lower, Carol. 2001. Searching for a home. *Toronto Star,* 28 October: A6.

Luccasen, Leo. 1998. The Great War and the origins of migration control in Western Europe and the United States (1880–1920). In *A regulation of migration,* ed. Anita Böcker, Kees Groenendijk, Tetty Havinga, and Paul Minderhoud, 45–72. Amsterdam: International Experiences.

Lynch, John. 2008. Geography, genealogy and genetics: Dialectical substance in newspaper coverage of research on race and genetics. *Western Journal of Communication* 72(3): 259–79.

MacCharles, Tonda. 2002. Terror suspects to learn fate today. *Toronto Star,* 11 January: 7.

Mahtani, Minelle. 2001. Representing minorities: Canadian media and minority identities. *Canadian Ethnic Studies* 33(3): 99–133.

Mahtani, Minelle, and Alison Mountz. 2002. Immigration to British Columbia: Media representations and public opinion. *Research on Immigration and Integration in the Metropolis Working Paper Series,* no. 02-15.

Maier-Albang, Monika, and Doris Näger. 2001. München braucht Tausende Ausländer. *Süddeutsche Zeitung,* Munich, 18 August: 49.

Mandel-Campbell, Andrea. 2002. New laws leave best shut out. *National Post*, FP (Financial Post), 24 June: 1.
Marchetti, Dominique. 2005. Subfields of specialized journalism. In *Bourdieu and the journalistic field*, ed. Rodney Benson and Erik Neveu, 64–82. Cambridge, UK: Polity.
Marcuse, Herbert. 1964. *One-dimensional man: Studies in the ideology of advanced industrial society*. Boston: Beacon Press.
Marlière, Philippe. 1998. The rules of the journalistic field: Pierre Bourdieu's contribution to the sociology of the media. *European Journal of Communication* 13(2): 219–34.
Marshall, Andy. 1999a. Calgary family fears mom may be deported. 19 February: B8.
– 1999b. Justice system too lax on immigrants. *Calgary Herald*, 22 March: A1.
Martin, Lawrence. 1999. But not because of the Centennial. *Ottawa Citizen*, 27 April: A13.
Martinez, Francisco. 1999. Canada is a human rights violator. 5 April: A14.
Marx, Karl. 1964 [1845]. Thesen über Feuerbach. In *Marx-Engels Werke*, vol. 3. Berlin: Dietz Verlag. www.mlwerke.de.
– 2001 [1867]. *Das Kapital: Kritik der politischen Ökonomie. Erstes Buch, der Produktionsprozeß des Kapitals*. In *Marx-Engels Werke*, vol. 23, 20th edition. Berlin: Karl Dietz Verlag.
Marx, Karl, and Friedrich Engels. 1953. *Die deutsche Ideologie*. Berlin: Dietz Verlag.
McGowan, William. 2003. *Postscript 9/11: Media coverage of terrorism and immigration*. Backgrounder, April. Washington: Center for Immigration Studies.
Meier-Braun, Karl-Heinz. 2002. *Deutschland, Einwanderungsland*. Surkamp: Frankfurt am Main.
Merrill, John C. 1989. *The dialectic in journalism: Towards a responsible use of press freedom*. Baton Rouge: Louisiana State University Press.
Mertl, Steve. 1996. Abuse of deportation laws feared: Canadian lawyers warn of arbitrary, secretive process. *Calgary Herald*, 28 August: A 9.
Migration und Bevölkerung. 2006. Deutschland: 15 Mio. Einwohner mit 'Migrationshintergrund.' Issue 5. http://www.migration-info.de.
Mitchell, Don. 1995. There is no such thing as culture: Towards a reconceptualization of the idea of culture in geography. *Transactions of the Institute of British Geographers* 20: 102–6.
– 1996. *Lie of the land: Migrant workers in the Californian landscape*. Minneapolis: University of Minnesota Press.
Mofina, Rick. 1996. Woman's ordeal over. *Calgary Herald*, 15 September: A2.
– 1998. Six years of torment in the pursuit of justice. *Calgary Herald*, 4 April: A6.

– 2001. Caplan admits concerns about immigration bill. *Vancouver Sun,* 9 May: 4.

Mommsen, Wolfgang J. 1990. Die Idee der deutschen Nation in Geschichte und Gegenwart. *Gewerkschaftliche Monatshefte* 5(6): 263–73.

Morris, Lydia. 2002. *Managing migration: Civic stratification and immigrants' rights.* London: Routledge.

Müller, Martin. 2008. Reconsidering the concept of discourse for the field of critical geopolitics: Towards discourse as language *and* practice. *Political Geography* 27: 322–38.

Müller, Peter. 2005. Das Zuwanderungsgesetz – Instrumentarium für eine effektive Steuerung und Begrenzung von Migration. *Zeitschrift für Staats- und Europawissenschaften* 3(2): 245–57.

Münz, Rainer, Wolfgang Seifert, and Ralf E. Ulrich. 1999. *Zuwanderung nach Deutschland: Strukturen, Wirkungen, Perspektiven.* 2nd ed. Frankfurt am Main: Campus Verlag.

Münz, Rainer, and Kristof Tamas. 2006. *Labour migrants unbound? EU enlargement, transitional measures and labour market effects.* Stockholm: Institute for Future Studies.

Münz, Rainer, and Ralf E. Ulrich. 1998. Zuwanderung und Staatsbürgerschaft: Was will die Mehrheit der Deutschen? *Migration und Bevölkerung* 7(98) (September): 1–2.

– 2000. Migration und zukünftige Bevölkerungsentwicklung in Deutschland. In *Migrationsreport 2000: Fakten-Analysen-Perspektiven,* ed. Klaus Bade and Rainer Münz, 23–57. Bonn: Bundeszentrale für politische Bildung.

Nathans, Eli. 2004. *The politics of citizenship in Germany: Ethnicity, utility and nationalism.* Oxford: Berg.

National Post. 1998. Immigrant admitted he was trained to kill. 8 July: A5.

– 2000a. Human cargo. 3 April: A17.

– 2000b. $5M might work where Canada failed. 7 April: A19.

– 2001. Rewriting our social contract. 26 November: A13.

Naumetz, Tim. 2001. 'All kinds' here illegally, Ottawa says. *Vancouver Sun,* 29 September: A9.

Nevins, Joseph. 2002. *Operation Gatekeeper: The rise of the 'illegal alien' and the making of the U.S.-Mexico boundary.* New York: Routledge.

Nicol, Heather. 2005. Resiliency or change? The contemporary Canada-US border. *Geopolitics* 10(4): 767–90.

Niehr, Thomas, and Karin Böke, eds. 2000. *Einwanderungsdiskurse: Vergleichende diskurslinguistische Studien.* Wiesbaden: Westdeutscher Verlag.

Nossek, Hillel, and Dan Berkowitz. 2006. Telling 'our' story through news of terrorism: Mythical newswork as journalistic practice in crisis. *Journalism Studies* 7(5): 691–707.

Nowak, Peter. 2004. Vorteil: Stammtisch – Der Fall Kaplan als Spielball konservativer Medien und Politiker. *Die Tageszeitung*, Medien, 3 June: 19.

Nyers, Peter. 2003. Abject cosmopolitanism: The politics of protection in the anti-deportation movement. *Third World Quarterly* 24(6): 1069–93.

Oates, Sarah. 2006. Comparing the politics of fear: The role of terrorism news in election campaigns in Russia, the United States and Britain. *International Relations* 20(4): 425–37.

Oberndörfer, Dieter. 1992. *Der Wahn des Nationalen: Die Alternative der offenen Republik.* Freiburg: Herder Verlag.

– 2007. Zuwanderung nach Deutschland – eine Bilanz. *Politische Essays zu Migration und Integration* 2/2007. Rat für Migration. www.rat-fuer-migration.de.

Oboler, Suzanne. 1995. *Ethnic labels, Latino lives: Identity and the politics of (re)presentation in the United States.* Minneapolis: University of Minnesota Press.

O'Connor, Elaine. 2002. The security certificate in action. *Ottawa Citizen*, 22 December: A4.

Oestreich, H. 2001. Wenn Otto Schily zweimal klingelt. *Die Tageszeitung*, 6 November: 3.

Office of the Auditor General of Canada. 1997. Citizenship and Immigration Canada and Immigration and Refugee Board. *News release*, 2 December. http://www.oag-bvg.gc.ca.

– 2000. *Citizenship and Immigration Canada – The economic component of the Canadian immigration program.* http://www.oag-bvg.gc.ca/internet/English/mr_20030527_e_15311.html.

Olmedo, Carlos, and Dennis L. Soden. 2005. Terrorism's role in re-shaping border crossings: 11 September and the US border. *Geopolitics* 10(4): 741–66.

Oltmer, Jochen. 2005. *Migration und Politik in der Weimarer Republik.* Göttingen: Vanderhoek & Ruprecht.

O'Reilly, Finbarr. 2000a. Chinese migrant children spared deportation. *National Post*, 21 December: A4.

– 2000b. Technicality saves drug dealer from deportation: Danger to public. *National Post*, 28 November: A6.

Ottawa Citizen. 2001. Immigrant, refugee screening 'a shocking, scandalous mess.' 30 October: A1.

Ouston, Richard, and Marina Jimenéz. 1998. Latinos still haunted by ghosts of war. *Vancouver Sun*, 23 February: A1.

Ouston, Rick. 1998. The life of a gangster. *Vancouver Sun*, 18 July: A1.

Park, Byong-Chul. 1998. Wittgenstein's use of the word 'Aspekt.' *Synthese* 115(1): 131–40.

Pellerin, Helene. 1999. Regionalisation of migration policies and its limits: Europe and North America compared. *Third World Quarterly* 20(5): 995–1011.

Piore, Michael J. 1979. *Birds of passage: Migrant labor and industrial societies.* Cambridge: Cambridge University Press.

Pohl, E. [no year]. *Beschneidung bei Frauen ist schwere Körperverletzung.* Ausländerbeauftragte von Berlin: Pamphlet.

Pratt, Geraldine. 2004. *Working feminism.* Edinburgh: Edinburgh University Press.

Prantl, Heribert. 2001a. Das erste Gesetz frißt das zweite. *Süddeutsche Zeitung,* 7 November: 4.

– 2001b. Geänderte Vorzeichen: Wie Schily bei der Zuwanderung die Union gewinnen will. *Süddeutsche Zeitung,* Nachrichten, 10 December: 1.

– 2001c. Otto Schilys Denkmal. *Süddeutsche Zeitung,* 4 August: 4.

– 2002. Ein einstmals heißes Thema spielt in diesem Wahlkampf keine Rolle. *Süddeutsche Zeitung,* 14 September: 8.

– 2004a. Einigung über das Zuwanderungsgesetz. *Süddeutsche Zeitung,* 18 June: 2.

– 2004b. Otto Potemkins Gesetz. *Süddeutsche Zeitung,* Meinungsseite, 5 May: 4.

– 2004c. 'Den Rechtsstaat schützen, nicht opfern.' *Süddeutsche Zeitung,* Meinungsseite, 22 March: 4.

Preuss, Ulrich. 2003. Citizenship and the German nation. *Citizenship Studies* 7(1): 37–55.

Pritchett, Jennifer. 1999. Somali community outraged by 'racist' legislation. *Ottawa Citizen,* 10 August: B3.

Rancière, Jacques. 2002. *Das Unvernehmen: Politik und Philosophie.* Frankfurt am Main: Surkamp.

Rath, Christian. 2003. Die CDU will einen deutschen Sonderweg. *Die Tageszeitung,* 13 March: 7.

Rath, Christian, and Sead Husic. 2001. Zur Zustimmung zwingen geht nicht. *Die Tageszeitung,* 14 March: 6.

Reitz, Jeffrey, Joachim R. Frick, Tony Calabrese, and Gert G. Wagner. 1999. The institutional framework of ethnic inclusion and exclusion: A cross-national analysis of the earnings of foreigners in Germany and immigrants in Canada. *Journal of Ethnic and Migration Studies* 25: 397–443.

Renner, Günter. 2004. Vom Ausländerrecht zum Zuwanderungsrecht. *Zeitschrift für Ausländerrecht und Ausländerpolitik* 8: 266–74.

Renshon, Stanley A. 2008. Emotional attachment: Continuation of a dialogue. *Migrations & Identities* 1(2): 193–202.

Riaño, Yvonne, and Doris Wastl-Walter. 2006. Immigration policies, state discourses on foreigners, and the politics of identity in Switzerland. *Environment and Planning A*, 38: 1693–1713.
Rose, Gillian. 1997. Situating knowledges: Positionality, reflexivities and other tactics. *Progress in Human Geography* 21: 305–20.
Rostock, Petra, and Sabine Berghahn. 2008. The ambivalent role of gender in redefining the German nation. *Ethnicities* 8(3): 345–64.
Rubner, Jeanne. 2002. Hoffen auf einen neuen Anlauf: Verbände zum Karlsruher Urteil. *Süddeutsche Zeitung*, Themen des Tages, 19 December: 2.
Said, Edward W. 1978. *Orientalism*. New York: Pantheon Books.
Samuel, John. 1998. Australia's treatment of natives holds some lessons for Canada. *Toronto Star*, 28 July: 1.
Sassen, Saskia. 1988. *The mobility of labor and capital: A study in international investment and labor flows*. Cambridge: Cambridge University Press.
Satzewich, Vic. 1991. *Racism and the incorporation of foreign labour: Farm labour migration to Canada since 1945*. London: Routledge.
Schiller, Bill. 1999. On Pier 21, Canada opened its doors. *Toronto Star*, 23 January: 1.
Schimmeck, Tom. 2009. *Am besten nichts Neues*. Frankfurt: Westend-Verlag.
Schlottmann, Antje. 2005. *Raumsprache: Ost-West-Differenzen in der Berichterstattung zur deutschen Einheit*. Stuttgart: Franz Steiner Verlag.
Schmidt, Ulrich. 2004. Deutschland wirft kluge Köpfe raus. *Frankfurter Allgemeine Zeitung*, Wirtschaft, 16 May: 42.
Schmidtke, Oliver. 2010. Einwanderer als Ware: Wie die Marktlogik Migranten aussortiert. *Blätter für deutsche und internationale Politik* 10: 51–7.
Schneider, Jan. 2009. *Die Organisation der Asyl- und Zuwanderungspolitik in Deutschland*. Working paper 25 of Forschungsgruppe des Bundesamtes. Nuremberg: Bundesamt für Migration und Flüchtlinge.
Schöneberg, Kai. 2002. Böse in der Bredouille: Innensenator soll sich für Bremer Ja im Bundesrat einsetzen. *Die Tageszeitung*, Bremen Aktuell, 16 February: 25.
Schudson, Michael. 2002. The news media as political institutions. *Annual Review of Political Science* 5: 249–69.
Schultz, Ida. 2007. The journalistic gut feeling: Journalistic doxa, news habitus and orthodox news values. *Journalism Practice* 1(2): 190–207.
Schultze, Günther, ed. 1994. *Einwanderungspolitik Kanada's und der USA: Beispiele für die Bundesrepublik Deutschland?* Bonn: Forschungsinstitut der Friedrich-Ebert-Stiftung, Apt. Arbeits- und Sozailforschung.
Sharma, Nandita. 2006. *Home economics: Nationalism and the making of migrant workers in Canada*. Toronto: University of Toronto Press.

Shattel, Mona M., and José Villalba. 2008. Anti-immigration rhetoric in the United States: Veiled racism? *Issues in Mental Health Nursing* 29: 541–3.

Sheehan, James. 1992. State and nationality in the Napoleonic period. In *The State of Germany,* ed. John Breuilly, 47–59. New York: Longman Publishing.

Shephard, Michelle. 2004. Branded as terrorist threat, men languish in Toronto jail. *Toronto Star,* 17 July: A1.

Sibley, David. 1995. *Geographies of exclusion: Society and difference in the West.* London: Routledge.

Simmons, Alan B. 1999a. Economic integration and designer immigrants: Canadian policy in the 1990s. In *Free markets, open societies, closed borders? Trends in international migration and immigration policy in the Americas,* ed. Max J. Castro, 53–69. Miami, Florida: North-South Center Press.

– 1999b. Immigration policy: Imagined futures. In *Immigrant Canada: Demographic, economic and social challenges,* ed. Shiva S. Halli and Leo Driedger, 21–50. Toronto: University of Toronto Press.

Simmons, Alan B., and Kieran Keohane. 1992. Canadian immigration policy: State strategies and the quest for legitimacy. *Canadian Review of Sociology and Anthropology* 29(4): 421–52.

Simon, Rita J., and Keri W. Sikich. 2007. Public attitudes towards immigrants and immigration policies across seven nations. *International Migration Review* 41(4): 956–62.

Skelton, Chad. 1999a. Early release possible for boat people. *Vancouver Sun,* 27 July: A1.

– 1999b. Sweeping changes planned to policy on immigration. *Vancouver Sun,* 7 January: A1.

– 2000a. Hondurans able to stay, thanks to lack of pact. *Vancouver Sun,* 3 February: A1.

– 2000b. Woman gets refugee status despite no fear of persecution. *Vancouver Sun,* 2 June: A4.

Smith, Allan. 1994. *Canada – an American nation? Essays on continentalism, identity, and the Canadian frame of mind.* Montreal and Kingston: McGill-Queen's University Press.

Snow, David A., Rens Vliegenthart, and Catherine Corrigall-Brown. 2007. Framing the French riots: A comparative study of frame variation. *Social Forces* 86(2): 385–415.

Soja, Edward W. 1996. *Thirdspace: Journeys to Los Angeles and other real-and-imagined places.* Malden, MA: Blackwell.

Soysal, Yasemin Nuhoğlu. 1994. *Limits of citizenship: Migrants and postnational membership in Europe.* Chicago: University of Chicago Press.

Spannbauer, Andreas. 2003. Nach der Green Card bleibt nur die Heirat. *Die Tageszeitung,* Inland, 7 August: 8.

SPD and BÜNDNIS 90/DIE GRÜNEN. 1998. *Aufbruch und Erneuerung – Deutschlands Weg ins 21. Jahrhundert: Koalitionsvereinbarung zwischen der Sozialdemokratischen Partei Deutschlands und BÜNDNIS 90/DIE GRÜNEN,* Bonn, 20 October 1998, http://www.datenschutz-berlin.de/doc/de/koalo/index.htm.

Spencer, Christina. 2009. Poor marks for warding off criminals. *Ottawa Sun.* 24 February. http://ottawasun.com.

Spiegel, Der. 2008. Allah im Abendland: Der Islam und die Deutschen. *Spiegel Special* 2.

Spiegel Online. 2004. Diskussion um Leitkultur: Schröder warnt vor Kampf der Kulturen. Rev. 22 November, http://www.spiegel.de.

– 2006. Wachsende Kluft zwischen Deutschen und Muslimen. February 2008. http://www.spiegel.de.

Spijkerboer, Thomas, and Sarah van Walsum. 2007. *Women and immigration law: New variations on classical feminist themes.* Abingdon: Routledge-Cavendish.

Statistics Canada. 2006. Table 292-0002: Labour force survey estimates (LFS), by sex and detailed age group, annual. *E–STAT Data.* Available from http://estat.statcan.ca.

– 2009. *2006 Census: Highlight tables.* Ottawa. http://www12.statcan.ca/census-recensement/2006/dp-pd/hlt/index-eng.cfm.

Stemler, Steve. 2001. An overview of content analysis. *Practical Assessment, Research & Evaluation* 7(17): no page. http://pareonline.net.

Sternberger, Dolf. 1990. *Verfassungspatriotismus* Frankfurt am Main: Insel Verlag.

Stoffman, Daniel. 2002. *Who gets in: What's wrong with Canada's immigration program – and how to fix it.* Toronto: Macfarlane Walter & Ross.

Storr, Christian, and Rainer Albrecht. 2005. *Kommentar zum Zuwanderungsgesetz.* Stuttgart: Boorberg.

Stuttgarter Zeitung. 2001. Rot-Grün ebnet Weg für Zuwanderungsgesetz. 3 November: 1.

– 2002. Union: Abschiebung erleichtern. Politik, 27 August: 2.

– 2006. Integration: Keine Strafen für Ausländer. 15 July: 1.

Stüwe, H. 2001. Zuwanderungsgesetz bleibt notwendig. *Frankfurter Allgemeine Zeitung,* Wirtschaft, 28 September: 18.

Suárez-Navaz, Liliana. 2007. Immigration and the politics of space allocation in rural Spain: The case of Andalusia. *Journal of Peasant Studies* 34(2): 100–18.

Süddeutsche Zeitung. 2001. Warten auf das Zuwanderungsgesetz. Allein dem Arbeitsamt sind 25 000 offene Stellen gemeldet. Munich, 18 August: 49.

– 2002a. Gerhard Schröder umwirbt die Wirtschaft. 13 March: 25.

– 2002b. Rot-Grün setzt Zuwanderungsgesetz im Bundestag durch. 2 March: 1.

– 2005. Zank über Einsatz der Bundeswehr. 16 July: 6.

Südwestrundfunk. 2006. Allensbach-Umfrage: Angst vor dem Islam – Die Einstellung der Deutschen zum Islam. 18 October. http://www.swr.de/islam/konflikte.

Suelman, Zool. 1997. Who can give immigrants the best advice? *Vancouver Sun*, 22 August: A19.

Sumara, Dennis, Brent Davis, and Linda Laidlow. 2001. Canadian identity and curriculum theory: An ecological, postmodern perspective. *Canadian Journal of Education* 26(2): 144–63.

Süssmuth, Rita. 2008. 13th International Metropolis Conference: Mobility, integration and development in a globalised world. Plenary session: Immigrant Germany: Policies and perspectives for the future. 29 October. Bonn, Germany.

Tageszeitung. 2001. Kein Wahlkampf gegen Ausländer. 8 December: 4.

– 2004a. Es gibt Flüchtlinge, die wollen zurück in ihr Land. 16 March: 7.

– 2004b. Kaplan holt sich die Papiere. Aktuelles, 2 June: 2.

– 2005. Mehr Schatten als Licht. 10 August: 24.

Takle, Marianne. 2007a. EU citizens: Challenging the notion of German national political community, 1990–2005. *International Journal of the Sociology of Law* 35: 178–91.

– 2007b. *German policy on immigration – From ethnos to demos?* Frankfurt am Main: Peter Lang.

Tanner, Adrienne. 1999. Illegals used as cheap labour. *National Post*, 16 August: A6.

Taylor, S. 2001. Locating and conducting discourse analytic research. In *Discourse as data: A guide to analysis*, ed. Margaret Wetherell, Stephanie Taylor, and Simeon J. Yates, 5–48. London: Sage.

Terwey, Michael. 2003. Ethnocentrism in Germany: Worldview connections and social context. In *Germans or foreigners? Attitudes towards ethnic minorities in post-reunification Germany*, ed. Richard Alba, Peter Schmidt, and Martina Wasmer, 69–94. New York: Palgrave Macmillan.

Thobani, Sunera. 2007. *Exalted subjects: Studies in the making of race and nation in Canada*. Toronto: University of Toronto Press.

Thomas, Alfred. 2002. Rege Debatten am Stammtisch: Das rot-grün-schwarze Zuwanderungsgesetz. *Süddeutsche Zeitung*, 25 March: 18.

Thomas, Dominic. 2007. *Black France: Colonialism, immigration and transnationalism*. Bloomington: Indiana University Press.
Thompson, Allan. 1997. Canada jails Saudi linked to bombing: Suspect in attack on U.S. base seeks refugee status here. *Toronto Star,* 23 March: A5.
– 2001a. Immigration bill called 'un-Canadian,' *Toronto Star,* 16 March: A6.
– 2001b. Immigration bill tough on criminals. *Toronto Star,* 14 June: A7.
– 2001c. We need the brightest, best. *Toronto Star,* 20 December: A1.
Tibbetts, Janice. 2001a. High court to decide if suspected terrorists can stay. *Vancouver Sun,* 22 May: A3.
– 2001b. Justices may be asked to rehear case of Tamil, Iranian. *National Post,* 20 September: A8 (also published in *Ottawa Citizen*).
– 2001c. Rehearing may be sought in suspected terrorists' case. *Ottawa Citizen,* 20 September: C5.
– 2001d. Top court hears pleas for refugee terrorists. *Ottawa Citizen,* 23 May: A5 (also published in *Calgary Herald*).
Toronto Star. 1998. Another half-baked idea from Lucienne Robillard. 12 May: 1.
– 1999. A mismanaged immigration department. 12 August: 1.
– 2000. Immigration reforms strike right balance. 9 April: 1.
– 2001a. Immigration act to face tough review. 14 September: A23.
– 2001b. Terrorist remains years after deportation order. 4 October: A8.
– 2002. Wrong balance. 1 May: A20.
– 2011. Halifax memorial. 21 January: A20.
Travers, James. 2001. Canada faces hard choices in relationship with U.S. *Toronto Star,* 13 September: A10.
Triadafilopoulos, Triadafilos. 2004. Building walls, bounding nations: Migration and exclusion in Canada and Germany, 1870–1939. *Journal of Historical Sociology* 17(4): 385–427.
– 2006. A model for Europe? An appraisal of Canadian integration policies. In *Politische Steuerung von Integrationsprozessen: Intentionen und Wirkungen,* ed. Sigrid Baringhorst, Uwe Hunger, and Karen Schönwälder, 79–94. Wiesbaden: VS Verlag für Sozialwissenschaften.
Tsoukala, Anastassia. 2008a. Boundary-creating processes and the social construction of threat. *Alternatives* 33: 137–52.
– 2008b. Defining the terrorist threat in the post-September 11 era. In *Terror, insecurity and liberty: illiberal practices of liberal regimes after 9/11,* ed. Didier Bigo and Anastassia Tsoukala, 49–99. London: Routledge.
Tuchman, Gaye. 1978. *Making news: A study in the construction of reality.* New York: Free Press.
United Nations High Commissioner for Refugees. 1998. 'Comments on *Not just numbers: A Canadian framework for future immigration.*' Report of the

Immigration Legislative Review Advisory Group. http://www.web.net/~ccr/hcrlegr.htm.

Vancouver Sun. 1996. The immigration minister and the not-so-law-abiding. 12 June: A5.

– 1998. Memories of pioneer toil, trouble motivate immigrant-fluency foes. 12 March: A19.

– 2000a. Ottawa is missing the boat on refugees. 20 March: A8.

– 2000b. Send an S O S to fill skilled labour pool. 27 September: A22.

– 2004. Provinces must co-operate on private language schools. 30 January: A14.

van Dijk, Teun A. 1987. *Communicating racism: Ethnic prejudice in thought and talk*. Newbury Park: Sage.

– 1991. *Racism and the press*. London: Routledge.

van Dijk, Teun A., ed. 1997a. *Discourse as social interaction. Discourse studies: A multidisciplinary introduction*, vol. 2. London: Sage.

– 1997b. *Discourse studies: A multidisciplinary introduction*. London: Sage.

Van Leeuwen, Theo, and Ruth Wodak. 1999. Legitimizing immigration control: A discourse-historical analysis. *Discourse Studies* 1(1): 83–118.

Veugelers, John W.R. 2000. State–society relations in the making of Canadian immigration policy during the Mulroney era. *Canadian Review of Sociology and Anthropology* 37 (1): 95–110.

Vienneau, David. 1996. Ottawa to 'update' Immigration Act to be modernized for 21st century, minister says. *Toronto Star*, 26 November: A2.

Vincent, Donovan. 1999. Refugee claimant accused of lying. *Toronto Star*, 26 August: 1.

Voigt, Claudius. 2004. Illegalität als eine Alternative. *Die Tageszeitung*, Ruhr regional, 21 July: 4.

Vukov, Tamara. 2003. Imagining communities through immigration policies: Governmental regulation, media spectacles and the affective politics of national borders. *International Journal of Cultural Studies* 6(3): 335–53.

Waever, Ole. 1995. Securitization and desecuritization. In *On security*, ed. Ronnie D. Lipschutz, 46–86. New York: Columbia University Press.

Wagner, Jonathan. 2006. *A history of migration from Germany to Canada, 1850–1939*. Vancouver: UBC Press.

Wallraff, Lukas. 2001. Kein Wahlkampf gegen Ausländer. *Tageszeitung*, 8 December: 4.

– 2002. Ausländer gut für Jobmarkt. *Die Tageszeitung*, Inland, 17 Jaunuary: 7.

– 2003. Besser gar nicht als schlecht. *Die Tageszeitung*, Meinung und Diskussion, 6 February: 12.

Walsh, James. 2008. Navigating globalization: Immigration policy in Canada and Australia, 1945–2007. *Sociological Forum* 23(4): 786–813.

Walton, Douglas. 2007. *Media argumentation: Dialectic, persuasion, and rhetoric.* Cambridge: Cambridge University Press.

Walzer, Michael. 1983. Spheres of justice: A defense of pluralism and equality. Oxford: Martin Robertson.

Ward, Ian. 2002. Identifying the European other. *International Journal of Refugee Law,* 14(2/3): 219–37.

Ward, Kevin. 2000. Britain's refugee debate offends UN agency. *Vancouver Sun,* 14 April: 14.

Wasmer, Martina, and Achim Koch. 2003. Foreigners as second-class citizens? Attitudes towards equal civil rights for non-Germans. In *Germans or foreigners? Attitudes towards ethnic minorities in post-reunification Germany,* ed. Richard Alba, Peter Schmidt, and Martina Wasmer, 95–118. New York: Palgrave Macmillan.

Weber, Robert P. 1990. *Basic content analysis,* 2nd ed. Newbury Park, CA: Sage.

Weikert, Eva. 2004a. Abschiebebock wird Integrationsgärtner. *Die Tageszeitung,* Hamburg Aktuell, 24 April: 26.

– 2004b. Helfer atmen durch. *Tageszeitung,* Hamburg Aktuell, 5 May: 22.

Welter, Patrick. 2004. Zuwanderer stehlen keine Arbeitsplätze. *Frankfurter Allgemeine Zeitung,* Wirtschaft, 6 June: 34.

Wengeler, Martin. 1995. Multikulturelle Gesellschaft oder Ausländer raus? Der sprachliche Umgang mit der Einwanderung seit 1945. In *Kontroverse Begriffe: Geschichte des öffentlichen Sprachgebrauchs in der Bundesrepublik Deutschland,* ed. Georg Stötzel, Martin Wengeler, and Karin Böke, 711–49. Berlin: Walter de Gruyter.

– 2000. Von 'Belastungen,' 'wirtschaftlichem Nutzen' und 'politischen Zielen.' Die öffentliche Einwanderungsdiskussion in Deutschland, Österreich und der Schweiz Anfang der 70er Jahre. In *Einwanderungsdiskurse: Vergleichende diskurslinguistische Studien,* ed. Thomas Niehr and Karin Böke, 135–57. Wiesbaden: Westdeutscher Verlag.

– 2003. *Topos und Diskurs: Begründung einer argumentationsanalytischen Methode und ihre Anwendung auf den Migrationsdiskurs (1960–1985).* Tübingen: Niemeyer.

– 2006. Zur historischen Kontinuität von Argumentationsmustern im Migrationsdiskurs. In *Massenmedien, Migration und Integration: Herausforderungen für Journalismus und politische Bildung,* ed. Christoph Butterwegge and Gudrun Hentges, 11–34. Wiesbaden: Verlag für Sozialwissenschaften.

Wetherell, Margaret, Stephanie Taylor, and Simeon J. Yates, eds. 2001. *Discourse as data: A guide to analysis.* London: Sage.

Whitaker, Reg. 1998. Refugees: The security dimension. *Citizenship Studies* 2(3): 413–34.

Wildenthal, Lora. 1997. Race, gender, and citizenship in the German colonial empire. In *Tensions of empire: Colonial cultures in a bourgeois world,* ed. Ann Laura Stoler and Frederick Cooper, 263–81. Berkeley: University of California Press.

Williams, Raymond. 1966. *Communication.* Harmondsworth: Penguin Books.

– 1983. *Keywords: A vocabulary of culture and society,* rev. ed. New York: Oxford University Press.

Wilson, William Julius. 1987. *The truly disadvantaged: The inner city, the underclass and public policy.* Chicago: University of Chicago Press.

Wimmer, Andreas, and Nina Glick Schiller. 2002. Methodological nationalism and beyond: Nation-state building, migration and the social sciences. *Global Networks* 2(4): 301–34.

Winter, Elke. 2001. National unity versus multiculturalism? Rethinking the logic of inclusion in Germany and Canada. *International Journal of Canadian Studies – Revue internationale d'études canadiennes* 24: 171–95.

– 2009. Die Dialektik multikultureller Identität: Kanada als Lehrstück. *Swiss Political Science Review* 15 (1): 133–68.

Wittgenstein, Ludwig. 2001 [1945/6]. *Philosophische Untersuchungen.* Kritisch-genetische Edition), ed. Joachim Schulte. Frankfurt: Suhrkamp.

Wodak, Ruth. 2001. The discourse-historical approach. In *Methods of critical discourse* analysis, ed. Ruth Wodak and Michael Meyer, 63–94. London: Sage.

– 2006. Dilemmas of discourse. *Language in Society* 35: 595–611.

Wodak, Ruth, Rudolf de Cillia, Martin Reisigl, and Karin Liebhart. 1999. *The discursive construction of national identity.* Translated by Angelika Hirsch and Richard Mitten. Edinburgh: Edinburgh University Press.

Wodak, Ruth, and Florian Menz, ed. 1990. *Sprache in der Politik – Politik in der Sprache: Analysen zum öffentlichen Sprachgebrauch.* Klagenfurt/ Celovec: Drava.

Wodak, Ruth and Michael Meyer, eds. 2001. *Methods of critical discourse analysis,* London: Sage.

Wöhrle, Christoph. 2006. Erster Integrationsgifel. *Migration und Bevölkerung Newsletter* 6: 1–2.

Wolfsfeld, Gadi. 1997. *Media and political conflict: News from the Middle East.* Cambridge: Cambridge University Press.

Wynnyckyj, Andrij Kudla. 1998. Canada's Immigration Act under legislative review; 'Not Just Numbers' report examined at hearings. Toronto Press Bureau. http://www.ukrweekly.com/Archive/1998/149802.shtml.

Yaffe, Barbara. 2000. Immigration Act has been a disaster for Canada. *Calgary Herald*, 25 May: A22 (also published in *Vancouver Sun*).

Yasmeen, Gisèle. 2004. Citizens of the world with Canadian passports? *PERCII Working Paper Series* no. WP05-04.

Ziedler, Christoph. 2002. Als Härtefall kann nun keiner mehr gelten. *Stuttgarter Zeitung*, 19 December: 2.

– 2003. Schily mauert in Brüssel, um Beckstein zu imponieren. *Stuttgarter Zeitung*, 25 July: 5.

Zinterer, Tanja. 2004. *Politikwandel durch Politikberatung? Die kanadische Royal Commission on Aboriginal Peoples und die Unabhängige Kommission 'Zuwanderung' im Vergleich*. Wiesbaden: Verlag für Sozialwissenschaften.

Žižek, Slavoj. 2006. *The parallax view*. Cambridge: Cambridge University Press.

Index

www.ingramcontent.com/pod-product-compliance
Lightning Source LLC
LaVergne TN
LVHW090805070826
844660LV00022B/1082

* 9 7 8 1 4 4 2 6 1 0 7 6 7 *